EASY EVERYDAY LOW-FAT COOKING

Patricia J. Stephenson, M.S., R.D.
William T. Stephenson, M.D.

Pat Stephenson

Hearth
PUBLISHING

Easy, Everyday Low-Fat Cooking
© 1992 by Patricia J. Stephenson, M.S., R.D.
and William T. Stephenson, M.D.

Fifth Printing, 1996 – Revised edition
Printed in the United States of America
Produced by Hearth Publishing, Hillsboro, Kansas

Library of Congress Catalog Card Number: 96-79361
ISBN 1-882420-28-4

Illustration — Patricia J. Stephenson, Author

Dear Reader/Fellow Cooks:

When we decided to collaborate on a cookbook, we established a major goal: to offer busy people easy ways to prepare tasty and healthy foods.

As a dietitian and a physician, we know the importance of proper nutrition for overall health and well being. And as busy family members (we're a mom and son team) we know that hectic schedules can make meal preparation seem like an impossible chore. In selecting our favorite healthy recipes, we adhered to our guidelines:

- *Each one is heart healthy and nutritionally sound. That means the recipes are relatively low in fat and rich in necessary nutrients. We analyzed our recipes to include information on calories, protein, carbohydrate, fats, cholesterol, sodium, potassium, fiber, vitamins and minerals.*

- *The recipes presented in our book are moderately low in sodium; severe restriction of salt is avoided, based upon the knowledge that strict reduction of salt and sodium is needed only for people with special medical needs.*

- *Each recipe is fairly easy to make and includes readily available ingredients. A sound nutritional philosophy is one that encourages moderation and variety, not faddish diets that call for hard-to-find foods. You will see that many of the foods you are already eating are right on track.*

- *Good healthy recipes need to be backed by good health advice. That is why we have carefully explained the "whys" behind a low-fat, heart-healthy diet. We have also included handy low-fat cooking tips you can incorporate in your everyday cooking routine.*

We hope you will keep this book in a handy place. Open it to the sections that interest you and as you are ready, make the low-fat, nutritional changes we suggest. When you feel comfortable, move on to another section and make those changes. Remember: slow, steady changes are successful changes.

Happy Eating,
Pat and William Stephenson

Acknowledgements

The idea for our cookbook rumbled through our heads for years but became a reality only because many people gave us continuing support, valuable criticism and encouragement. Our son Steve (William Thomas Stephenson, II, M.D.), who is co-author, gave freely of his time and expertise. Steve has a degree in nutrition from Brigham Young University and, while deep into the residency years of his medical training, took time to read, review and rewrite the informational sections.

My children, Barbara, Betsy and Steve, were my captive diners through many years of low-fat meal preparation, eating both the successes and the failures. In spite of it all, they grew into healthy, active, slender adults.

As retirement time neared, the desire to share our quick and easy recipes and low-fat cooking methods became stronger. My mother, Clara May Evanhoe, R.D. provided seed money. My husband gave hundreds of hours doing computerized nutritional analyses and word processing. My good neighbor, Betty Simpson, contributed valuable ideas and suggestions as did my long-time friend and co-worker, Bernita Olson, R.D. Amy Stephenson, Steve's wife, spent many, many hours setting up the original computerized layout and formatting for the cookbook. My friend, Julia Conaway, was always helpful and understanding in her support. My art teacher, Diane Lawrence, lead me through the joys and intricacies of colored-pencil drawings, one of which forms a part of the cover of our book. Writers Dena Wallace and Nancy Stoetzer smoothed and clarified our written material.

We hope our efforts will speed you toward tasty and successful everyday low-fat eating enjoyment.

Pat Stephenson

Preface

For most of us, our usual meals are based on meats and grains accompanied by plenty of desserts and snacks. We think vegetables are best with some kind of sauce or fat added. But this is the kind of diet that promotes heart disease, strokes, certain cancers, diabetes and other maladies that follow too many calories, fats and sweets and too few fruits and vegetables along with not enough exercise.

Here is a book written for you by an experienced dietitian and her physician son. They show you just how to eat better using the kinds of things you have in the kitchen while conserving your time, energy, and money.

Pat and William explain what you need to know about nutrition without overkill. This book includes the latest, scientifically-based information about fat and cholesterol, sodium, fiber and complex carbohydrates. Besides the tried and true favorites slimmed down to fit current Dietary Guidelines, it includes less popular alternatives such as tofu and yogurt and the new government-released Food Guide Pyramid that replaces the outdated Basic Four that's been around since the early 1950s. In fact, the book is arranged according to the Pyramid beginning with the foundation of healthful diets, the grains i.e. all the breads and cereals with their complex carbohydrates, vitamins, minerals and fiber.

For my part, I am pleased to recommend this factually based, practical, time and energy saving cookbook that puts into practice what I have been suggesting for fifteen years. I invite you to try some of the recipes. You'll find that they're not very different from what you like now.

For diet changes to be permanent, they should be made gradually and one at a time. To begin with, you might find the turkey sausage and potato skillet main dish on page 166 to be a good tasting substitute for that high fat, salty hot dog casserole you now serve.

To your good health as well as good eating!
Mary P. Clarke, PhD, RD, LD, CHE
Extension Specialist, Nutrition Education
Kansas Cooperative Extension Service
Kansas State University and
Past-President, Kansas Dietetic Association

Contents

Quick Recipe Finder

Main Dishes & Entrees

Main Dishes & Entrees

Main Dishes & Entrees

Fish and Seafood (Continued)

Pork and Ham

Tofu

Main Dishes & Entrees

Gravies and Sauces

Gravies and Sauces

Herbs, Marinades, Spices and Toppings

Pasta

Pasta *(Continued)*

Rice

Potatoes

Vegetables

Vegetables *(Continued)*

Salads

Fruit

Main Dish

Vegetable

Salad Dressings

Salad Dressings *(Continued)*

Fruits and Desserts

Fruit

Fruit-based Desserts

Desserts

Beverages *(Continued)*

Snacking, Low-Fat

See suggestions on pages 258 and 259

Why Eat a Low-Fat Diet?

T hat is a tough question, especially if you are sitting in front of a plate of crispy fried chicken, mashed potatoes smothered in gravy and a thick piece of chocolate cake with ice cream.

Culinarily speaking, fats boost taste. Fats and oils pick up flavors and blend them throughout the food. That is why high-fat dishes can seem particularly satisfying to the palate and why so many Americans derive 40 to 50 percent of their calories from fat, much more than the recommended 30 percent.

Unfortunately, a constant stream of fats, especially saturated fats, will clog arteries the way hard minerals gradually clog water pipes. Scientists around the world have presented volumes of evidence linking a high-fat, high cholesterol diet to an increased risk of coronary heart disease. Surprisingly, trimming saturated fat from the diet is more important than avoiding the cholesterol containing foods. While both of these measures are effective, reducing saturated fat in the diet will lower the blood cholesterol level more than will eating less cholesterol.

Calories and fat:

Calories come from four sources: carbohydrates, proteins, fats and alcohol. While no more than 30 percent of your total calories should be comprised of fat, amounts aren't the only important thing to remember. You also need to be aware of what *kinds* of fat you are eating.

The three basic types of fats are saturated, monounsaturated and polyunsaturated. Of these three, saturated fats warrant the greatest concern because they cause more cholesterol to be produced in the body, which in turn can block the arteries. Examples of saturated fats that should be limited are beef fat and tropical oils such as coconut and palm kernel.

Saturated fats should be limited to less than 10 percent of your daily calories. The remaining 20 percent can be divided between polyunsaturated fats, such as corn oil and safflower oil and monounsaturated fats, such as canola oil and olive oil. The best kind of fat to consume is monounsaturated because it lowers Low Density Lipoproteins (LDLs) which are high in cholesterol and carry cholesterol to the body tissues. Monounsaturated fats, however, have no effect on one's High Density Lipoproteins (HDLs) which pick up cholesterol from all over the body and carry it back to the liver. The liver then converts excess cholesterol to bile which is collected in the gallbladder. The gallbladder secretes the bile into the intestine to aid in digestion. Since LDLs deposit cholesterol in body tissues, they are often considered "bad" while HDLs pick up cholesterol and are considered "good". To check the differences between vegetable oils and animal fats, consult the fat comparison chart on page 260.

Figuring fat calories:

Foods high in fat often create a pleasing feeling of fullness. As a result, a diet very low in fat usually leaves a person feeling vaguely dissatisfied. For this reason, we recommend that you ease your way into a low-fat diet. At least in the beginning, make sure that 30 percent, and no fewer, of your calories come from fat.

To figure a desirable daily fat intake, follow this simple formula: multiply 0.3 (30 percent) times the number of calories you need each day. For example, if you need 2,000 calories, you could safely consume 600 of those calories from fat.

There are nine calories in every gram of fat. To find out how many grams of fat you can consume daily, divide your allotted fat calories, in this case 600, by 9 (the number of calories in every gram of fat). So, on a 2,000 calorie diet, you can consume about 67 grams of fat.

To determine if a dish is low-fat, establish a guideline of allowing three grams of fat per 100 calories. Three grams of fat provides 27 calories per 100 calories or just under 30 percent of the calories from fat. Desserts, main dishes and meats may have a higher fat content if your total fat calories average out at thirty percent over several days.

A little fat can be good.

It is unfortunate that our daily eating patterns, as well as party, picnic and celebration dining, are filled with fat-rich foods. High-fat snack foods fill a nibbling niche in our stress-filled lives. As a result, a fat-free diet often seems monotonous and lacking in flavor and appeal.

Motivation is essential to following a low-fat lifestyle. Moderation, however, is the key to success and good health. Along with many other needed nutrients, fats and oils have a vital role in a balanced diet. Food should add pleasure to life, not boredom.

The sample breakfasts, lunches and suppers provided in the section, Healthful Eating Every Day (see pages 236-257), will help illustrate how a low-fat diet can be easily established.

Tips to reducing fat calories and saturated fat include:

- *Use low-fat or skim milk, cheese, yogurt and frozen yogurt.*
- *Eat fish several times a week.*
- *Use skinless chicken or turkey and cut out all the other fat you can see. Half the fat in poultry is in or directly under the skin.*
- *Select lean meats and trim all visible fat before cooking.*
- *Bake, grill, roast, microwave, steam or broil meats to allow fats to drip out.*
- *Use nonstick pans, or spread a very thin film of vegetable oil in the pan to prevent sticking.*
- *Use vegetables, fruits, breads, grains and cereals generously. They are high in nutrients and are almost fat-free.*
- *Choose oils that are low in saturated fat for cooking and in salad dressings. Canola oil and olive oil are wise selections. Reserve your saturated fat intake for lean meat and cheese where making substitutions is more difficult.*
- *Use margarines that have liquid vegetable oil listed as the first ingredient. Choose soft tub margarines because they contain less saturated fat. Stick margarines are firm because the monounsaturated and polyunsaturated fats have been converted to saturated fat by the process of hydrogenation to give the margarine a more firm consistency.*

Making Sense of the Alphabet Soup with the Food Guide Pyramid

T rying to sort through all the recommended vitamins and minerals is a lot like trying to make sentences out of alphabet soup. RDAs is an abbreviation of the term, the Recommended Dietary Allowances. When we talk about the RDAs, we are talking about the amounts of various nutrients in foods that are needed to maintain good health.

In 1992 the United States Department of Agriculture produced a new Food Guide Pyramid (see back cover) which makes it easy to select a nutritious, low-fat diet. When we eat the recommended servings of foods from the food groups shown in the pyramid, we are assured of getting the RDAs. As the base of the pyramid graphically shows, the foundation for good eating is composed of grains such as breads, cereals, pastas and rices. The next level up the pyramid encourages eating vitamin-rich and mineral-rich fruits and vegetables. As the pyramid narrows, dairy products, dried beans, fish, poultry, nuts, meats and eggs are recommended. The top tier of the pyramid clearly shows that fats, oils and sweets are to be eaten sparingly.

Our cookbook simplifies the proper selection of foods. The book begins with foods and recipes from the grain base of the pyramid and follows the pyramid upward through the basic food groups while giving easy, low-fat cooking methods and recipes.

Sample breakfast, lunch and supper menus on pages 238 to 257 show how to combine tasty foods into quick-to-the-table meals.

Select recipes from the hundreds listed in our Quick Recipe Finder on pages vi to xvi.

No matter what your age, you need to consume the proper foods to give you a healthy, fit body. A proper diet provides us with 50 necessary nutrients including water, glucose from starches and sugars, fats and fatty acids, eight to 10 amino acids from proteins, 16 vitamins and 20 to 25 minerals. But foods give us more than nutrients and that is why we need to eat real food, not just vitamin-mineral supplements. Foods naturally contain many other compounds that can be cancer-fighters and components such as fibers and antioxidants that may have very important effects upon health.

The Food Guide Pyramid makes it easy to select healthy, satisfying foods each day:

- *Breads, Cereals, and other Grain Products, preferably whole grain*
  6 to 11 servings (include several servings of whole grain products daily)

- *Fruits*
  2 to 4 servings (include citrus and fruits high in Vitamins A and C)

- *Vegetables*
  3 to 5 servings (include dark green leafy and dark yellow vegetables once each day)

- *Dried beans and peas, Fish, Poultry, Meat, Eggs, Nuts and Seeds*
  2 to 3 servings (use 3 to 6 ounces, after cooking; limit egg yolks to 3 or 4 each week)

- *Milk, Yogurt and Cheese*
  2 to 3 servings (use 3 to 4 servings for women who are pregnant or breastfeeding and for teens)

- *Fats and Sweets*
  Use fats and sweets sparingly. If you drink alcoholic beverages, do so in moderation

No matter what your dietary goal, one simple rule of thumb remains. Each day, eat a wide variety of foods in moderation.

The Nutrient Analysis

A nutrient analysis is provided for each recipe, based on one serving. The analysis includes a count of:

- *Calories*
- *Grams of protein, carbohydrate and total fat*
- *Grams of saturated and monounsaturated fat*
- *Milligrams of cholesterol, sodium and potassium*
- *Grams of fiber*
- *The percentages of U.S. Recommended Daily Allowances of vitamins and minerals, if two percent or more*

You will find the format of the analysis very familiar as it is similar to what you see listed on many containers purchased at the supermarket. It is helpful to know that 1,000 milligrams = 1 gram; 28 grams = 1 ounce. The Recommended Dietary Allowances were calculated to provide a comforting safety factor and the requirements may be met over a period of several days, rather than each day.

All foods shown in the ingredient list are included in the analysis. Optional ingredients are omitted, however. When a choice of ingredients is shown, as in "dried or fresh parsley", the analysis is based upon the ingredient listed first.

Nutritional composition of a single food item can vary widely due to factors such as variety, maturity at harvest and length of time in storage. A nutrient analysis of a food item is based on hundreds of analyses conducted by food scientists, the food industry and by the food analysts of the United States Department of Agriculture. Therefore, the actual nutrients in a recipe may vary from those shown in our nutritional analysis tables.

The nutritional analysis is provided for people who, while able to observe normal diet outlines, have decided to select lower fat, healthier diets. If you follow a diet prescribed by a physician, consult a registered dietitian for help in adjusting these recipes to your special needs.

6

Salt, Sodium, Herbs and Spices

Flavor enhancers, such as salt, herbs and spices, are powerful little items in any kitchen. A twist of just the right flavoring can unleash a food's natural taste, turning a dish from blah to bravo. If a meal isn't tasty unless accompanied by a salt shaker, it may be time to give the taste buds a break and try some other seasonings. Unleashing the culinary magic of herbs and spices on common foods can reap some delicious surprises. The key to healthy seasoning is to use more herbs and spices and less salt.

Why do we need to reduce our salt and sodium intake? The typical American diet contains from 3,000 to 6,000 milligrams of sodium per day, and a high sodium diet can increase blood pressure in many people. High blood pressure is a concern because atherosclerosis (hardening of the arteries) occurs at a much faster rate, leading to strokes and heart attacks at younger ages.

Salt can cause high blood pressure partly because the sodium pulls water into the blood vessels and raises blood pressure. It also affects the body's hormone balance. There may be other ways salt causes high blood pressure, too. Salt is comprised of 40 percent sodium and 60 percent chloride. One teaspoon of table salt contains about 2,000 milligrams of sodium. The body's average requirement is less than 500 milligrams of sodium per day. Using our suggestions, you can follow a moderately low sodium diet of 2,000 to 4,000 milligrams of sodium per day. Many health organizations recommend a sodium range of 2,000 to 3,000 milligrams.

As you read labels, you will notice many low-fat ready-to-eat foods are quite high in sodium. Food producers have learned that foods low in fat *and* sodium do not sell well, as this is too much of a flavor change for many people. We also know the hurried cook must get food into the lunch bag, or on the table, fast. Time simply is not available to home-prepare the lower sodium versions. Don't despair; getting your family switched to lower fat foods is your first goal. Throughout our cookbook we suggest ways to reduce the amount of salt and sodium in your meals. You can gradually ease into lower sodium foods and keep the total sodium per meal at 700 to 900 milligrams, by diluting the sodium with generous usage of unprocessed foods.

Salt is hidden in many foods. Many processed foods use salt and sodium compounds to intensify flavor or to preserve the foods. They can be found in most canned foods and some frozen vegetables, smoked and cured meats, pickles and catsup. Salt is used in cheeses, sauces, soups, salad dressings and many breakfast cereals. Sodium is even found in instant puddings and bakery items.

Because most people have learned to prefer salty flavors, reducing the daily intake should be a gradual process. It is not easy, but many former heavy salters are now enjoying the subtle, more natural flavor of foods.

Reducing sodium starts with buying fresh vegetables, poultry, fish and meats. We know how handy processed foods can be for the hurried cook; many of the recipes in this book include such items. Processed foods extended with fresh vegetables, fruit, poultry, meat, pasta and grains have less salt and sodium per serving.

The ideal, of course, is to grow accustomed to the flavors provided by herbs and spices. They are practically sodium-free and they can create some exciting tastes. Most people can easily become accustomed to using significantly less salt over a two to three month period.

For those who still want to enjoy a salty flavor, a half sodium chloride, half potassium chloride, light salt is available. This reduces the sodium per teaspoon from 2,000 to 1,000 milligrams. The additional potassium may be beneficial for many people, but check with your physician before using such an item, particularly those with liver or kidney problems or those taking medicines for high blood pressure.

Herb and spice mixtures are available at supermarkets, but can be expensive. Our Make-Your-Own Herb Blend recipe offers a less costly alternative (see page 10). Experiment with your own combinations, making several different flavors D one for poultry, one for fish, etc.

Keep in mind the following flavor hints when cooking:

- *Lemon juice, lemon rind, tomato juice, low salt broths, vinegars and herbed vinegars add back the tang many people miss when they lower the salt in their diet.*

- *Peppers and onions are a tried and true seasoning method used by cooks all over the world. Try this combination with beef or vegetables.*

- *Herbs come in versions that are fresh, dried, flaked, finely ground, as pastes and liquid hot sauces. Remember, the fresher the herb the more potent the flavor.*

- *Most of an herb's flavor comes from aromatic essential oils which can evaporate at warm temperatures or are destroyed by oxygen. With that in mind, keep containers tightly sealed and away from a warm stove. Spices and herbs are best when stored in the refrigerator or freezer and when used within a year of purchasing.*

- *There is often very little difference between more expensive herbs and spices and the cheaper, generic varieties. Whatever is cheaper will usually work just as well.*

- *Chopped fresh vegetables add color, flavor, fiber and very little sodium: try chopped carrots, green onions, white, yellow and red onions, celery, chives, parsley and peppers.*

- *A small amount of sugar can bring out other flavors.*

- *See page 150 on how to reduce sodium in recipes.*

Make-Your-Own Herb Blend

A sprinkle of herb seasoning is calorie, sodium, cholesterol and fat-free.

1 teaspoon dry mustard

2 teaspoons basil leaves

1 teaspoon ground thyme

2 teaspoons celery seed

2 teaspoons ground cumin

2 teaspoons dill weed

2 teaspoons ground marjoram

2 teaspoons dried lemon or orange peel (optional)

Nutrients per serving:

calories	*0*
protein	*0 gm*
carbohydrate	*0 gm*
total fat	*0 gm*
saturated fat	*0 gm*
monounsat'd fat	*0 gm*
cholesterol	*0 mg*
sodium	*0 mg*
potassium	*0 mg*
fiber	*0 gm*

% US-RDA

vitamin A	***
vitamin C	***
thiamin	***
riboflavin	***
vitamin B$_6$	***
folacin	***
iron	***
zinc	***
calcium	***

Measure all ingredients into a small bowl. Stir to mix thoroughly. Spoon or funnel into an emptied-out herb shaker with wide holes. (If you prefer a finer blend, crush with a mortar and pestle or blender and pour into salt shaker.) Makes 12 teaspoons of seasonings.

Use this mild blend for fish, poultry and vegetables. Double or triple recipe, seal in an air-tight container and freeze.

Start with this, or the Oniony-Peppery Herb Seasoning recipe. Open an herb or spice container; smell, taste and imagine what foods you feel would be enhanced. Keep careful notes of the changes you make. Use small amounts, then add more as needed. Rely upon your own flavor-aroma sense to develop your own special blends.

Oniony-Peppery
Herb Seasoning

In 15 minutes the herb blend is ready to use.

2 teaspoons garlic powder

2 teaspoons onion powder

1 teaspoon dry mustard

1 teaspoon basil leaves

1/2 teaspoon ground marjoram

1 teaspoon ground thyme

1 teaspoon dill weed

2 teaspoons dried parsley flakes

1/2 teaspoon ground nutmeg

1 teaspoon black or white pepper

1/2 teaspoon red pepper

1 or 2 teaspoons dried lemon or orange
peel (optional)

Measure all ingredients into a small bowl. Stir to mix thoroughly. Spoon or funnel into herb shaker with wide holes. If you prefer a finer blend, crush with a mortar and pestle or blender and pour into salt shaker. Makes 12 teaspoons of seasonings.

Use this rather strong, robust blend for beef, herbed breads and soups.
Double or triple the recipe, seal in an air-tight container, and freeze.

Nutrients per serving:

calories	0
protein	0 gm
carbohydrate	0 gm
total fat	0 gm
saturated fat	0 gm
monounsat'd fat	0 gm
cholesterol	0 mg
sodium	0 mg
potassium	0 mg
fiber	0 gm

% US-RDA

vitamin A	***
vitamin C	***
thiamin	***
riboflavin	***
vitamin B$_6$	***
folacin	***
iron	***
zinc	***
calcium	***

Herbed Breading for Fish, Chicken and Meat

In 10 minutes this handy breading is ready to use.

1 can (10 oz.) plain dry bread crumbs

4 teaspoons paprika

3 teaspoons garlic powder

1/2 teaspoon black or white pepper

2 teaspoons onion powder

1 teaspoon lite salt

**1/2 cup cornmeal or cornflake crumbs
   (optional)**

other herbs to your taste

Combine all ingredients in storage container. Mix with fork until well blended. Use immediately or cover and refrigerate to preserve flavors. To assure the breading adheres to food surfaces, dip first into egg white and/or low-fat milk. Pour breading into pie pan and coat food by turning or by shaking the food and breading together in a bag. Makes twenty-eight 2-tablespoon portions.

The attractive golden brown crust holds in flavor and moistness. Paprika in the breading turns a pleasing brown in a 325 to 350° oven. This breading can be used as is to top casseroles or a small amount of vegetable oil may be added for a more crumbly and moist topping.

Nutrients per serving:

calories	50
protein	2 gm
carbohydrate	10 gm
total fat	0 gm
saturated fat	0 gm
monounsat'd fat	0 gm
cholesterol	0 mg
sodium	100 mg
potassium	35 mg
fiber	0 gm

% US-RDA

vitamin A	***
vitamin C	***
thiamin	***
riboflavin	***
vitamin B_6	***
folacin	***
iron	3
zinc	***
calcium	***

Improving Flavor With Sauces, Gravies, Marinades and Salad Dressings

We have trained our palates to prefer foods that are heavy with fats such as fried meats, mayonnaise, sour cream, butter, margarine and cheeses. And we have grown to like salty seasonings, too. Somehow we were led to believe an equivalent flavor could be achieved while changing to baked foods, low-fat milk and cheese, while also cutting back on fats, oils and salt.

The truth is that low-fat cooking does taste different than high-fat fare. It does take time to adjust to the new flavor treats that you will learn to find more pleasing and satisfying. And you won't miss that overloaded sensation you once felt after a high-fat meal.

Sauces, gravies, marinades and salad dressings improve flavor and moistness in every food from low-fat fish and poultry, to starches and vegetables, salads and desserts. Featured are a variety of low-fat quick to fix sauces to complement a wide range of dishes. Because these sauces are low-fat, they may be used generously. Some sauces are created from low-fat canned soups. To reduce sodium content, select reduced or low sodium varieties. Also included is a chart showing the fat and sodium content in commonly used portions of commercially produced low-fat sauces and vinegars. Those high in sodium should be used in smaller amounts.

Beef or Pork Pan Gravy

Low in fat, high in flavor.

10 to 16 ice cubes

1/2 teaspoon bouillon granules or 1/2 cube (beef flavor for beef gravy, chicken for pork gravy)

3 tablespoons all-purpose or crystallized flour

1/2 teaspoon garlic powder

1 teaspoon onion powder

1 can (4 oz.) mushroom pieces with liquid

1/2 teaspoon lite salt

black pepper to taste

Nutrients per serving:

calories	18
protein	0 gm
carbohydrate	4 gm
total fat	0 gm
saturated fat	0 gm
monounsat'd fat	0 gm
cholesterol	0 mg
sodium	135 mg
potassium	90 mg
fiber	0 gm

% US-RDA

vitamin A	***
vitamin C	***
thiamin	***
riboflavin	***
vitamin B6	***
folacin	***
iron	***
zinc	***
calcium	***

Remove the roast to a platter and place in warm oven (200°) while preparing gravy. In roasting pan, add ice cubes to meat drippings and allow ice cubes to congeal fat. Stir to remove drippings adhering to pan bottom. Remove fat and ice cubes. Add flour (2 tablespoons per cup of liquid) to the remaining drippings and water; stir gently. Add remaining ingredients, bring to a simmer and cook at least 5 minutes, stirring gently, to assure no raw flour taste remains. Makes six 1/4-cup servings.

Use a wooden spoon and stir gently to prevent breaking down the gravy. Add any finely-chopped vegetables such as onions, carrots or celery.

Quick Chicken and Meat Gravy

Keeps the food moist and flavorful during baking or use for an easy to serve gravy.

1 tablespoon tub margarine

¼ teaspoon garlic powder

2 tablespoons all-purpose or crystallized flour

1 cup canned bouillon or 1 teaspoon bouillon granules dissolved in 1 cup boiling water (chicken flavor for chicken and pork, beef flavor for beef)

herbs, catsup or chili sauce

Melt margarine in one-quart saucepan. Sprinkle in garlic powder and flour and stir until blended. Using a wooden spoon, gently stir in the bouillon liquid and seasonings. Bring to a boil, stirring gently but constantly, for 4 to 5 minutes to assure the flour is well cooked. Pour over poultry or meat before roasting, or use as a gravy. Makes 1 cup or four ¼-cup servings.

Packaged instant soups and gravies are faster, very low in fat, but high in sodium. By eliminating the salt used in preparing the meat and starch, the total sodium for the meal can be kept in the 1,000 milligram range.

Nutrients per serving:

calories	*41*
protein	*0 gm*
carbohydrate	*3 gm*
total fat	*3 gm*
saturated fat	*1 gm*
monounsat'd fat	*2 gm*
cholesterol	*0 mg*
sodium	*255 mg*
potassium	*10 mg*
fiber	*0 gm*

% US-RDA

vitamin A	*2*
vitamin C	***
thiamin	*4*
riboflavin	*5*
vitamin B_6	***
folacin	***
iron	***
zinc	***
calcium	***

15

Golden Mushroom Sauce

10-minute sauce for fish, poultry or red meats.

1 tablespoon tub margarine

Any or all of these to make 1 cup:
   1/3 cup chopped green pepper or celery
   1/3 cup chopped onion
   1/3 cup thinly sliced carrots

1 can (10 1/2 oz.) golden mushroom soup

Melt margarine in one-quart saucepan; add vegetables and stir until soft, about 4 minutes. Add soup and heat together for 3 minutes. Makes 1 1/2 cups of sauce or six 1/4-cup servings.

Many canned soups are low in fat. Select those with 3 grams of fat or less per serving, as shown on the can. Sauces, like this one, can be made with tomato, zesty tomato and cream of potato soups. Other fresh vegetables to add are mushrooms, parsley, tomatoes and summer squash. Refer to page 250 for a listing of low-fat canned soups.

Nutrients per serving:

calories 40
protein . . . . 0 gm
carbohydrate . . . . 3 gm
total fat . . . . 3 gm
saturated fat . . . . 1 gm
monounsat'd fat . . . . 1 gm
cholesterol . . . . 0 mg
sodium . . . . 240 mg
potassium . . . . 55 mg
fiber . . . . 1 gm

% US-RDA

vitamin A 30
vitamin C 12
thiamin . . . . ***
riboflavin . . . . ***
vitamin B$_6$ . . . . ***
folacin . . . . ***
iron . . . . ***
zinc . . . . ***
calcium 4

Quick Tomato Salsa

Your choice — hot or mild.

1 can (15 oz.) tomatoes, chopped but not
   drained

1 can (4 oz.) tomato puree

1 medium green pepper, chopped

1/4 cup dried onion flakes (or 1 small
   onion, chopped)

2 teaspoons chili powder

1/2 teaspoon cumin

1/4 teaspoon black pepper or to taste

1/4 teaspoon hot pepper sauce or to taste

1 can (4 oz.) chopped green chilies,
   drained

Combine all ingredients in jar. Cover tightly and
shake well. Chill at least 1 hour before serving.
Refrigerated salsa improves in flavor and keeps well for
several weeks. Makes 2½ cups or ten ¼-cup servings.

Serve on Mexican foods or as a sauce for cold meats.
To lower sodium levels, use fresh tomatoes.
For a tangy seafood dip, combine ½ cup salsa, ½ cup
salad dressing and ½ cup mock sour cream or low-fat yogurt.

Nutrients per serving:

calories	22
protein	1 gm
carbohydrate	5 gm
total fat	0 gm
saturated fat	0 gm
monounsat'd fat	0 gm
cholesterol	0 mg
sodium	80 mg
potassium	185 mg
fiber	1 gm

% US-RDA

vitamin A	13
vitamin C	36
thiamin	3
riboflavin	2
vitamin B_6	3
folacin	***
iron	6
zinc	11
calcium	3

Creole Sauce

Spicy sauce for fish, seafood, rice or beans.

1 tablespoon tub margarine

1 medium onion, chopped

1 medium green pepper, chopped

1 teaspoon garlic powder

**1 can (15 oz.) tomatoes, chopped, not drained
   or 5 medium tomatoes, peeled, chopped**

**1 tablespoon dried parsley flakes or 1/4 cup
   chopped fresh parsley**

2 teaspoons paprika

1 teaspoon sugar

1/8 teaspoon red pepper

1 bay leaf

1 cup fresh or frozen okra

1 tablespoon cornstarch

2 tablespoons cold water

Melt margarine in one-quart saucepan. Add onions, green pepper and garlic powder, heat and stir about 4 minutes until soft. Add remaining vegetables and herbs, bring to boil. Reduce heat, cover and simmer 30 minutes. Remove bay leaf. Mix cornstarch with cold water. Stirring constantly, slowly add cornstarch to sauce and cook until sauce is clear. Makes 1 1/2 cups or six 1/4-cup servings.

When using fish or seafood, add 1-inch pieces and cook about 5 minutes, or until fish flakes easily with a fork and serve over steamed rice.

Nutrients per serving:

calories	*54*
protein	*1 gm*
carbohydrate	*8 gm*
total fat	*2 gm*
saturated fat	*0 gm*
monounsat'd fat	*1 gm*
cholesterol	*0 mg*
sodium	*35 mg*
potassium	*265 mg*
fiber	*2 gm*

% US-RDA

vitamin A	*31*
vitamin C	*50*
thiamin	*7*
riboflavin	*5*
vitamin B₆	*5*
folacin	*8*
iron	*10*
zinc	*****
calcium	*2*

Medium White Sauce

White sauce is easy to make and is a real meal stretcher.

2 tablespoon tub margarine

4 tablespoons all-purpose or crystallized flour (see comment below)

2 cups ¹/₂% low-fat or skim milk

1 teaspoon lite salt

black pepper to taste

Melt margarine over low heat in one-quart saucepan. Add flour and cook for 4 minutes, stirring constantly to remove raw flour taste. Slowly and gently stir in milk, lite salt and pepper; continue stirring to prevent sticking. Simmer until sauce has thickened and is smooth and hot. The gentle use of a wire whip or wooden spoon and steady blending prevents the sauce from thinning down or lumping. Makes two 1-cup servings.

Crystallized flour is especially formulated to blend easily into liquids and water without lumping.

In 10 to 12 minutes you have a base for cream soups, tuna casserole or creamed meat over toast. Omit salt when a salty food is used. Vary the flavor by adding nutmeg or lemon juice, dried chopped onion or chopped chives or chopped parsley. Make your own cream soup by adding cooked potatoes, onions, carrots, celery, mushrooms and other vegetables.

Nutrients per serving:

calories	258
protein	10 gm
carbohydrate	23 gm
total fat	14 gm
saturated fat	3 gm
monounsat'd fat	6 gm
cholesterol	7 mg
sodium	600 mg
potassium	1000 mg
fiber	0 gm

% US-RDA

vitamin A	15
vitamin C	***
thiamin	6
riboflavin	11
vitamin B₆	***
folacin	3
iron	5
zinc	6
calcium	31

19

All About Marinades

M arinades are savory concoctions that bring out flavors, tenderize and moisturize. Even the beginning cook can become an expert. By mastering these simple steps, tasty fish, poultry or meat can be created for grilling, broiling or pan frying. On the following pages are recipes for basic seafood, beef and citrus marinades. Spice them up to suit your taste.

- *Three basic ingredients are:*

    1) Acid to tenderize: vinegar, soy sauce, yogurt, citrus juice, wine or beer.

    2) Oil to moisturize: use 2 parts acid to 1 part oil.

    3) Seasoning to dress up flavors.

- *Avoid salt because it pulls moisture from the meat.*

- *Always marinate in glass, porcelain or stainless steel. Don't use cast iron or aluminum as the acid reacts with the metal and gives an unpleasant appearance and flavor.*

- *Marinate fish fillets and vegetables up to 30 to 60 minutes, thick fishsteaks, chicken and chops up to 1 to 2 hours, large pieces of meat and less tender cuts of beef for 4 to 24 hours. Cut large chunks into smaller ones, score the surface to allow the marinade to penetrate and season.*

- *Do not marinate more than 24 hours because meat fibers will break down and the meat surface will become mushy.*

- *To prevent bacterial contamination,* DO NOT LEAVE AT ROOM TEMPERATURE MORE THAN 2 HOURS. *It is best to cover and marinate the food for the entire time in the refrigerator.*

Bring the left-over marinade to a boil before using as a basting sauce. Always discard any left-over marinade.

Basic Seafood Marinade

An easy way to improve flavors.

1/2 cup lemon juice

3 tablespoons canola or olive oil

1 teaspoon garlic powder

1/2 teaspoon marjoram or thyme

Combine all ingredients and mix well in a large glass baking dish. Turn and coat all surfaces of fish with marinade. Arrange fish or seafood in a single layer. Cover and refrigerate for 30 to 60 minutes. Makes 3/4 cup or marinates 6 servings.

Refer to fish cookery section for the best ways to bake, broil or grill fish.

To vary the recipe, use a total of 1 1/2 to 2 teaspoons of dried herbs such as parsley, tarragon, dill weed, chives, basil or rosemary. For a spicier flavor, add a dash of red pepper or Italian seasoning. Because only a small amount of marinade remains on the seafood, very few calories are added.

Nutrients per serving:

calories	10
protein	0 gm
carbohydrate	0 gm
total fat	1 gm
saturated fat	0 gm
monounsat'd fat	1 gm
cholesterol	0 mg
sodium	0 mg
potassium	6 mg
fiber	0 gm

% US-RDA

vitamin A	***
vitamin C	***
thiamin	***
riboflavin	***
vitamin B6	***
folacin	***
iron	***
zinc	***
calcium	***

Basic Beef Marinade

Great flavor! Especially for less tender cuts.

2/3 cup wine vinegar

1/3 cup canola or olive oil

1 tablespoon dried parsley flakes

1 teaspoon marjoram

1 teaspoon dry mustard

1 teaspoon paprika

1 teaspoon garlic powder

1 tablespoon dried onion flakes

Combine all ingredients and mix well in a large glass baking dish. Cut tougher meats into smaller pieces. Turn and coat all surfaces of meat with marinade. For flank or other less tender steaks, cut the surface with 1/4-inch deep slits at a 90° angle and work marinade into surface. Cover and marinate 4 to 24 hours. Makes 1 cup or marinates 6 servings.

Variations:
Add 1/4 to 1/2 teaspoon of one or some of these herbs: basil, ginger, red pepper, oregano, black pepper or thyme.
For a soy-flavored marinade, substitute 1/3 cup of lower sodium soy sauce for 1/3 cup wine vinegar.

Nutrients per serving:

calories	14
protein	0 gm
carbohydrate	1 gm
total fat	1 gm
saturated fat	0 gm
monounsat'd fat	1 gm
cholesterol	0 mg
sodium	0 mg
potassium	10 mg
fiber	0 gm

% US-RDA

vitamin A	***
vitamin C	***
thiamin	***
riboflavin	***
vitamin B6	***
folacin	***
iron	***
zinc	***
calcium	***

Citrus Marinade

A versatile one for fish, poultry, beef or pork.

1/2 cup orange juice

1/4 cup lemon or lime juice

1/4 cup canola or olive oil

1 tablespoon honey

1 teaspoon garlic powder

1 teaspoon dry mustard

black pepper to taste

2 teaspoons grated orange peel (optional)

Combine all ingredients and mix well in glass baking dish. Turn and coat all surfaces with marinade. To marinate, cover and refrigerate as follows:

Fish or seafood	30 to 60 minutes
Poultry	1 to 2 hours
Beef, pork and lamb	4 to 24 hours

Makes 1 cup or marinates 6 servings.

Marinade may be thickened with cornstarch or flour and used with cooked meat for a tasty sauce.

For a soy-flavored marinade, substitute 2 tablespoons lower sodium soy sauce for 2 tablespoons orange juice and add 1/2 teaspoon ginger or onion powder.

Nutrients per serving:

calories	*8*
protein	*0 gm*
carbohydrate	*2 gm*
total fat	*1 gm*
saturated fat	*0 gm*
monounsat'd fat	*1 gm*
cholesterol	*0 mg*
sodium	*0 mg*
potassium	*10 mg*
fiber	*0 gm*

% US-RDA

vitamin A	***
vitamin C	*5*
thiamin	***
riboflavin	***
vitamin B6	***
folacin	***
iron	***
zinc	***
calcium	***

Herbed Oil-and-Vinegar Dressing

Oil-vinegar-herb salad dressings are ready in 10 minutes.

$^1/_2$ cup canola or olive oil

$^1/_4$ cup water

$^1/_4$ cup vinegar

$^1/_2$ teaspoon lite salt

1 teaspoon paprika

1 teaspoon dry mustard

2 teaspoons dried parsley flakes

$^1/_2$ teaspoon garlic powder or 1 thinly sliced garlic clove

black pepper to taste

Nutrients per serving:

calories	*85*
protein	*0 gm*
carbohydrate	*1 gm*
total fat	*9 gm*
saturated fat	*1 gm*
monounsat'd fat	*7 gm*
cholesterol	*0 mg*
sodium	*75 mg*
potassium	*95 mg*
fiber	*0 gm*

% US-RDA

vitamin A	*8*
vitamin C	*4*
thiamin	*****
riboflavin	*****
vitamin B$_6$	*****
folacin	*****
iron	*4*
zinc	*****
calcium	*****

Combine all ingredients in glass container. Cap tightly and shake vigorously. Chill until ready to use. Flavor mellows when chilled at least 24 hours. Makes 1 cup or ten 1$^1/_2$-tablespoon servings.

In addition to giving flavor, paprika and mustard keeps the oil and vinegar mixed when shaken. Add herb powders to your taste. Soaking a thinly sliced garlic clove in oil and vinegar strengthens the garlic flavor.

Honey-Dijon Dressing

A thinner, tangier dressing that is lower in fat.

¹/₂ cup water

¹/₂ cup canola or olive oil

¹/₂ cup Dijon mustard

¹/₂ cup honey

1 cup white vinegar

Combine all ingredients in glass container. Cap tightly and shake vigorously. Chill until ready to use. Flavor improves when chilled at least 24 hours. Makes 3 cups or twenty-four 2-tablespoon servings.

Especially tasty over torn lettuces and greens. Try torn dark green, romaine, or red lettuce, torn fresh spinach leaves and thinly sliced radishes.

Making your own salad dressings is easy. Use canola or olive oil and herbs or packaged salad dressing mix.

Excellent reduced-fat and fat-free bottled salad dressings are available.

Nutrients per serving:

calories	*60*
protein	*0 gm*
carbohydrate	*5 gm*
total fat	*5 gm*
saturated fat	*1 gm*
monounsat'd fat	*3 gm*
cholesterol	*0 mg*
sodium	*60 mg*
potassium	*20 mg*
fiber	*0 gm*

% US-RDA

vitamin A	***
vitamin C	***
thiamin	***
riboflavin	***
vitamin B₆	***
folacin	***
iron	*2*
zinc	***
calcium	***

Creamy French Dressing

Always colorful and tasty on tossed vegetable salads.

1 cup salad dressing

2 tablespoons cider vinegar

2 tablespoons 1/2% low-fat or skim milk

1/2 teaspoon paprika

1/2 teaspoon dry mustard

1/2 teaspoon lite salt

Combine ingredients in glass container. Stir until well blended. Chill until ready to use. Makes 1 1/4 cups or ten 2-tablespoon servings.

Low-fat variations:
  Russian: Add 1/2 cup catsup, 2 teaspoons lemon juice, 2 teaspoons grated onion and a dash of horseradish.
  Thousand Island: Add 1/4 cup catsup or chili sauce, 1/4 cup finely chopped green pepper and 2 finely chopped egg whites or eggs.

Nutrients per serving:

calories	40
protein	1 gm
carbohydrate	4 gm
total fat	2 gm
saturated fat	1 gm
monounsat'd fat	1 gm
cholesterol	12 mg
sodium	205 mg
potassium	75 mg
fiber	0 gm

% US-RDA

vitamin A	***
vitamin C	***
thiamin	***
riboflavin	***
vitamin B$_6$	***
folacin	***
iron	2
zinc	***
calcium	2

Easy and Tart
Salad Dressing

Keep the smoothness and flavor without the fat!

1 cup plain low-fat yogurt

¹/₂ cup salad dressing

Combine ingredients well. Use immediately or keep as a base to use for other salad dressings. Makes 1¹/₂ cups or twelve 2-tablespoon servings.

Regular mayonnaise contains 11 grams of oil per tablespoon, while salad dressing has only 5 grams. This tangy dressing can be used as is or in salads needing an acid flavor such as coleslaw, pasta or potato salad.

Nutrients per serving:

calories	50
protein	1 gm
carbohydrate	4 gm
total fat	4 gm
saturated fat	1 gm
monounsat'd fat	1 gm
cholesterol	4 mg
sodium	80 mg
potassium	45 mg
fiber	0 gm

% US-RDA

vitamin A	***
vitamin C	***
thiamin	***
riboflavin	3
vitamin B_6	***
folacin	***
iron	***
zinc	***
calcium	4

Salad Topping Mix

A versatile, flavorful blend.

6 tablespoons sesame seeds

1 teaspoon celery seed

4 tablespoons onion powder

1 tablespoon garlic powder

4 teaspoons paprika

3 tablespoons poppy seeds (optional)

$^{1}/_{4}$ teaspoon black or white pepper

$^{1}/_{2}$ teaspoon lite salt

Combine all ingredients. Spoon into shaker, cap and refrigerate until ready to use. Makes 1 cup or thirty-two $^{1}/_{2}$-tablespoon servings.

Toasting the sesame seeds before combining adds a nutty flavor. Nutrient-laden seeds and herbs make a delicious and crunchy topping over vegetable salads, greens, sliced tomatoes, cottage cheese or baked potatoes.

Nutrients per serving:

calories	18
protein	1 gm
carbohydrate	2 gm
total fat	1 gm
saturated fat	0 gm
monounsat'd fat	1 gm
cholesterol	0 mg
sodium	20 mg
potassium	50 mg
fiber	0 gm

% US-RDA

vitamin A	3
vitamin C	***
thiamin	2
riboflavin	***
vitamin B$_6$	***
folacin	***
iron	3
zinc	2
calcium	2

Tartar Sauce

Always good with fish and seafood.

1/2 cup low-fat cottage cheese

1/2 cup salad dressing

1/4 cup finely chopped onion

1/4 cup sweet pickle relish

3 tablespoons dried parsley flakes or
  chopped fresh parsley

Blend together all ingredients. Can be used immediately or covered and kept for up to 3 days in coldest part of refrigerator. Do not freeze as the salad dressing will break down. Makes 1 1/2 cups sauce or eighteen 1 1/2-tablespoon servings.

The sauce is smoother if the cottage cheese is first creamed in the blender. Then, stir in the remaining ingredients.

Other flavorful additions include a dash of Dijon mustard or horseradish, chopped, hard cooked egg whites or egg, lemon juice or chopped dill pickles.

Nutrients per serving:

calories	47
protein	1 gm
carbohydrate	4 gm
total fat	3 gm
saturated fat	1 gm
monounsat'd fat	1 gm
cholesterol	2 mg
sodium	110 mg
potassium	15 mg
fiber	0 gm

% US-RDA

vitamin A	9
vitamin C	5
thiamin	2
riboflavin	***
vitamin B6	***
folacin	***
iron	2
zinc	***
calcium	***

Yogurt Dressing

A low-fat and tangy dressing for lettuce, vegetable salad, crackers, bread or meat.

1 cup plain low-fat yogurt

2 tablespoons canola or olive oil

2 tablespoons lemon juice

¹/₂ teaspoon lite salt

In the storage container, mix all ingredients together and blend until smooth. Cover and refrigerate for 3 hours to allow flavors to blend and mellow. Makes 1¹/₄ cups or thirteen 1¹/₂-tablespoon servings.

For horseradish sauce: add 2 tablespoons horseradish and/or ¹/₂ cup chili sauce.

For dill sauce: add 1 cup chopped cucumber (press and blot with paper towel to remove excess liquid), 2 teaspoons minced onion, ¹/₂ teaspoon dill weed and ¹/₂ teaspoon garlic powder.

Look carefully at the label. There is nonfat and low-fat plain yogurt. There is also plain vanilla yogurt, which is sweetened, and is best used with fruits and sweet foods. Some devoted yogurt-lovers prefer to use their yogurt without any herb or vegetable additions for salads, meats, breads and fruits.

Nutrients per serving:

calories	34
protein	1 gm
carbohydrate	4 gm
total fat	2 gm
saturated fat	1 gm
monounsat'd fat	1 gm
cholesterol	1 mg
sodium	50 mg
potassium	95 mg
fiber	0 gm

% US-RDA

vitamin A	***
vitamin C	2
thiamin	***
riboflavin	3
vitamin B₆	***
folacin	***
iron	***
zinc	***
calcium	4

Mock Sour Cream

A fast, tasty dressing for baked potatoes or base for dips.

½ cup ½% low-fat buttermilk

1 tablespoon canola oil

1 cup low-fat cottage cheese

or, for a more tart dressing:

½ cup ½% low-fat yogurt

1 tablespoon canola oil

1 cup low-fat cottage cheese

Combine all ingredients and blend until smooth. Makes 1½ cups, or eight 3-tablespoon servings.

Because commercial buttermilk has salt added, none needs to be added to the buttermilk recipe. Yogurt has a tangier flavor but has no added salt, so you may wish to add some. This low-fat dressing has a thick, full-bodied texture that can be used in place of sour cream in any cold recipe. In hot dishes, add just before serving to prevent break down or separation.

Nutrients per serving:

calories	34
protein	2 gm
carbohydrate	2 gm
total fat	2 gm
saturated fat	1 gm
monounsat'd fat	1 gm
cholesterol	1 mg
sodium	65 mg
potassium	25 mg
fiber	0 gm

% US-RDA

vitamin A	8
vitamin C	***
thiamin	2
riboflavin	5
vitamin B$_6$	2
folacin	2
iron	***
zinc	2
calcium	10

Buttermilk Ranch Dressing

Thick and rich but moderate in fat.

1¹/₄ cups ¹/₂% low-fat buttermilk

1 package (0.4 oz.) buttermilk ranch dressing

³/₄ cup salad dressing

Measure buttermilk into a storage container which has a lid. Sprinkle dressing mix on top of buttermilk and stir to blend. Add salad dressing and mix well. Cover tightly and shake vigorously. Refrigerate at least 30 minutes to allow dressing to thicken. Makes 2 cups or sixteen 2-tablespoon servings.

When made with fresh buttermilk (check the date on container), the refrigerated dressing will taste fresh for 2 to 3 weeks.

The original boiled salad dressing of yesteryear resembled mayonnaise but was made with a cooked cornstarch, egg and milk base and contained less fat than mayonnaise. Mayonnaise was almost pure egg yolk and oil. The commercial salad dressing available today is even lower in fat than the older versions and does not contain cholesterol laden egg yolk.

Nutrients per serving:

calories	86
protein	1 gm
carbohydrate	7 gm
total fat	6 gm
saturated fat	1 gm
monounsat'd fat	3 gm
cholesterol	10 mg
sodium	450 mg
potassium	45 mg
fiber	0 gm

% US-RDA

vitamin A	***
vitamin C	***
thiamin	***
riboflavin	3
vitamin B₆	***
folacin	***
iron	***
zinc	***
calcium	4

Fresh Citrus Dressing

Delicious five-minute dressing for fruit salads.

¹/₄ **cup lemon juice**

²/₃ **cup orange juice**

2 tablespoons honey

1 tablespoon canola or olive oil

3 teaspoons grated orange peel

dash of white pepper (optional)

Combine all ingredients in glass container. Cap tightly and shake vigorously. Chill until ready to use. Makes 1 cup or five 3-tablespoon servings.

Use this dressing over fresh melon cubes, orange and kiwi slices or banana chunks with mandarin sections or cottage cheese and fruit salads. To frame your salad, serve on bright green lettuce or spinach leaves.

Nutrients per serving:

calories	54
protein	0 gm
carbohydrate	9 gm
total fat	2 gm
saturated fat	0 gm
monounsat'd fat	2 gm
cholesterol	0 mg
sodium	3 mg
potassium	62 mg
fiber	0 gm

% US-RDA

vitamin A	***
vitamin C	20
thiamin	2
riboflavin	***
vitamin B₆	***
folacin	8
iron	2
zinc	***
calcium	***

Cranberry-Orange Sauce

A fast, do-ahead sauce that keeps well frozen or refrigerated.

1 medium naval orange, unpeeled, cut into eighths

1 medium apple, unpeeled, cut into eighths

1 package (12 oz.) fresh or frozen cranberries

1/2 cup orange juice

1 1/4 cups sugar

Combine all ingredients in food processor or food grinder. If a blender is used, grind half of ingredients at one time. Place in refrigerator for 4 hours for blending of flavors. Keeps several weeks in refrigerator. Makes 3 1/2 cups or eighteen 3-tablespoon servings.

Cranberry-orange sauce is delicious hot or cold with lean chicken, turkey or pork.

Or, make a colorful, fat-free molded salad with red raspberry gelatin (3 oz. package). Follow package directions. Allow the gelatin to thicken, then add 1 cup cranberry-orange sauce. Refrigerate at least 4 hours for gelatin salad to set.

Nutrients per serving:

calories	50
protein	0 gm
carbohydrate	13 gm
total fat	0 gm
saturated fat	0 gm
monounsat'd fat	0 gm
cholesterol	0 mg
sodium	13 mg
potassium	26 mg
fiber	1 gm

% US-RDA

vitamin A	***
vitamin C	9
thiamin	***
riboflavin	***
vitamin B$_6$	***
folacin	***
iron	***
zinc	***
calcium	***

Fruit Sauce

Instant, delicious nonfat topping.

1 cup fruit jam (plum, cherry, raspberry
    orange marmalade, strawberry,
    blackberry or grape)
3/4 cup light corn syrup

In a storage container with lid, mix jam and corn syrup to a well blended consistency. Use immediately, or cover and refrigerate for up to two weeks. Makes 1³/4 cups or fourteen 2-tablespoon servings.

The perfect topping for biscuits, pancakes, waffles, french toast, angel food cake, low-fat frozen yogurt or sherbet.
Another favorite is chocolate sauce, which can also be fat-free. Make your own sauce from our cocoa recipe (see page 205), or read the label and purchase the one with no added fat. Fudge sauces contain fats and oils.

Nutrients per serving:
calories *104*
protein . . . . *0 gm*
carbohydrate . . . . *26 gm*
total fat . . . . *0 gm*
saturated fat . . . . *0 gm*
monounsat'd fat . . . . *0 gm*
cholesterol . . . . *0 mg*
sodium . . . . *11 mg*
potassium . . . . *25 mg*
fiber . . . . *0 gm*

% US-RDA
vitamin A . . . . *****
vitamin C . . . . *****
thiamin . . . . *****
riboflavin . . . . *****
vitamin B_6 . . . . *****
folacin . . . . *****
iron . . . . *****
zinc . . . . *****
calcium . . . . *****

Rum Hard Sauce

For the sweet tooth, an easy to make dessert topping.

2 cups powdered sugar, unsifted

2 tablespoons tub margarine

2 tablespoons hot water

2 teaspoons rum or brandy extract

1 teaspoon vanilla

Combine all ingredients in small mixing bowl. Beat at high speed until well blended. Cover and keep at room temperature until serving time. This sauce becomes too firm when refrigerated. Makes 1¹/₄ cups sauce or ten 2-tablespoon servings.

For a special touch, serve over gingerbread or cold desserts.

Nutrients per serving:

calories	*123*
protein	*0 gm*
carbohydrate	*24 gm*
total fat	*3 gm*
saturated fat	*1 gm*
monounsat'd fat	*1 gm*
cholesterol	*0 mg*
sodium	*40 mg*
potassium	*4 mg*
fiber	*0 gm*

% US-RDA

vitamin A	*3*
vitamin C	*****
thiamin	*****
riboflavin	*****
vitamin B₆	*****
folacin	*****
iron	*****
zinc	*****
calcium	*****

Ready to use Seasonings, Sauces and Vinegars

	Amount	Fat gm	Sodium mg	Calories
Sauce:				
Barbecue	1 tablespoon	*	120	13
Catsup	1 tablespoon	*	150	16
Chili Sauce	1 tablespoon	*	200	16
Horseradish	1 tablespoon	*	17	10
Mustard, Dijon	1 tablespoon	*	195	15
Mustard, Yellow	1 tablespoon	*	190	15
Pickles, Dill	2 slices	*	186	1
Salsa (Picante)	¼ cup	*	320	27
Pickle Relish, Sweet	1 tablespoon	*	107	15
Soy sauce	1 tablespoon	*	1030	14
Soy sauce, lower sodium	1 tablespoon	*	515	14
Steak	1 tablespoon	*	150	18
Sweet and Sour	¼ cup	*	320	131
Spaghetti	½ cup	4	925	80
Tabasco	1 teaspoon	*	0	0
Taco, Hot/Mild	2 teaspoons	*	100	4
Teriyaki	1 tablespoon	*	690	15
Worcestershire	1 tablespoon	*	147	12
Mushrooms:				
Fresh, sliced	¼ cup	*	9	5
Canned, sliced	¼ cup	*	450	20
Pimentos, canned	2 tablespoons	*	0	15
Vinegars:				
All vinegars; distilled, cider, red wine, white wine and herbed	1 tablespoon	*	1	2

*Less than one gram
(continued)

Sauces (continued)

	Amount	Fat gm	Sodium mg	Calories
Juices:				
Lime	1 tablespoon	*	0	4
Orange	1 tablespoon	*	0	7
Tomato, salted	1 tablespoon	*	35	3
Tomato, salt free	1 tablespoon	*	1	3

A common question is, "what can I substitute for wine?" Depending upon the recipe, you might try a tart fruit juice, or use half as much vinegar as wine; substitute broth, or use some combination of these liquids.

*Less than one gram

Understanding Complex Carbohydrates

T he world is full of myths and the world of food is no exception. One myth we would like to dispel is that carbohydrate foods are fattening and should be avoided.

Carbohydrates are actually healthy and delicious mainstays in a well-rounded diet.

Epidemiologic studies have shown that populations eating high carbohydrate diets rich in rice, dried beans, soybeans, grain, pasta, breads and potatoes are healthier than those eating high animal food diets. High carbohydrate eaters weigh less and have lower rates of coronary heart disease and diabetes.

Why? Carbohydrates are burned for quick energy while fat passes through a more complicated cycle before it is converted to energy. This, in part, may be why fat sticks to the body and is so difficult to lose.

In our culture, we assume overweight people are gluttonous eaters of rich, calorie laden foods. The truth of the matter is that many obese people take in fewer calories than people of normal weight! However, they expend fewer calories. Research has shown overweight people engage in less physical movement and spend more time reclining and sitting. Muscle movement is needed to burn calories and to prevent foods from being turned into fat.

Before we delve into the savory foods high in carbohydrates, let us take a look at where they come from and what they do. Carbohydrates are the movers and shakers of the food world. Think of them as Type A personalities, the ones who like to get up and go! Though they have a lofty responsibility, their roots are rather humble — starting with a simple plant and a glistening ray of sunshine.

Carbohydrates are made when the leaves of a plant absorb carbon dioxide from the air and the roots soak up water from the soil. Energy from sunlight is harnessed by green chlorophyll in plant leaves, which enables them to make sugar. Sugars are the building blocks of carbohydrates. Starches (the everyday name for complex carbohydrates) are made up of more than ten sugar molecules. More complex carbohydrates are made from several hundred sugar molecules. Some of these complicated molecules become fibers that are not digestible by the body.

One major misconception about nutrition is that high-starch foods are fattening. Foods such as bread and potatoes aren't the culprit. It is the company they keep — calorie-rich toppings such as butter, sour cream and gravy. Remember, pure starches provide only about 110 calories per ounce while pure fat provides 250. Eating more starchy foods is a good way to fill up with fewer calories, provided you watch those additions. A medium potato provides only 3/4 ounce of starch (85 carbohydrate calories) and is about 80 percent water.

Any food derived solely from a plant, such as a high-carbohydrate food like potatoes, is cholesterol-free. That is because plants are cholesterol-free; only animal products contain cholesterol.

Most parts of a plant are nutrient rich. For example, whole grains and dried beans and peas are the nutrient-laden seeds of plants. The seed germ is packed with B vitamins, iron, zinc and other trace minerals required to start the new plant. The grains, legumes and starchy vegetables are such efficient packages of nutrition that you can get most of the calories, proteins, vitamins, minerals and dietary fiber you need from them.

Also, it is now known that plant protein tends to reduce blood cholesterol levels. This may help explain why vegetarians have lower blood cholesterol in spite of their higher intake of eggs and cheese.

In the following selection of recipes, you will find many high-carbohydrate dishes that will leave your palate and tummy more than satisfied. These foods can be quite hearty, so try eating some of them as a main dish, accompanied by your favorite vegetable.

Typically, we eat four to eight ounces of meat with three to four ounces of starch per meal. A more wholesome and less expensive way is to reverse this pattern by eating two servings of fiber-rich carbohydrate foods and a three ounce portion of cooked fish, poultry or lean red meat.

For example:

- *Eat a larger serving of pasta with less meat in your spaghetti sauce.*
- *Enjoy both potatoes and a roll with your meal.*
- *Have a large serving of breakfast cereal with a slice of toast instead of eggs and bacon.*
- *Work a 1/3 cup serving of beans into soups, casseroles, salads and sandwich spreads.*
- *Include more pasta, rice or potatoes and smaller amounts of fish, poultry and meat in casseroles and mixed dishes.*

In the following recipe sections we have grouped these high carbohydrate foods according to the way most people use them:

- *Breads, grains and cereals, purchased ready-to-eat or prepared from scratch, are delicious additions to most any meal.*
- *Pasta and rice are typically used to accompany the main dish or are combined into casseroles.*
- *Although potatoes are a rich carbohydrate food, they are primarily a vegetable and are explained in that section.*
- *Dried beans are often used as a main dish item and are grouped with those foods.*

Don't Forget Your Fiber

For years, fiber was a forgotten item. The menu prescription of the past advised us to eat diets high in protein with generous servings of meat and eggs, neither of which provide any fiber. Then, research in the 1970s began to show that food fibers not only aid healthy intestinal functioning, but have some beneficial effects on gastrointestinal problems, cardiovascular disease, diabetes mellitus and in the possible prevention of colon cancer.

Now that is a lofty case for fiber.

Dietary fiber generally refers to parts of fruits, vegetables and grains that can't be digested by humans. Meats and dairy products don't contain fiber; the fiber-like substances in meat are digestible connective tissue. The two basic types of fiber are soluble and insoluble. Most foods containing fiber feature both, but one type or the other often predominates.

Soluble fibers are found within plant cells. The gummy texture of oat bran and the mushy center of a cooked bean reflect both the soluble fiber content of those foods and the ability of those fibers to soak up water. The gel-like substance adds to fecal bulk and increases its water content. A diet low in fat and high in soluble fiber may reduce blood cholesterol by three to six percent by binding cholesterol in the digestive tract and then eliminating it.

The water insoluble dietary fibers are the structural parts of plants. These retain water, increase the volume of bowel movements, soften the stool and cause the intestine to move the food along quickly. Insoluble fibers, such as bran, seem to have the greatest effect on the colon or large intestine. The best-established benefit of a high insoluble fiber diet is the treatment and prevention of constipation. If you have diarrhea, fiber will slow down the frequency of bowel movements, too.

For a healthy, fiber-rich diet, try to increase your dietary fiber intake to the recommended 25 to 35 grams a day. Do this by eating a variety of foods and not by relying on fiber supplements. Mother Nature had wonderful reasons for creating fiber-laden foods and we should take advantage of them rather than using substitutes.

How do you know if you are getting enough fiber? "Floaters" and "Sinkers" will tell you. The bowel movement containing plenty of fiber is large, soft, contains gas bubbles from the normal, healthy fermentation of fiber that occurs in the colon, and will float. Sinkers are hard and small, the result of eating highly refined (fiber removed) white breads, crackers and cereals and very little fruits and vegetables. A high protein, low carbohydrate diet will also produce sinkers.

Increase your fiber consumption slowly. Gradually increase high fiber foods in your diet and accompany this new addition with plenty of liquids. Water is an excellent choice.

The chart below shows rich sources of soluble and insoluble fiber. Consult pages 262 to 267 for a comprehensive listing in grams, of total dietary fiber in common foods.

Sources of Fiber

Higher in Soluble Fiber	Contain Both Soluble and Insoluble Fiber	Higher in Insoluble Fiber
Barley	Dried beans/peas	Wheat bran
Citrus fruits	Oat bran	Corn bran
Psyllium	Oatmeal	Rice bran
Pectin	Apples	Nuts
	Potatoes	Whole wheat products
	Broccoli	Brown rice
	Carrots	Bananas
		Cauliflower
		Green beans
		Green peas

Whole Grains — The Staff of Life

Using breads and cereals.

Look in any supermarket and you will find aisles bountifully heaped with luscious bakery items and cereals. Such items originated, however, from nutrient-laden whole grains that are very low in fat, but high in fiber, complex carbohydrates, B vitamins, iron and zinc. Include six or more servings of whole grains each day. Health-wise ways to do it are:

- *One serving consists of one slice or one ounce of bread or roll, 1/2 to 2/3 cup cooked cereal or one ounce of ready-to-eat cereal.*

- *Choose loaf breads, rolls and crackers made from whole wheat, whole grain mixtures, rye or enriched flours.*

- *Bake your own bread from frozen dough. A simple method is on page 45.*

- *Add variety with English muffins, tortillas, pita and bagels.*

- *Eat low-fat crackers and breads such as matzo, bread sticks, Swedish and rye wafers, zwieback and unsalted crackers.*

- *Read labels and choose items made with unhydrogenated vegetable oils and containing only one to two grams of fat per serving.*

- *Use the basic Quick Mix recipe on page 47 for making fragrant hot-to-the-table breads. Avoid packaged muffin, biscuit and quick breads which are high in fat and saturated fat.*

- *Before purchasing packaged cereal, consult the Ready-to-Eat Cereals chart on page 55. Also refer to the information on hot quick-cooking cereals on page 57 and the suggestions for enhancing cereal with fruit and nuts on page 58.*

Home Baked Bread

Everyone loves the aroma and taste of freshly baked bread.

Once you try use this easy method, you will use it often.

1 (16 oz.) frozen bread loaf. One to four loaves can be prepared and baked at the same time. Baking time will be 8 to 15 minutes longer with more loaves.

tub margarine

Preheat oven to 200°; turn off oven. While oven is warming, heat 2 quarts water to rolling boil in a large saucepan; place pan in oven. The moist heat keeps the oven warm and makes covering the bread unnecessary. Oil 8½x4x3-inch loaf pan and frozen loaf with tub margarine. Place bread in oven, close the door, and allow to rise until dough is one inch above pan, about one to three hours. *SET THE TIMER TO REMIND YOURSELF THE BREAD IS RISING.* The rising time will vary with the warmth of the oven and room. To speed up the rising process, reheat the pan of water and return it to oven. Remove bread and water from oven.

Preheat oven to 375°. Bake 25 to 30 minutes or until top is golden brown and sounds hollow when tapped on crusty surface. Remove baked loaf from pan immediately, turn on side and cool on wire rack. For a soft crust, brush hot bread with margarine. For easier slicing, let bread cool thoroughly. Loaf should be placed on side and sliced with a serrated or electric knife to prevent crushing. Makes 16 slices.

Nutrients per serving:

calories	*70*
protein	*2 gm*
carbohydrate	*12 gm*
total fat	*1 gm*
saturated fat	*0 gm*
monounsat'd fat	*1 gm*
cholesterol	*0 mg*
sodium	*120 mg*
potassium	*27 mg*
fiber	*0 gm*

% US-RDA

vitamin A	***
vitamin C	***
thiamin	*5*
riboflavin	*5*
vitamin B_6	***
folacin	*6*
iron	*5*
zinc	***
calcium	***

Herbed Breads

Make breads special with a variety of toppings!

1 thick slice of bread

1 teaspoon softened tub margarine

sprinkle of herbs

Spread a thin layer of softened tub margarine on bread. Add flavor with herbs instead of fat. Serve immediately or warm the bread, uncovered, in 350° oven for 5 to 7 minutes. Makes 1 serving.

Bread
Whole wheat, rye, French, Italian, sourdough, English muffins, white loaf bread, split bagels, left-over dinner rolls

Herbs
Garlic powder, Italian herb mixture, onion powder, parsley, chives, thyme, dill, celery, caraway or poppy seed, basil, marjoram, oregano

Eating generous amounts of bread lightly spread with margarine and herbs is a delightful and satisfying low-fat way to get your complex carbohydrates, B vitamins iron and varying amounts of fiber.

Nutrients per serving:

calories	128
protein	3 gm
carbohydrate	20 gm
total fat	4 gm
saturated fat	1 gm
monounsat'd fat	2 gm
cholesterol	0 mg
sodium	260 mg
potassium	30 mg
fiber	1 gm

% US-RDA

vitamin A	3
vitamin C	***
thiamin	7
riboflavin	7
vitamin B$_6$	***
folacin	10
iron	7
zinc	***
calcium	***

Quick Mix

From start to clean up, this mix takes 30 minutes.

5¹/₂ cups all-purpose flour

5 cups whole wheat flour

¹/₄ cup baking powder

1 tablespoon lite salt

¹/₂ cup wheat germ (optional)

In a large bowl, sift together all ingredients except wheat germ. Blend in wheat germ but do not sift. Place in large air-tight container. Label with current date; store in cool dry place. Use within 10 to 12 weeks. Makes 11 cups of mix.

Versatile Quick Mix recipes are included for biscuits, cornbread, sugar and molasses cookies, hot fudge pudding and fruit cobbler (See Quick Recipe Finder on pages vi to xvi).

Whole wheat flour, all-purpose flour or any combination of flours for a total of 10¹/₂ cups may be used.

Nutrients per 1 cup mix:

calories	433
protein	15 gm
carbohydrate	91 gm
total fat	1 gm
saturated fat	0 gm
monounsat'd fat	1 gm
cholesterol	0 mg
sodium	550 mg
potassium	680 mg
fiber	9 gm

% US-RDA

vitamin A	***
vitamin C	***
thiamin	61
riboflavin	23
vitamin B_6	14
folacin	22
iron	25
zinc	12
calcium	7

Homemade Biscuits

Ready for the oven in 10 minutes.

2 cups Quick Mix (see page 47)

1/3 cup canola oil

2/3 cups 1/2% low-fat or skim milk

Preheat oven to 425°. Measure mix into large bowl. Pour oil and milk into measuring cup, don't stir. Dump oil and milk into mix and stir with a fork to form a ball. A dry dough mixture makes a dry biscuit; a moist dough, a moist one. Add a little more liquid if the ball does not hold together. Knead ball in bowl 10 times. On an unoiled cookie sheet, press the ball into a 7x7x1/2-inch thick square and cut into 16 squares. Separate squares leaving about 1-inch between biscuits. Bake for 12 to 15 minutes until golden brown. Makes 16 biscuits.

Variations:

Low-fat buttermilk may be used in the same amount (with 1/4 teaspoon baking soda first stirred into mix) for a more tender biscuit.

For drop biscuits, increase milk or buttermilk to 1 cup. Oil the cookie sheet.

For herbed biscuits, mix in dried minced onion or onion powder, garlic bits or powder, parsley, chives or other herbs to your liking.

For cinnamon biscuits, knead and roll each one in cinnamon-sugar mixture before baking on oiled cookie sheet.

Nutrients per serving:

calories	100
protein	2 gm
carbohydrate	12 gm
total fat	5 gm
saturated fat	1 gm
monounsat'd fat	3 gm
cholesterol	0 mg
sodium	100 mg
potassium	150 mg
fiber	1 gm

% US-RDA

vitamin A	***
vitamin C	***
thiamin	8
riboflavin	3
vitamin B6	4
folacin	4
iron	3
zinc	2
calcium	2

Buttermilk Cornbread

*Two recipes and both are quick
and easy to prepare.*

1 egg or 2 egg whites or ¼ cup egg substitute

1½ cups low-fat buttermilk or skim milk

1½ cups cornmeal

½ cup all-purpose flour

1 teaspoon sugar (optional)

2 teaspoons baking powder

½ teaspoon baking soda

1 teaspoon lite salt

¼ cup canola oil

Preheat oven to 450°. Combine egg and buttermilk. Add remaining ingredients and mix well. Pour batter into lightly oiled skillet or 9x9-inch pan. Bake 20 to 25 minutes. Makes 12 servings.

Quick Mix Cornbread:

1 egg or 2 egg whites or ¼ cup egg substitute
1¼ cup ½% low-fat or skim milk (do not use buttermilk).
1½ cups Quick Mix (see page 47)
¾ cup cornmeal
⅓ cup canola oil
½ teaspoon baking powder

Combine and bake as for buttermilk cornbread. Nutritional analysis is approximately the same for both recipes.

Nutrients per serving:

calories	*150*
protein	*4 gm*
carbohydrate	*20 gm*
total fat	*6 gm*
saturated fat	*1 gm*
monounsat'd fat	*3 gm*
cholesterol	*18 mg*
sodium	*200 mg*
potassium	*200 mg*
fiber	*1 gm*

% US-RDA

vitamin A	*3*
vitamin C	*****
thiamin	*9*
riboflavin	*6*
vitamin B₆	*10*
folacin	*4*
iron	*6*
zinc	*2*
calcium	*6*

Buttermilk Pancakes

Pancake mixes can speed preparation. Or, try this homemade variation from an old Wisconsin logger, Eric Soderberg.

1¼ cups ½% low-fat buttermilk

1 egg or ¼ cup egg substitute

1 tablespoon canola oil

½ cup whole wheat flour

½ cup all-purpose flour

½ teaspoon baking powder

½ teaspoon baking soda

½ teaspoon lite salt

Nutrients per serving:

calories.....................*74*
protein...................*3 gm*
carbohydrate...........*11 gm*
total fat...................*2 gm*
saturated fat..............*1 gm*
monounsat'd fat.........*1 gm*
cholesterol.............*22 mg*
sodium................*240 mg*
potassium.............*160 mg*
fiber.......................*1 gm*

% US-RDA

vitamin A..................*****
vitamin C...................*****
thiamin....................*7*
riboflavin...................*7*
vitamin B6................*3*
folacin....................*4*
iron......................*3*
zinc.......................*2*
calcium....................*6*

Preheat griddle (see temperature test below). Spread griddle with thin film of canola oil. Whip together buttermilk, egg and oil. Mix in flours, baking powder, baking soda and lite salt. Pour onto hot griddle. When bubbles break on the surface, turn and brown the other side. Makes ten 4-inch pancakes.

To test griddle for the right temperature, let a few drops of cold water fall on it. If the water bounces and sputters, the griddle is ready to use. Pour the batter from the tip of a spoon, close to griddle surface. The batter should round out at the edges and not run. Batter that is too thick makes a dry and high pancake.

Silver Dollar Pancakes

A delightful treat for any meal.

¾ **cup all-purpose flour**

1 **tablespoon sugar**

½ **teaspoon lite salt**

1 **cup ½% low-fat or skim milk**

1 **egg**

3 **egg whites or ⅓ cup egg substitute**

2 **tablespoons canola oil**

6 **tablespoons tart jelly or jam**

powdered sugar

Preheat oven to 250°. Mix flour, sugar and lite salt together in a mixing bowl. In another bowl whip milk, eggs and egg whites; add dry ingredients and beat until smooth. Brush griddle surface with a film of canola oil. Heat griddle until a drop of water dances on the hot surface. Re-oil griddle after each batch. For each cake, pour 2 teaspoons of batter on griddle. Cook until surface of each cake looks set and continue cooking until lightly browned on bottom. Turn browned side up, dot each cake with jelly and stack on warmed plate. Keep in oven until all are cooked. Move to heated serving plates, dust cakes with powdered sugar. Makes 60 cakes or 4 servings.

Serve with lean Canadian bacon or crisp turkey bacon, a large glass of orange juice and low-fat milk for breakfast, lunch or supper.

Nutrients per serving:
calories *303*
protein .... *9 gm*
carbohydrate .... *46 gm*
total fat .... *9 gm*
saturated fat .... *2 gm*
monounsat'd fat .... *5 gm*
cholesterol .... *55 mg*
sodium .... *190 mg*
potassium .... *340 mg*
fiber .... *1 gm*

% US-RDA

vitamin A 15
vitamin C .... ***
thiamin 15
riboflavin 16
vitamin B₆ 16
folacin 6
iron 9
zinc 4
calcium 12

Easy French Toast

And better than ever!

3/4 cup egg substitute or 6 egg whites

1/4 cup 1/2% low-fat milk or skim milk

1/2 teaspoon lite salt

1 teaspoon sugar

1/2 teaspoon vanilla (optional)

1/4 teaspoon cinnamon (optional)

4 large slices day old bread or French bread

Preheat griddle to medium heat, about 325°. Spread thin film of canola oil over griddle surface. Pour egg substitute and milk into pie pan; add lite salt, sugar, vanilla and cinnamon. If using egg whites, blend well with milk. Whip with fork to mix all ingredients. Dip bread one slice at a time into egg mixture, coating both sides evenly, and immediately place on hot griddle. Brown 3 to 4 minutes; turn and brown 3 to 4 minutes on other side. Makes 2 servings.

French toast isn't just for breakfast. Try it for brunch, lunch or supper. Use a variety of breads: white, wheat and oatmeal are good. Top with fruit, fruit sauces (see Quick Recipe Finder on pages xiv and xv), jams, jellies or syrup.

Nutrients per serving:

calories	*320*
protein	*15 gm*
carbohydrate	*38 gm*
total fat	*12 gm*
saturated fat	*2 gm*
monounsat'd fat	*7 gm*
cholesterol	*0 mg*
sodium	*835 mg*
potassium	*590 mg*
fiber	*2 gm*

% US-RDA

vitamin A	*30*
vitamin C	*****
thiamin	*30*
riboflavin	*41*
vitamin B$_6$	*18*
folacin	*14*
iron	*46*
zinc	*11*
calcium	*24*

Oat Bran Muffins

Delicious way to get 10 percent of your daily fiber requirement.

1 cup whole wheat flour

1 cup oat bran or whole grain uncooked cereal

1/2 cup brown sugar, firmly packed

1/2 teaspoon baking soda

2 1/2 teaspoons baking powder

1 teaspoon lite salt

1 teaspoon cinnamon

2 egg whites, well beaten, or 1/4 cup egg substitute

3/4 cup 1/2% low-fat or skim milk

1/4 cup canola oil

1 cup applesauce, unsweetened or sweetened

Preheat oven to 350°. Oil 12-cup muffin tin. In large bowl combine dry ingredients, blending well with fork. In a small bowl, whip egg whites until frothy, add milk and oil and mix well; stir in applesauce. Combine applesauce mixture with flour-bran mixture, stir until just blended. Do not over mix. Fill each muffin cup almost full. Bake 20 minutes or until golden brown. Makes 12 servings.

Double the recipe. Sealed in air-tight containers, frozen muffins will keep a month. To make pancakes with the same batter, increase milk to 1 1/2 cups.

Nutrients per serving:

calories	145
protein	4 gm
carbohydrate	21 gm
total fat	5 gm
saturated fat	1 gm
monounsat'd fat	3 gm
cholesterol	0 mg
sodium	190 mg
potassium	230 mg
fiber	3 gm

% US-RDA

vitamin A	***
vitamin C	***
thiamin	9
riboflavin	3
vitamin B$_6$	3
folacin	6
iron	7
zinc	***
calcium	5

Honey Fruit Granola

Delicious as a breakfast cereal or a crunchy topping for fruit or yogurt.

1 tablespoon canola oil

1²/₃ cups uncooked oat bran

1 cup quick uncooked oatmeal

¹/₃ cup instant nonfat dry milk

2 teaspoons grated orange peel

1¹/₂ teaspoon lite salt

2 medium apples, unpeeled and chopped

1 teaspoon vanilla

¹/₂ cup honey

²/₃ cup chopped almonds or walnuts

¹/₂ cup raisins or chopped dates

Nutrients per serving:

calories	*264*
protein	*8 gm*
carbohydrate	*40 gm*
total fat	*8 gm*
saturated fat	*1 gm*
monounsat'd fat	*5 gm*
cholesterol	*0 mg*
sodium	*70 mg*
potassium	*815 mg*
fiber	*7 gm*

% US-RDA

vitamin A	***
vitamin C	***
thiamin	*10*
riboflavin	*9*
vitamin B₆	*4*
folacin	*4*
iron	*33*
zinc	*4*
calcium	*9*

Preheat oven to 350°. Spread oil over bottom of 9x13x2-inch heavy-bottomed baking pan. In same pan, combine oat bran, oatmeal, nonfat dry milk, orange peel, lite salt, apples and vanilla. Mix repeatedly by mounding in center of baking pan, then making a "volcano" hole and spreading the walls of the "volcano" evenly to sides of pan. Repeat mixing method until thoroughly mixed. Drizzle honey in a thin stream over entire granola surface. Bake 10 minutes and mix again. Repeat mixing at 10 to 15 minute intervals until golden brown. Mix in almonds and dried fruit. Cool. Store, tightly covered, in refrigerator for up to one week or freeze for up to two months. Makes ten ¹/₂-cup (2 ounce) servings.

Most granola cereals are high in fat. Not only is this one moderate in fat, it is mostly the desirable monounsaturated fat. Eat and enjoy this delicious, high fiber dish.

Ready-To-Eat Cereals

Choosing a wholesome cereal is easy.

Use these guidelines to evaluate the nutrition information on labels. Most people prefer to eat two ounces — not the one ounce usually referred to on package labels. Without added milk, one ounce should contain:

- *Whole grain or bran as first ingredient*
- *Two grams or more of dietary fiber*
- *Two grams or less of fat and contain no palm, coconut or hydrogenated fats or oils*
- *Seven grams (1¹/₂ teaspoons) or less of sugar or sweeteners*
- *350 milligrams or less of sodium*
- *70 to 115 calories*

Many cereals meet these criteria. Examples are:

One Ounce	Vol.	Cal.	Bran/Grain	Dietary Fiber gm	Fat gm	Sugar[a] gm	Sodium mg
All Bran	¹/₃ cup	71	wheat bran	2.0	0.5	5	320
Bran, 100%	¹/₂ cup	76	wheat bran	5.0	1.4	5	195
Cheerios	1 cup	110	whole oats	3.0	2.0	1	300
Health Valley Fruit and Nut Bran	³/₄ cup	90	oats, oat bran	3.0	2.0	0	3
Fiber Cereal with Fruit	¹/₂ cup	87	whole grains	4.0	0.3	3	195
Grape-Nuts	¹/₄ cup	110	wheat, barley	3.0	0.3	0	170

One Ounce	Vol.	Cal.	Bran/Grain	Dietary Fiber gm	Fat gm	Sugar[a] gm	Sodium mg
Nutri-Grain Wheat Flakes	3/4 cup	102	whole wheat	2.5	0.3	2	195
Wheat Chex	2/3 cup	104	whole wheat	2.5	0.6	2	190
Shredded Wheat	1 biscuit	83	whole wheat	3.0	0.3	0	0
Wheaties	1 cup	99	whole wheat	2.5	0.5	3	350
Quaker Oat Squares	1/2 cup	100	whole oats	2.0	2.0	5	160
Post Oat Flakes	2/3 cup	110	whole oats	2.0	1.0	6	140

[a] *or Sugary Sweeteners*

Hot, Quick Cooking Cereals

Freshly ground cereals are the most flavorful, but they need 30 to 50 minutes of cooking time. Fast-cooking cereals, ready in five to 10 minutes, are ideal for the busy family. Try the whole grain cereals or add wheat germ, oat bran, fresh or dried fruits to increase fiber. One ounce uncooked dry cereal makes six ounces of cooked cereal.

Six Ounces Cooked Cereal (³/₄ cup):

	Calories	Bran/Grain	Dietary Fiber gm	Fat gm	Sugar gm	Sod-ium[a] mg
Corn Grits	110	cracked corn starch	1.4	0.5	0	0
Cream of Rice	95	cracked rice starch	0.8	0.1	0	1
Cream of Wheat	100	cracked wheat starch	0.8	0.4	0	2
Farina	90	cracked wheat starch	0.8	0.1	0	1
Maltex	130	cracked whole grains	3.0	0.8	0	7
Malt-o-Meal	90	cracked wheat starch	0.8	0.2	0	2
Oatmeal	110	rolled whole oats	3.0	1.8	0	1
Ralston	100	cracked whole wheat	3.5	0.6	0	3
Roman Meal	110	cracked whole grains	3.5	0.7	0	2
Quaker Whole Wheat	110	rolled whole wheat	3.5	0.7	0	1

[a] *¹/₄ teaspoon lite salt per serving adds 250 milligrams sodium and 375 milligrams potassium*

Cereal Enhancers

Increase flavor and fiber in both ready-to-eat and hot cooked cereal with:

Item	Quantity	Cal.	Dietary Fiber gm	Fat gm	Sugar gm	Sodium mg
Almonds	12 chopped	90	1.0	4.0	0	0
Apples	1/2 cup chopped	80	1.5	0.5	4	1
Dates	5 chopped	114	1.8	0.4	10	2
Fruit, dried	2 tbsp. chopped	40	1.0	0.2	6	3
Raisins	2 tablespoons	25	1.3	0.2	5	0
Oat Bran	2 tablespoons	40	4.4	1.5	0	0
Wheat Germ	2 tablespoons	50	1.5	0.7	0	1

A Pasta for Every Occasion

P asta, especially thin varieties, are ideal for a quick meal. They are tasty with plain or herbed margarine, or are easily combined in a main dish. Pasta is fat free, high in complex carbohydrates and is a good source for B vitamins, iron and protein. Pasta digests slowly giving a lasting, satisfied feeling. Perfect pasta is easy to cook.

- *Pasta doubles in quantity during cooking. One fourth cup (2 ounces dry) becomes a 1/2 cup serving of 100 calories.*

- *For each eight ounces of pasta, heat three quarts of water and one teaspoon of lite salt to boiling in a large pot. To prevent boiling over, add one teaspoon vegetable oil. Add pasta gradually so the water doesn't stop boiling.*

- *Most pasta shapes can be interchanged by substituting them ounce for ounce in recipes.*

- *Cook pasta uncovered, stirring occasionally to separate until it is* al dente, *which is Italian for "firm to the bite". Al dente pasta is tender but still firm in the middle, with no raw taste.*

- *Use a long handled wooden fork or pronged pasta server for stirring and lifting strands from the pot to test for doneness.*

- *Follow the package directions for cooking times. If pasta is being used in a casserole and will be cooked longer than the recommended time, reduce cooking time by one third.*

- *For long pasta, such as vermicelli and spaghetti, place ends in boiling water. As pasta softens, coil it around the pan until it is completely under water.*

- *Drain immediately in colander or strainer. Add a teaspoon of vegetable oil to prevent sticking. If you are a pasta connoisseur, drop pasta in a second pot of boiling water to remove the starch film and drain again.*

- *To store left-over pasta, add another teaspoon of oil and keep in a tightly sealed container for up to four days in the refrigerator. Reheat by adding to boiling water for two minutes and then serving immediately. The microwave is great for warming up left-over pasta.*

- *The mild flavor of pasta blends well with cooked sauces, meats and vegetables or cold with crisp, fresh vegetables.*

Only a few years ago, pasta meant noodles, spaghetti and macaroni. Today, our pasta consumption includes a multitude of shapes eaten in dozens of luscious ways. Nearly 150 pasta shapes are produced in the United States using superior durum and other hard wheats under the strictest of manufacturing standards. Varieties include:

- *Long strands — linguine, fettuccine and spinach fettuccine, vermicelli, thin and regular spaghetti.*

- *Noodle shapes — thin, medium and wide noodles; lasagna.*

- *Tube shapes — small, medium and large elbow macaroni; manicotti, cannelloni and grooved rigatoni.*

- *Fun shapes — stars, alphabets, ditalini, wagon wheels, bow ties, small, medium and large shells; rotini spirals.*

Herb and Lemon Spaghetti

Thin spaghetti is a quick-cooking side dish.

½ pound thin spaghetti or vermicelli

2 tablespoons tub margarine

1 teaspoon dried or chopped fresh parsley

½ teaspoon garlic powder

½ teaspoon marjoram flakes (optional)

½ teaspoon lite salt

½ to 1 tablespoon lemon juice

Boil noodles in Dutch oven, using lite salt or no salt, as directed on package. Place ends in boiling water; as pasta softens, coil it around until it is completely under water. Cook about 7 minutes or until done to taste. Drain. Rinse under hot water and drain well; return to Dutch oven. Add margarine, herbs, lite salt, lemon juice and blend gently while reheating. Makes 4 servings.

Pasta will taste raw or starchy unless boiled in a large quantity of water.
Make this a main attraction by adding chunks of cooked fish or chicken.

Nutrients per serving:

calories	*234*
protein	*7 gm*
carbohydrate	*38 gm*
total fat	*6 gm*
saturated fat	*1 gm*
monounsat'd fat	*3 gm*
cholesterol	*0 mg*
sodium	*280 mg*
potassium	*125 mg*
fiber	*3 gm*

% US-RDA

vitamin A	*7*
vitamin C	*3*
thiamin	*19*
riboflavin	*10*
vitamin B_6	*5*
folacin	*8*
iron	*12*
zinc	*5*
calcium	*3*

Noodles with Vegetable Sauce

Colorful, flavorful, easy.

1 tablespoon tub margarine

1/2 medium onion, chopped

1 medium zucchini, thinly sliced

1/2 teaspoon garlic powder

1 can (15 oz.) whole tomatoes, drained (save liquid)

tomato liquid from above plus enough water to make 1 1/2 cups

2 tablespoons all-purpose flour or crystallized flour

1 teaspoon Italian seasoning

1/2 teaspoon lite salt

8 ounces uncooked noodles or fettucini noodles

1/4 cup parmesan cheese

Melt margarine in skillet. Cook onion, zucchini and garlic powder for 2 minutes. Drain tomatoes, reserving liquid. Add water to tomato liquid to make 1 1/2 cups. Moisten flour with 3 tablespoons tomato-water liquid to make a paste; stir paste into tomato-water liquid in skillet. Cut tomatoes in quarters and add to the skillet along with Italian seasonings and lite salt. Cover and simmer 15 to 20 minutes, stirring occasionally. Boil noodles, using lite salt or no salt, as directed on package. Drain. Toss noodles with sauce and serve immediately, sprinkled with parmesan cheese. Makes 4 servings.

For a quicker variation, add bottled spaghetti sauce to onion, garlic powder and zucchini. Omit tomatoes, flour and seasonings. Stir to prevent sticking; serve over pasta and sprinkle with parmesan cheese.

Nutrients per serving:

calories	*278*
protein	*11 gm*
carbohydrate	*45 gm*
total fat	*6 gm*
saturated fat	*2 gm*
monounsat'd fat	*2 gm*
cholesterol	*4 mg*
sodium	*390 mg*
potassium	*710 mg*
fiber	*4 gm*

% US-RDA

vitamin A	*23*
vitamin C	*45*
thiamin	*29*
riboflavin	*15*
vitamin B_6	*16*
folacin	*22*
iron	*16*
zinc	*8*
calcium	*16*

Noodles Romanoff

An easy gourmet main dish.

6 ounces uncooked wide egg noodles

1½ cups low-fat cottage cheese

½ cup low-fat yogurt

4 green onions, chopped

¼ teaspoon garlic powder

½ teaspoon lite salt

Topping: (or use Herbed Breading recipe
on page 12)

   ¼ cup plain dry bread crumbs

   1 tablespoon tub margarine

   ¼ teaspoon paprika (optional)

   1 teaspoon steak sauce

Preheat oven to 350°. Boil noodles in Dutch oven, using lite salt or no salt, as directed on package, reducing cooking time by one-third. Drain and rinse noodles in hot water. Save washing a pot by lightly oiling the Dutch oven, then add noodles, cottage cheese, yogurt, onions, garlic powder and lite salt. In a small bowl, combine topping ingredients and blend well. Spoon over noodle mixture. Bake 25 to 30 minutes until well heated and crumbs are golden brown. Makes 4 servings.

For a faster version, serve without baking; spoon crumbs over top.
Earn your family's accolades by serving this dish with a bright green vegetable and/or salad, a whole grain roll and a light fruit dessert. A highly nutritious meal!

Nutrients per serving:

calories	278
protein	19 gm
carbohydrate	37 gm
total fat	6 gm
saturated fat	2 gm
monounsat'd fat	2 gm
cholesterol	9 mg
sodium	600 mg
potassium	465 mg
fiber	2 gm

% US-RDA

vitamin A	20
vitamin C	14
thiamin	18
riboflavin	25
vitamin B_6	8
folacin	14
iron	11
zinc	8
calcium	18

Hearty Pasta and Bean Soup

A popular, rich Italian soup easy to cook and eat now or prepare the evening before for an even faster dinner.

5 strips thin sliced bacon

2 stalks celery, sliced

1 medium onion, chopped

2 cans (15 oz.) small white beans, not drained

4 cups water

2 teaspoons beef granules

1 can (8 oz.) tomato sauce

1/2 teaspoon lite salt

1/2 teaspoon garlic powder

1/4 teaspoon black pepper or crushed hot pepper flakes

1/2 teaspoon basil or oregano

3 ounces ditalini or other tiny pasta

1/4 cup dried or fresh chopped parsley

Fry bacon in Dutch oven until crisp; drain on paper towels. In Dutch oven containing small amount of bacon drippings, cook celery and onions for 3 minutes or until soft. Add undrained beans, water, beef granules, tomato sauce, lite salt, garlic powder, pepper, basil and crumbled bacon. Simmer for 20 minutes. Add ditalini, stir to prevent sticking until pasta is tender. Serve immediately topped with parsley, or cool and store in refrigerator. Makes 8 servings.

Hearty soups, thick with vegetables, beans and pasta provide a nutritious all-in-one main dish. Serve with hot, herbed bread, fruit salad and a glass of milk for a satisfying meal.

Nutrients per serving:

calories	*303*
protein	*15 gm*
carbohydrate	*36 gm*
total fat	*11 gm*
saturated fat	*4 gm*
monounsat'd fat	*6 gm*
cholesterol	*18 mg*
sodium	*1000 mg*
potassium	*700 mg*
fiber	*5 gm*

% US-RDA

vitamin A	*17*
vitamin C	*35*
thiamin	*30*
riboflavin	*16*
vitamin B$_6$	*12*
folacin	*8*
iron	*31*
zinc	*12*
calcium	*9*

Creamy Fettuccine

A main dish cooked in one pot.

8 ounces fettuccine or linguine

1 tablespoon olive or canola oil

4 green onions, chopped

1/2 teaspoon basil

1/4 teaspoon dried or fresh grated lemon peel

1/2 teaspoon garlic powder

1/8 teaspoon black or white pepper

1/3 cup parmesan cheese

1 cup low-fat yogurt or evaporated skim milk

1/4 cup parmesan cheese

Boil pasta in Dutch oven according to package instructions, using lite salt or no salt. Drain; immediately return to Dutch oven. Add oil and gently toss to coat. Add green onions and seasonings. In small bowl, combine 1/3 cup parmesan cheese and low-fat yogurt; stir into pasta. Cook over medium heat until just bubbly, stirring constantly. Sprinkle with 1/4 cup parmesan cheese and serve immediately. Makes 4 servings.

Other creamy substitutions for the yogurt are low-fat cream sauce (see page 19) or mock sour cream (see page 31). Do not let yogurt or mock sour cream boil; they will separate into curds and liquid.

Nutrients per serving:

calories	297
protein	15 gm
carbohydrate	39 gm
total fat	9 gm
saturated fat	3 gm
monounsat'd fat	4 gm
cholesterol	14 mg
sodium	275 mg
potassium	275 mg
fiber	1 gm

% US-RDA

vitamin A	9
vitamin C	7
thiamin	17
riboflavin	18
vitamin B_6	9
folacin	44
iron	11
zinc	11
calcium	38

Be Creative
Vegetable Pasta Salad

A do-ahead, low-fat, nutrition-plus main dish.

8 ounces pasta (small shells, elbow macaroni or corkscrews)

1/3 cup olive or canola oil

1 cup cooked turkey, cut in 1/2-inch cubes, or water packed tuna

2 to 3 cups raw and/or cooked vegetables (see below)

1/4 cup sliced ripe olives

1/3 cup wine or cider vinegar

1/2 teaspoon garlic powder

1/2 teaspoon basil

2 teaspoons Dijon mustard or dry mustard

1 teaspoon sugar

1/2 teaspoon lite salt

1/4 teaspoon black pepper

Cook pasta according to package directions, using lite salt or no salt; rinse with cold water and drain well. Pour into large glass or plastic bowl with cover. Drizzle oil over pasta but do not stir. Top with turkey, vegetables and olives but do not stir. Combine vinegar, herbs, sugar, lite salt and pepper. Pour over pasta and turkey. Mix gently, cover and marinate in refrigerator for 12 to 24 hours. Stir occasionally. Makes 6 servings.

Choose raw vegetables such as thin, diagonally sliced carrots, broccoli florets, thinly sliced cucumbers, sliced green or red onions, red and green pepper strips, chopped parsley, chopped tomatoes, yellow or zucchini squash. Select cooked vegetables such as green beans, peas, pimentos or Italian green beans. Two-thirds cup Italian dressing may be substituted for vinegar, oil and herbs.

Nutrients per serving:

calories	*286*
protein	*11 gm*
carbohydrate	*29 gm*
total fat	*14 gm*
saturated fat	*2 gm*
monounsat'd fat	*9 gm*
cholesterol	*13 mg*
sodium	*345 mg*
potassium	*585 mg*
fiber	*3 gm*

% US-RDA

vitamin A	*40*
vitamin C	*50*
thiamin	*15*
riboflavin	*9*
vitamin B$_6$	*11*
folacin	*18*
iron	*12*
zinc	*7*
calcium	*7*

Versatile Rice

The supermarket sports an array of rice: aromatic, long grain, parboiled, instant, quick or long cooking. These fine complex-carbohydrates are fat free, very low in sodium and supply B vitamins and protein. The vigorous health of the Oriental people attests to these nutritional values. Rice is moderate in cost with a long shelf life. It does lose moisture with age, so the older the rice the more additional liquid will be needed for cooking.

Brown rice has the added advantage of having extra vitamin E and fiber because only the outer hull is removed during processing, leaving the brown bran layer. Longer cooking time is needed because of the firmer texture, which is chewier, with a nutlike flavor.

For regular white rice, the hull and bran have been removed during processing. A thin coating of vitamins is applied to each grain to restore nutrients. So, avoid rinsing unless specified on the package. Shorter grained rice is softer and stickier. Long grain rice is best for all purpose use.

Parboiled or converted rice is treated before milling to retain the natural vitamin and mineral content. It takes a little longer to cook than regular rice.

Wild rice actually isn't rice but a seed from an American aquatic grass, the zizania plant. Follow package directions for the longer cooking times.

For best results when cooking rice:

- *Use a heavy-bottomed pan with a tight fitting lid.*
- *Follow package directions, but use no salt or lite salt.*
- *Don't peek, as lifting the lid during cooking can cause gumminess.*
- *After cooking, fluff with a fork. Let stand covered for five minutes.*
- *Cooked rice can be covered and stored in the refrigerator for up to a week. To reheat, add two teaspoons canola oil, two to four tablespoons of water and stir while heating, about five to 10 minutes. For even faster reheating, use a microwave oven.*

Shrimp and Rice

Or use chicken, tuna or scallops.

1 tablespoon canola or olive oil

1 medium green pepper, cut in thin slices

1 medium onion, chopped

8 ounces cooked shrimp, peeled and
   deveined

1 teaspoon garlic powder

1 medium tomato, peeled and chopped

3 drops hot pepper sauce

2¹/₂ cups cooked rice

2 tablespoons cider vinegar

¹/₂ teaspoon lite salt

Nutrients per serving:

calories	263
protein	6 gm
carbohydrate	44 gm
total fat	7 gm
saturated fat	2 gm
monounsat'd fat	4 gm
cholesterol	48 mg
sodium	290 mg
potassium	435 mg
fiber	3 gm

% US-RDA

vitamin A	15
vitamin C	90
thiamin	19
riboflavin	4
vitamin B₆	42
folacin	18
iron	31
zinc	4
calcium	16

Heat oil in heavy bottomed skillet; cook green pepper and onion until soft, about 3 minutes. Add shrimp, garlic powder, tomato and hot sauce. Stir and heat together 2 to 3 minutes. Add rice, vinegar and lite salt to mixture. Heat and serve immediately. Makes 3 servings.

Fresh shrimp and shellfish should be cooked soon after purchase, the same day is best.

Substitute or add a variety of vegetables. Brown rice adds a chewier texture, a nutlike flavor, vitamin E and fiber.

Confetti Rice

Colorful, nutritious and delicious.

2¹/₂ cups water

1 tablespoon tub margarine

1 teaspoon chicken flavor bouillon
   granules

1 cup uncooked long grain rice

1 medium carrot, thinly sliced

1 stalk celery, sliced in crescents

¹/₂ small onion, chopped

¹/₂ cup frozen peas, thawed

In a two-quart saucepan heat water, margarine and bouillon granules to boiling. Add rice, carrots, celery and onion. Stir to mix evenly. Bring to a boil; reduce to a simmer. Cover and simmer 20 minutes or until rice is tender and liquid is absorbed. Add peas and heat together an additional 5 minutes. Makes 4 servings.

Use quick-cooking rice for a faster meal. Cooking vegetables and rice together makes a tasty side dish and saves washing two pans.

Nutrients per serving:

calories	175
protein	4 gm
carbohydrate	33 gm
total fat	3 gm
saturated fat	1 gm
monounsat'd fat	1 gm
cholesterol	0 mg
sodium	290 mg
potassium	150 mg
fiber	3 gm

% US-RDA

vitamin A	76
vitamin C	7
thiamin	17
riboflavin	3
vitamin B₆	31
folacin	14
iron	9
zinc	4
calcium	3

Brown Rice Pilaf

This rice casserole holds well for a do-ahead meal.

5 slices thin-sliced bacon, diced

1 medium onion, chopped

1¹/₂ cup uncooked brown rice

1¹/₂ teaspoons chicken bouillon granules

3 cups water

3 tablespoons light soy sauce

¹/₂ teaspoon garlic powder

Brown bacon in heavy bottomed skillet until almost crisp; add onion and saute for 2 minutes. Do not drain bacon drippings. Add rice and stir while browning, about 4 minutes. Stir in remaining ingredients, bring to boil. Cover, bring to a simmer until done, about 30 to 40 minutes. Or bake covered in 350° oven for 1¹/₂ hour. Makes 6 servings.

The fat in pork and bacon has more monounsaturated and polyunsaturated fat and less saturated fat than beef. This allows the occasional use of bacon and bacon fat in modest amounts.

Add a three ounce serving of lean fish or poultry, a colorful vegetable and/or a salad and you have a delightful, simple meal!

Nutrients per serving:

calories	208
protein	5 gm
carbohydrate	20 gm
total fat	12 gm
saturated fat	3 gm
monounsat'd fat	6 gm
cholesterol	9 mg
sodium	600 mg
potassium	180 mg
fiber	1 gm

% US-RDA

vitamin A	***
vitamin C	5
thiamin	12
riboflavin	3
vitamin B₆	21
folacin	5
iron	7
zinc	4
calcium	***

Fried Rice and Vegetables

A colorful, satisfying meal in 30 minutes.

1 tablespoon canola oil

2 cups cooked rice

1/2 cup egg whites or egg substitute

1 tablespoon canola oil

1/2 small onion, chopped

1 stalk celery, thinly sliced

2 medium green peppers, cut in thin slices

1 medium fresh or frozen yellow or zucchini
   squash, sliced

1 cup fresh or frozen, defrosted, broccoli cuts

1 teaspoon ground ginger

1 teaspoon lite salt

Preheat oven to 200°. Heat 1 tablespoon oil in heavy bottomed skillet; add cooked rice and stir while heating. Pour egg whites over hot rice, place skillet in oven and allow to congeal. Heat a second skillet over medium high heat until hot. Add 1 tablespoon oil. Add vegetables slowly to keep vegetables sizzling; sprinkle with ginger and lite salt, stirring constantly to prevent sticking. Cook 3 to 4 minutes until tender crisp. Serve rice on hot plate, arrange stir-fried vegetables over fried rice. Makes 2 generous servings.

Add 1 cup (4 ounces) cubed lean ham or tofu to rice before stir-frying. This adds 100 calories and 4 grams of fat per serving. The technique of stir-frying in a small amount of very hot oil, is a quick, easy and low-fat cooking method.

Nutrients per serving:

calories	*392*
protein	*14 gm*
carbohydrate	*48 gm*
total fat	*16 gm*
saturated fat	*1 gm*
monounsat'd fat	*9 gm*
cholesterol	*0 mg*
sodium	*665 mg*
potassium	*1500 mg*
fiber	*6 gm*

% US-RDA

vitamin A	*56*
vitamin C	*210*
thiamin	*34*
riboflavin	*23*
vitamin B$_6$	*54*
folacin	*44*
iron	*30*
zinc	*13*
calcium	*13*

Fast and Easy Onion Rice

A tasty side dish, ready in minutes.

1 tablespoon tub margarine

1 medium onion, chopped

1½ cups quick-cooking rice

1½ cups water

¼ teaspoon lite salt

⅛ teaspoon black pepper

1 tablespoon dried or fresh chopped
   parsley

In a two-quart saucepan, melt margarine and add onion; cook until tender, about 3 minutes. Add rice and stir until rice is lightly browned. Add water, lite salt and pepper; bring to boil. Cover, remove from heat and let stand 5 minutes. Stir in parsley. Makes 4 servings.

Plain cooked rice is delicious. Its delicate flavor blends well with mushrooms, vegetables, poultry, fish or red meats.

Nutrients per serving:

calories	195
protein	4 gm
carbohydrate	38 gm
total fat	3 gm
saturated fat	1 gm
monounsat'd fat	1 gm
cholesterol	0 mg
sodium	100 mg
potassium	120 mg
fiber	2 gm

% US-RDA

vitamin A	5
vitamin C	5
thiamin	17
riboflavin	***
vitamin B_6	5
folacin	10
iron	12
zinc	5
calcium	2

Nature's Vegetable Garden

Some of the richest food gifts come from nature's garden.

Vegetables provide us with all the flavor and nutrients we need to make an extraordinary meal. The health benefits derived from eating large quantities of vegetables are staggering. Eating three or more servings each day may protect one from atherosclerotic disease (hardening of the arteries) and some cancers. Frequent eating of deep green and deep yellow vegetables, rich in beta-carotene and often a good source of vitamin C and fiber, may help lower chances of developing cancers of the lung, stomach and large intestine.

Take advantage of the bounty during spring and summer, when nature is most generous with her gifts. Try eating vegetables raw. Those not accustomed to eating raw vegetables will be delightfully surprised by their flavor, freshness and crunchy texture. As an accompaniment to a hearty dish, or as the main attraction, vegetables are a must in your daily meal plan.

Make the most of the many nutrients vegetables offer. Cooking vegetables destroys some nutrients. To lessen the loss, cook vegetables only until tender in as little water as possible. Baking, steaming, stir-frying and microwaving are also excellent methods to use.

These hints will help you take advantage of the natural goodness found in vegetables:

- *A splash of vinegar added to steaming hot vegetables enhances the flavor. The acid evaporates leaving a tang. (Adding too much or while vegetables are cooking will darken the color.)*

- *During the off season, fulfill your vegetable craving in the frozen food aisle. Frozen vegetables are especially good when baked in a covered casserole with a dab of margarine.*

- *Because most people are accustomed to salty flavors, you might get better acceptance adding 1/2 teaspoon lite salt or salt per pound of vegetables.*

- *Chopped chives and parsley, sprinkled on just before serving, improve the flavor of many vegetables.*

- *Use herbs and spices in subtle amounts to avoid excessive flavors. Start with a small quantity of one herb — 1/8 to 1/4 teaspoon per pound of fresh or frozen vegetables. Let your taste buds decide if you want more or less.*
- *Herbs are a vegetable's best friend. The following chart offers suggestions as to which vegetable and herb pairings make the tastiest matches:*

White vegetables:

Cauliflower	white pepper, paprika, parsley, chives, rosemary
Potatoes	dill weed, nutmeg, paprika, parsley, white pepper

Red vegetables:

Beets	garlic powder, cloves, allspice, bay leaf
Tomatoes	basil, oregano, marjoram, black pepper, dill weed, thyme, garlic powder

Green vegetables:

Asparagus	nutmeg, dry mustard, black pepper
Broccoli	lemon & pepper seasoning, black pepper, ground red pepper, garlic powder, oregano
Cabbage	garlic powder, caraway seed, black pepper, thyme
Cucumbers	dill weed, basil, black pepper, chives
Green beans	garlic powder, black pepper, thyme, tarragon, dill weed
Peas	minced onion, mint flakes, basil, chives, black pepper
Spinach	nutmeg, mace, ginger
Zucchini	oregano, black pepper, basil, marjoram

Yellow vegetables:

Carrots	ginger, nutmeg, dry mustard, dill weed, chives, black pepper
Corn	chili powder, onion powder, chives, black pepper
Sweet potatoes or yams	cinnamon, nutmeg, allspice, mace, cardamon
Yellow squash	onion powder, basil, dill weed, parsley, paprika, chives, black pepper
Winter squash	cinnamon, nutmeg, pumpkin pie spice, thyme, marjoram

Tossed Green Salad

Raw, leafy, crisp vegetable salads yield only 20 calories per 3/4 cup! Try this easy method.

8 large leaves of dark green lettuce (romaine is great)

8 medium radishes, sliced

8 green onions, sliced

Tear lettuce into bite-sized pieces, place in individual salad bowls. Scatter sliced radishes and onions over lettuce. Cover and chill until serving time. Just before serving, add a low-fat salad dressing or a dash of vinegar and Salad Topping Mix (see page 28). Makes 4 servings.

The darker green the lettuce or vegetable, the richer it is in beta-carotene, which may be helpful in preventing cancer of the lung and throat.

Other additions may include broccoli florets or shredded carrots. In season, use tomatoes, raw zucchini, yellow summer squash, parsley, cucumbers and red and green peppers.

Speed up salad-making by washing salad greens as soon as you bring them home. Shake leaves vigorously to remove excess water, then store in cotton or plastic bags in refrigerator. You will have salads in minutes.

Nutrients per serving:

calories	20
protein	1 gm
carbohydrate	4 gm
total fat	0 gm
saturated fat	0 gm
monounsat'd fat	0 gm
cholesterol	0 mg
sodium	20 mg
potassium	275 mg
fiber	1 gm

% US-RDA

vitamin A	25
vitamin C	30
thiamin	***
riboflavin	***
vitamin B$_6$	3
folacin	26
iron	10
zinc	***
calcium	6

Cucumbers and Onions in Vinegar

Double or triple the recipe for a second meal and snacking.

1/2 cup water

1/3 cup cider or wine vinegar

3 teaspoons sugar

1 teaspoon lite salt

dash black pepper

1 medium cucumber, thinly sliced

1 medium onion, thinly sliced

In serving bowl, blend water, vinegar, sugar, salt, and pepper. Peel off about half of cucumber skin in long, narrow strips and discard. Gently stir sliced cucumbers and onions into vinegar-herb liquid. Cover and refrigerate for at least one hour before serving. Makes 4 servings.

Yogurt variation: substitute 2/3 cup low-fat yogurt for vinegar and water. Blot cucumber to remove excess moisture before adding to yogurt.

Nutrients per serving:

calories	20
protein	0 gm
carbohydrate	5 gm
total fat	0 gm
saturated fat	0 gm
monounsat'd fat	0 gm
cholesterol	0 mg
sodium	100 mg
potassium	200 mg
fiber	1 gm

% US-RDA

vitamin A	***
vitamin C	7
thiamin	2
riboflavin	***
vitamin B_6	3
folacin	6
iron	3
zinc	***
calcium	2

Creamy Coleslaw

Great with fish.

½ cup salad dressing

1 tablespoon vinegar (pickle juice is good)

1 teaspoon sugar

1 tablespoon grated onion

½ cup low-fat buttermilk or yogurt

½ teaspoon lite salt

black pepper to taste

4 cups finely shredded or chopped
    cabbage

½ cup finely chopped green pepper

In serving bowl, blend together salad dressing, vinegar, sugar, onion, buttermilk, lite salt and pepper. Add cabbage and green peppers and mix well; cover and chill. For a crisper coleslaw, add cabbage and green pepper just before serving. Makes 8 servings.

Master the use of the French knife for speedy chopping of cabbage and vegetables. Gourmet friends can show you this efficient method. Always remember to keep your knuckles curled against the blade while your other hand grips the knife handle. Or, keep the palm of your hand on top of the blade with your fingers curled up and away from the cutting edge.

Nutrients per serving:

calories	81
protein	1 gm
carbohydrate	8 gm
total fat	5 gm
saturated fat	1 gm
monounsat'd fat	2 gm
cholesterol	5 mg
sodium	150 mg
potassium	200 mg
fiber	1 gm

% US-RDA

vitamin A	3
vitamin C	53
thiamin	3
riboflavin	4
vitamin B$_6$	4
folacin	16
iron	3
zinc	2
calcium	7

Old-Fashioned Cabbage Slaw

An easy vinegar and oil dressed salad.

1 teaspoon lite salt

$1/4$ teaspoon black pepper

$1/2$ teaspoon dry mustard

$1/2$ teaspoon celery seed (optional)

$1/4$ cup finely chopped green pepper

1 tablespoon chopped pimento (optional)

2 teaspoons sugar

1 tablespoon grated onion

3 tablespoons canola or olive oil

$1/3$ cup cider vinegar

3 cups finely chopped cabbage

Place all ingredients except cabbage in large bowl; mix thoroughly. Stir in cabbage and mix well. Cover and chill. Garnish with bright green vegetable such as parsley sprigs or green pepper rings. Makes 6 servings.

Cabbage, broccoli, cauliflower, Brussels sprouts and kale are cruciferous (arrangement in florets in the form of a cross) vegetables rich in vitamin C and sulfur-containing compounds. Diets high in these vegetables may help protect against cancers of the esophagus, stomach and colon.

Nutrients per serving:

calories	107
protein	1 gm
carbohydrate	10 gm
total fat	7 gm
saturated fat	0 gm
monounsat'd fat	5 gm
cholesterol	0 mg
sodium	135 mg
potassium	300 mg
fiber	1 gm

% US-RDA

vitamin A	3
vitamin C	50
thiamin	3
riboflavin	***
vitamin B_6	4
folacin	14
iron	10
zinc	2
calcium	5

78

Marinated Vegetables

A beautiful do-ahead salad for guests or family.

4 medium carrots, sliced diagonally ¼-inch
   thick

½ medium cauliflower, separated into florets

2 cups broccoli florets

Marinade:

  ½ cup canola or olive oil

  ¼ cup vinegar, wine or cider

  1 teaspoon lite salt

  ½ teaspoon prepared mustard

  1 teaspoon sugar

  ½ teaspoon basil

  ¼ teaspoon black pepper

10 cherry tomatoes for garnish

Arrange vegetables, starting with carrots, on steamer rack and cook over boiling water until tender-crisp. Rinse in cold water. Place in glass or plastic bowl with cover. Mix marinade ingredients. Gently combine vegetables with marinade. Cover and chill at least 6 hours. Gently stir vegetables at least once to evenly distribute marinade. Garnish with cherry tomatoes before serving. Makes 8 servings.

For a faster marinade, use ¾ cup Italian salad dressing.
Green beans, peas and corn marinate well and are high on the list of favorite vegetables. Introduce new marinated vegetables, such as zucchini, small whole okra and yellow summer squash, when diners will be hungry or with a festive meal.

Nutrients per serving:

calories	78
protein	2 gm
carbohydrate	4 gm
total fat	6 gm
saturated fat	0 gm
monounsat'd fat	4 gm
cholesterol	0 mg
sodium	120 mg
potassium	450 mg
fiber	3 gm

% US-RDA

vitamin A	200
vitamin C	78
thiamin	7
riboflavin	5
vitamin B_6	12
folacin	20
iron	5
zinc	2
calcium	4

Tomatoes Vinaigrette

A bright, do-ahead summer tomato salad.

5 large, peeled, fresh sliced tomatoes

1 teaspoon basil

1/4 cup Herbed Oil-and-Vinegar Dressing (see page 24) or commercially prepared light Italian dressing

In a low, shallow dish, place a layer of sliced tomatoes and sprinkle with basil. Repeat, using all tomatoes. Pour oil-and-vinegar dressing over tomato slices. Gently lift tomato slices to allow dressing to flow between slices. Cover, refrigerate and marinate 1 to 3 hours. Makes 6 servings.

Tasty either chilled or at room temperature, this zesty salad goes well with a buffet or picnic. The juice and tomatoes make a tangy sauce for grilled meats. Try sliced, whole canned tomatoes in the winter months.

Nutrients per serving:

calories	48
protein	1 gm
carbohydrate	4 gm
total fat	3 gm
saturated fat	0 gm
monounsat'd fat	2 gm
cholesterol	0 mg
sodium	10 mg
potassium	210 mg
fiber	1 gm

% US-RDA

vitamin A	23
vitamin C	30
thiamin	5
riboflavin	4
vitamin B_6	3
folacin	4
iron	4
zinc	***
calcium	***

Savory Carrots

Carrots are one of the richest sources of beta-carotene.

¹/₂ cup water

¹/₂ teaspoon chicken flavor bouillon granules

4 medium, peeled or scrubbed carrots, cut in ¹/₄-inch thick slices or strips

1 teaspoon tub margarine

dash of nutmeg or herb of your choice

dash of black pepper (optional)

Bring water to boil in one-quart saucepan. Add bouillon granules, then carrots. Lower heat to a simmer; cover and cook until carrots are tender-crisp, about 8 to 10 minutes. Drain off all liquid and save for making soups or sauces. Add margarine and seasonings. Makes 4 servings.

Use bright yellow carrots at least once per week as a cooked vegetable, or mixed into a casserole or raw, as carrot sticks or in salads. Vitamin A not used by the body is stored in the liver for future use.

Potatoes, frozen lima beans, peas or summer squash are tasty when seasoned this low-fat way.

Nutrients per serving:

calories	*45*
protein	*1 gm*
carbohydrate	*8 gm*
total fat	*1 gm*
saturated fat	*0 gm*
monounsat'd fat	*1 gm*
cholesterol	*0 mg*
sodium	*145 mg*
potassium	*245 mg*
fiber	*2 gm*

% US-RDA

vitamin A	*400*
vitamin C	*12*
thiamin	*6*
riboflavin	*3*
vitamin B₆	*6*
folacin	*6*
iron	*3*
zinc	*****
calcium	*3*

Spinach with Onions

A fast, colorful treat.

2 teaspoons tub margarine

4 cups fresh or frozen loose leaf spinach or 10-ounce package frozen, chopped spinach, partially thawed

1 small onion, chopped

¼ teaspoon lite salt

black pepper to taste

Melt margarine in heavy bottomed skillet. Combine fresh or undrained frozen spinach, onion, lite salt and pepper over medium heat for 10 to 15 minutes until spinach liquid has evaporated. Stir frequently to cook spinach evenly. Serve immediately. Makes 4 servings.

Leafy fresh vegetables such as spinach, chard, mustard, collard and beet greens release liquid as they cook down to one-twelfth the original volume. Simmer vegetables in this natural liquid to retain flavor and nutrients.

The delicate use of herbs decreases the amount of margarine needed for seasoning. Refer to the herb chart on pages 73 to 74. If you use a complimentary vegetable-herb combination, less margarine will be needed.

Nutrients per serving:

calories	46
protein	2 gm
carbohydrate	5 gm
total fat	2 gm
saturated fat	0 gm
monounsat'd fat	1 gm
cholesterol	0 mg
sodium	150 mg
potassium	325 mg
fiber	2 gm

% US-RDA

vitamin A	110
vitamin C	16
thiamin	5
riboflavin	9
vitamin B₆	6
folacin	37
iron	10
zinc	***
calcium	10

Herbed Broccoli

Two for one recipe: steamed florets for the recipe and raw broccoli stalks for munching.

1 pound fresh broccoli or 10 oz. pkg. frozen broccoli cuts

2 teaspoons tub margarine

1 to 2 teaspoons lemon juice

sprinkle of garlic powder, oregano and basil

Thoroughly wash broccoli; cut off stalks. Divide heads into florets. Place on steamer rack in pan. Steam with lid partially off, until broccoli is bright green and feels tender-crisp with a fork. Remove steamer rack, drain off water. Melt margarine in pan with broccoli; sprinkle on herbs and lemon juice. Stir well to mix and serve immediately. Makes 4 servings.

Acid causes the bright green color to become an olive-drab. Acidic vapors from the broccoli and over cooking will cause it to darken. By leaving the lid partially off, the vapors can escape. For the same reason, don't add the acidic lemon juice and the herbs until just before serving.

Peel off the tough outer layers of the broccoli stalk. Slice the stalk into rounds for munching or for stir-fry cooking.

Nutrients per serving:

calories	*50*
protein	*3 gm*
carbohydrate	*5 gm*
total fat	*2 gm*
saturated fat	*0 gm*
monounsat'd fat	*1 gm*
cholesterol	*0 mg*
sodium	*55 mg*
potassium	*330 mg*
fiber	*3 gm*

% US-RDA

vitamin A	*32*
vitamin C	*150*
thiamin	*6*
riboflavin	*12*
vitamin B_6	*12*
folacin	*35*
iron	*6*
zinc	*2*
calcium	*6*

Oven Baked Onion Rings

Enjoy delicious, low-fat onion rings.

1 large white or yellow onion, sliced 1/4-inch thick and separated into rings

2 egg whites or 1/4 cup egg substitute

3/4 cup Herbed Breading (see page 12) or make breading:

> **3/4 cup dry bread crumbs**
>
> **1/2 teaspoon lite salt**
>
> **1/8 teaspoon black pepper**
>
> **1/2 teaspoon paprika**

Preheat oven to 450°. Oil a nonstick baking sheet or thick bottomed cookie sheet or pizza pan. Mix bread crumbs, lite salt and pepper. Beat egg whites until frothy. Dip each ring in egg white, then in breading; place on oiled pan. Bake on middle to upper oven rack to prevent burning bottom sides of onion rings. Bake 10 minutes or until golden brown. Makes 4 servings.

To prepare onions without tears:

- *Cut them under running water.*
- *Chill in freezer for 15 minutes before cutting.*
- *Use an enclosed chopper or food processor to make a lot and freeze.*
- *Buy frozen, raw onions.*
- *Shorten exposure time while chopping by using a French knife.*

Nutrients per serving:

calories	102
protein	3 gm
carbohydrate	18 gm
total fat	2 gm
saturated fat	0 gm
monounsat'd fat	1 gm
cholesterol	0 mg
sodium	200 mg
potassium	400 mg
fiber	1 gm

% US-RDA

vitamin A	***
vitamin C	10
thiamin	7
riboflavin	7
vitamin B$_6$	6
folacin	10
iron	6
zinc	***
calcium	3

Corn and Tomato Casserole

Sure to be a family favorite.

1 can (15 oz.) whole kernel corn, drained

1 can (15 oz.) tomatoes, chopped, drained

1/4 teaspoon basil

1/4 teaspoon garlic powder

1 teaspoon onion powder

2 tablespoons tub margarine

**1/3 cup dry bread crumbs or Herbed
    Breading mix (see page 12)**

1/4 cup parmesan cheese

Preheat oven to 375°. Combine corn, tomatoes, basil, onion and garlic powder in a shallow two-quart casserole dish. Melt margarine in small pan and blend in bread crumbs and parmesan cheese; sprinkle over vegetables. Bake for 20 minutes. Makes 4 servings.

When preparing ahead for a large gathering, this recipe can be doubled or tripled easily. Pre-mix the corn, tomatoes and herbs and refrigerate; mix bread crumbs and cheese ahead of time. Right before baking, melt margarine, make topping and sprinkle on. Bake 30 minutes, or until bubbly and brown.

Nutrients per serving:

calories	224
protein	7 gm
carbohydrate	31 gm
total fat	8 gm
saturated fat	2 gm
monounsat'd fat	3 gm
cholesterol	4 mg
sodium	670 mg
potassium	460 mg
fiber	5 gm

% US-RDA

vitamin A	24
vitamin C	42
thiamin	10
riboflavin	11
vitamin B_6	8
folacin	26
iron	10
zinc	5
calcium	10

Rae Bartunek's Corn Oysters

A faculty wife introduced this simple dish years ago.

1 can (15 oz.) whole kernel corn, drained or 1 can (12 oz.) vacuum packed

¹/₄ cup egg whites or egg substitute, or 1 egg

¹/₂ small onion, chopped

¹/₂ medium green pepper, chopped

¹/₄ cup all-purpose flour

³/₄ teaspoon baking powder

¹/₂ teaspoon lite salt

¹/₈ teaspoon black pepper

dash of paprika (optional)

Nutrients per serving:

calories 142
protein . . . . 5 gm
carbohydrate . . . . 26 gm
total fat . . . . 2 gm
saturated fat . . . . 0 gm
monounsat'd fat . . . . 1 gm
cholesterol . . . . 5 mg
sodium . . . . 540 mg
potassium . . . . 225 mg
fiber . . . . 5 gm

% US-RDA

vitamin A 10
vitamin C 15
thiamin 10
riboflavin 11
vitamin B₆ 6
folacin 6
iron 5
zinc 5
calcium 8

Stir together all ingredients and mix well. Preheat griddle or skillet until a drop of water dances on surface. Spread with thin film of vegetable oil. Drop batter from a tablespoon onto hot surface to form a 2 inch round oyster. Cook until underside is light brown, turn and cook other side. Makes 16 oysters, or 4 servings.

Chopped sweet red peppers, pimento, parsley, chives or grated carrots may be added to or substituted for the vegetables listed in the recipe. This has been a consistent winner with all age groups over many years!

Creamy Broccoli Soup

A filling soup that is simple to prepare.

1 pkg. (10 oz.) frozen chopped broccoli, thawed

2 cups 1/2% low-fat or skim milk

1 tablespoon tub margarine

1 pkg. (2 oz.) or 1 cup potato flakes

2 teaspoons dried onion flakes

1 can (10 1/2 oz.) chicken broth or 1 1/2 cups water and 2 teaspoons chicken flavor bouillon granules

1/4 teaspoon lite salt, if needed

black pepper to taste

Cook broccoli until tender and set aside. Combine milk and margarine in medium saucepan until thoroughly heated, but do not boil. Stir in potato and onion flakes. Mash broccoli well and blend into milk-potato mixture. (For a smoother consistency, place milk-potato mixture in blender, add broccoli and process 30 seconds. Scrape down sides and process another 30 seconds. Return to saucepan.) Stir in broth, salt and pepper. Simmer 10 minutes stirring frequently to prevent sticking. Makes 4 servings.

This basic method can be used with such vegetables as cauliflower, green beans, peas and carrots.

Nutrients per serving:

calories	117
protein	9 gm
carbohydrate	9 gm
total fat	5 gm
saturated fat	1 gm
monounsat'd fat	2 gm
cholesterol	4 mg
sodium	665 mg
potassium	730 mg
fiber	2 gm

% US-RDA

vitamin A	30
vitamin C	65
thiamin	6
riboflavin	9
vitamin B_6	33
folacin	31
iron	8
zinc	3
calcium	24

Stir-Fry Method

Stir-frying, an Oriental method of cooking, preserves the flavor, texture and nutrients of vegetables and meats. Learn the basics of this quick cooking method and then let your creative juices flow! The slow part of the process is the preparation of vegetables and meats. To practice this fun art you will need:

- *A heavy wok or skillet. The nonstick variety works well.*
- *Oil (preferably canola or peanut.)*
- *A wooden spatula or spoon to stir the vegetables.*
- *Fresh vegetables.*
- *Raw, skinless chicken or turkey, tofu, lean beef or pork.*
- *A cutting board and a sharp knife.*

To prepare stir-fry ingredients:

- *Vegetables and meats can be cut ahead of time, covered and kept refrigerated for up to 2 hours.*
- *Cut stringy vegetables such as celery, green onions or green beans on the diagonal.*
- *The thick stems of broccoli and ribs of leaf vegetables should be removed and thinly sliced separately.*
- *All vegetables should be bite-sized, or thin-sliced.*
- *Only one to three vegetables are needed to stir-fry a delightful meal, but you can use as many as you wish.*
- *One pound of vegetable makes three to four servings.*
- *If you are using fresh garlic or fresh ginger root to flavor the cooking oil, slice it very thin. These herbs are added to season the oil and are removed before adding meats or vegetables.*
- *Place raw chicken, turkey, pork or beef in freezer 15 to 20 minutes for easier, thin slicing.*
- *Quickly blot off extra moisture from meat and vegetables with paper towels to minimize splattering and to prevent unwanted steaming during cooking.*

- *If you are serving rice, check preparation method and required time on package. The rice should be ready just prior to stir-frying.*

Group vegetables according to cooking time:

5-8 Minutes	3-5 Minutes	Add at the very last
Very thin carrots	Cauliflower florets	Bean sprouts
Cabbage, Chinese cabbage	Broccoli florets	Chives
	Green or red pepper	Frozen peas (defrosted)
Celery	Tender green onion	Romaine lettuce
Onions/green onions		Snow peas
Tender green beans		Spinach or chard
Ribs from chard leaves, thin rounds of broccoli stalks		Zucchini or squash
		*Mushrooms and tofu are added just before serving

Stir-frying tips:

- *Place one tablespoon oil per serving in heavy wok or skillet. Heat oil until a drop of water dances on the surface. The objective of stir-frying is to sear the surfaces of food, so a very hot surface is used. Vegetables and meats should not bubble and simmer.*

- *If meat is used, add a few strips at a time; stir, to sear all surfaces; move partially cooked pieces to side of pan. Remove meat from pan just before it becomes done.*

- *Stir-fry vegetables in order shown in chart to insure that each vegetable will not be cooked beyond the tender-crisp stage.*

- *Stir in the pre-seared meat.*

- *If you like a sauce on your stir-fry, for each serving combine one tablespoon cornstarch, three tablespoons cold water and one tablespoon soy sauce. Stir vigorously and pour over hot vegetables, cooking one to two minutes or until sauce is clear and shiny.*

The process of stir-frying sounds complicated. But after a few trials, you will love this delightful, colorful, fast cooking method.

Surprising Potato Facts

The potato was first popularized in the American diet by the Irish, for whom the vegetable was a mainstay. During the mid-1840s disease destroyed the potato crop in Ireland, causing the Great Potato Famine. Thousands of Irish immigrated to America, and brought with them their love for potatoes. In the nineteenth and early twentieth centuries, complex carbohydrates (such foods as potatoes, rice, pastas, beans, cereals and grains) provided most of the calories for a lean and active population. As life styles changed, people became more sedentary, and therefore, more plump. The potato and other healthy starches were blamed since they were thought to be fattening.

Now, we are more nutrition-wise. It is not the potato that is fattening. It is the butter, cheese, sour cream and bacon bits we add to the potato that triples the fat and calories. A medium potato, with the skin on, has only 110 calories, three grams of protein, 25 grams of carbohydrates, three grams of fiber and *no fat or cholesterol.* It is low in sodium (only 10 milligrams) and high in potassium, with 500 milligrams. A potato supplies generous amounts of the RDAs with 24 percent of vitamin C and vitamin B_6, eight percent of thiamin and folacin and 10 percent of iron. The wonderful potato also contains riboflavin, zinc and small amounts of other vitamins and minerals. This is one of the very best foods to include in a healthy, low-fat diet!

Buy potatoes that are clean, firm and smooth. Avoid any that are wrinkled, have wilted skins, soft or dark areas, cut or rough surfaces or a green color. Store potatoes in a cool, dry, dark, well ventilated place. At 40° to 50°, potatoes will last several weeks; at warmer temperatures they will keep for at least a week. Don't refrigerate potatoes, however. At temperatures cooler that 40°, the starch content turns to sugar, the potato darkens in color and has an unpleasant sweet taste when cooked.

The wonderful, versatile and nutritious potato can be prepared in dozens of quick and easy ways, as you will see in the recipes that follow.

The Absolutely Perfect Baked Potato

1 medium potato: 150 grams or ¹/₃-pound
or 3x2¹/₂x2-inches or about the size of
a flattened baseball

Preheat oven to 400°. Carefully scrub potato. Pierce the skin in several places with tines of a fork before baking. This allows the steam to escape and prevents the potato from bursting. If you prefer a crisp skin, it is ready to bake. For a softer skin, rub with vegetable oil.

Bake directly on the oven rack or on a cookie sheet. Potatoes are well done in 40 to 45 minutes at 400° and will feel soft when covered with a hot pad and gently squeezed. A lower temperature may be used but cooking time is longer. Your 110 calorie medium potato can be topped with:

Two tablespoons:	Fat grams	Calories
Parmesan cheese	3	60
Mock sour cream	2	24
Low-fat cottage cheese	0.3	20
Plain low-fat yogurt	0.5	18
Chopped tomatoes, green pepper and green onions	0	5
Sliced mushrooms in fat-free salad dressing	0	5
Chives and parsley	0	0
Other herbs and spices	0	0

Make your own Baked Potato Bar by using these toppings and lean, cubed ham, fish or poultry. See the nutrients in a baked, skin-on potato in Surprising Potato Facts.

Notice that two tablespoons of margarine add 24 grams of fat and 200 calories!

Parsley Boiled Potatoes

Simple but good!

The inexperienced cook can easily master this important, basic method.

1 cup water

¹/₂ teaspoon lite salt

4 medium potatoes, cut in 1-inch pieces, skin-on or peeled

¹/₂ tablespoon dried or chopped fresh parsley

1 tablespoon tub margarine

Bring water and lite salt to a boil in a one-quart saucepan. Add potatoes, cover with a tight lid, and lower to a simmer. Stir once or twice to assure potatoes cook evenly. Cook until potatoes are fork-tender (see below). Drain. Add parsley and margarine to potatoes and toss lightly together. Makes 4 servings.

A medium whole potato cooks in about 30 to 40 minutes. Cut it in half and it cooks in 15 to 20 minutes. One-inch cubes cook in 10 to 15 minutes. New potatoes (1¹/₂-inches in diameter) cook in 10 to 15 minutes. New potatoes and thin-skinned potatoes taste best if skin is left on. Save liquids drained from potatoes and vegetables for tasty soup additions or for gravies.

Nutrients per serving:

calories	140
protein	3 gm
carbohydrate	25 gm
total fat	3 gm
saturated fat	1 gm
monounsat'd fat	1 gm
cholesterol	0 mg
sodium	300 mg
potassium	700 mg
fiber	3 gm

% US-RDA

vitamin A	10
vitamin C	25
thiamin	8
riboflavin	2
vitamin B₆	15
folacin	16
iron	8
zinc	2
calcium	***

Fluffy Mashed Potatoes

Always a favorite and surprisingly nutritious.

1 cup water

1/2 teaspoon lite salt

4 medium potatoes, peeled, cut into 1 to
　2-inch pieces

2 tablespoons tub margarine

1/2 teaspoon lite salt

black or white pepper to taste

1/2 cup potato water

1/4 cup instant nonfat dry milk

Bring water and lite salt to a boil in two-quart saucepan. Add potatoes, cover with tight lid and lower to a simmer; cook 12 to 15 minutes or until fork tender. Drain and save potato water. Leave potatoes in saucepan, mash with a potato masher or an electric mixer. Add margarine, lite salt and pepper. Slowly add back potato water and nonfat dry milk. Beat until potatoes are light and fluffy. The more potato water used, the thinner the mashed potatoes will be. Makes 4 servings.

Instant mashed potatoes are quicker and are preferred by some families. Nutrition-wise they are similar to fresh potatoes and both provide delicious complex carbohydrates.

Nutrients per serving:

calories	175
protein	6 gm
carbohydrate	25 gm
total fat	6 gm
saturated fat	2 gm
monounsat'd fat	2 gm
cholesterol	2 mg
sodium	260 mg
potassium	925 mg
fiber	0 gm

% US-RDA

vitamin A	8
vitamin C	30
thiamin	15
riboflavin	14
vitamin B_6	15
folacin	15
iron	9
zinc	3
calcium	10

Tic-Tac-Toe Potato

Children love this potato.

2 large potatoes

4 teaspoons tub margarine

dash of lite salt

dash of pepper

dash of paprika

dash of your favorite herbs (optional)

Preheat oven to 400°. Scrub potatoes but do not peel. Cut each potato in half lengthwise. With the point of knife, cut from the cut surface down to near the skin, making 1/2-inch "tic-tac-toe" squares. Blot surface dry. Heat margarine in a large skillet over low heat and cook potatoes cut side down for 10 minutes. Slide egg turner under potatoes occasionally to prevent sticking. Turn cut side up, sprinkle with seasonings and paprika. Place skillet in oven and bake for 30 minutes or until tender. Makes 4 servings.

Introduce the family to the enjoyment of eating high-fiber potato skins with this easy-to-fix method.

Nutrients per serving:

calories	136
protein	3 gm
carbohydrate	22 gm
total fat	4 gm
saturated fat	1 gm
monounsat'd fat	1 gm
cholesterol	0 mg
sodium	100 mg
potassium	315 mg
fiber	2 gm

% US-RDA

vitamin A	8
vitamin C	20
thiamin	8
riboflavin	2
vitamin B$_6$	15
folacin	10
iron	8
zinc	2
calcium	***

Escalloped Potato and Dried Beef Casserole

A filling dish ready to bake in 20 minutes.

1 package (2¹/₂ oz.) dried beef

2 teaspoons tub margarine

4 medium carrots, thinly sliced

1 medium onion, chopped

5 medium potatoes, unpeeled and thinly sliced

1 can (10¹/₂ oz.) mushroom soup

¹/₂ cup ¹/₂% low-fat milk or skim milk

¹/₄ teaspoon nutmeg (optional)

black pepper to taste

Preheat oven to 350°. Slice dried beef and soak in ¹/₂ cup warm water. Melt margarine in Dutch oven over low heat. Add carrots and onion; stir occasionally while preparing potatoes. Scrub potatoes, slice in half and lay flat on cutting board. Use French knife to cut thin slices of potato. Add to heated vegetables. Add drained dried beef, soup, milk and seasonings. Heat together only until it bubbles. Bake in oven 30 to 40 minutes or until potatoes are tender. Makes 4 servings.

Prepare and refrigerate for a ready-to-bake next-day meal. Dried beef is low-fat but high sodium. Sodium per serving is reduced by soaking dried beef in water and draining well. Fat and sodium per serving are lowered by the generous use of fresh potatoes, onions and carrots.

Nutrients per serving:

calories	340
protein	11 gm
carbohydrate	38 gm
total fat	16 gm
saturated fat	5 gm
monounsat'd fat	5 gm
cholesterol	18 mg
sodium	1000 mg
potassium	960 mg
fiber	3 gm

% US-RDA

vitamin A	240
vitamin C	50
thiamin	20
riboflavin	14
vitamin B₆	11
folacin	14
iron	23
zinc	9
calcium	12

95

Italian Potatoes and Zucchini

Add a pan-broiled Italian meat patty for a 35 minute meal.*

2 large potatoes

2 medium zucchini squash

2 tablespoons canola oil

1/2 teaspoon lite salt

dash of black pepper

dash garlic powder

dash of Italian herbs or basil and oregano

Nutrients per serving:

calories	172
protein	2 gm
carbohydrate	23 gm
total fat	8 gm
saturated fat	2 gm
monounsat'd fat	3 gm
cholesterol	0 mg
sodium	215 mg
potassium	435 mg
fiber	3 gm

% US-RDA

vitamin A	90
vitamin C	12
thiamin	10
riboflavin	***
vitamin B$_6$	14
folacin	10
iron	13
zinc	***
calcium	***

Scrub potatoes. Do not peel. Cut into 1/2-inch diagonal slices. Scrub zucchini and cut into lengthwise strips 1-inch wide. Blot surfaces of potatoes and zucchini dry; rub oil over all surfaces. Spread a thin film of vegetable oil in heavy bottomed skillet, add vegetables and sprinkle with seasonings. Cover with lid and cook over low heat 18 to 20 minutes or until tender. Slide egg turner under vegetables while cooking to prevent sticking. During last 10 minutes, remove lid to prevent steaming. Makes 4 servings.

For a browner, crispier vegetable, cover and steam potatoes and zucchini for 5 minutes on top of stove, remove lid, then bake in 350° oven for 30 minutes.

* Use the basic meatloaf recipe and add a small amount of garlic powder, basil and oregano. Brown patty in skillet with 1 teaspoon oil.

Green Potatoes

Children love broccoli this way!

4 medium potatoes

1 large broccoli stalk

1/4 cup 1/2% low-fat or skim milk

4 teaspoons tub margarine

4 tablespoons grated cheddar or
  mozzarella cheese

1 teaspoon lite salt

black pepper to taste

dash of paprika

Preheat oven to 400°. Scrub potatoes and make shallow slit around the middle as if you were cutting the potato in half, lengthwise. During baking, this forms a rim for each potato half. Bake until done, about 45 minutes. Peel off outer surface of broccoli stem, then cut stem and head into 1/2-inch pieces. Steam until just tender and bright green. Cut potato along rim; scoop out potatoes into pre-warmed bowl. Add milk, margarine, cheese, broccoli, lite salt and pepper; mash all together. Place potato shells on baking pan, pile filling into shells. Top with paprika and heat in 350° oven 10 to 15 minutes. Makes 4 servings.

Cooked peas, chopped green beans, chopped green onions or chives can be used in place of or in addition to broccoli.

Nutrients per serving:

calories	223
protein	6 gm
carbohydrate	34 gm
total fat	7 gm
saturated fat	2 gm
monounsat'd fat	2 gm
cholesterol	8 mg
sodium	250 mg
potassium	825 mg
fiber	4 gm

% US-RDA

vitamin A	11
vitamin C	70
thiamin	13
riboflavin	8
vitamin B$_6$	24
folacin	16
iron	16
zinc	5
calcium	10

Red Potato-Cottage Cheese Salad

Delicious, low-fat, high fiber potato salad that keeps well.

5 medium red, thin-skinned potatoes

1 cup water

1/2 teaspoon lite salt

1 medium onion, thinly sliced; red onion, if available

1 carton (12 oz.) 2% low-fat cottage cheese

1/3 cup salad dressing

1/2 teaspoon lite salt

black pepper to taste

Nutrients per serving:

calories	232
protein	10 gm
carbohydrate	30 gm
total fat	8 gm
saturated fat	3 gm
monounsat'd fat	2 gm
cholesterol	13 mg
sodium	550 mg
potassium	830 mg
fiber	4 gm

% US-RDA

vitamin A	5
vitamin C	19
thiamin	14
riboflavin	9
vitamin B_6	20
folacin	12
iron	4
zinc	3
calcium	8

Scrub potatoes; do not peel, cut into bite size pieces. Bring water and lite salt to a boil in a one-quart saucepan. Slip potatoes into water and cook until almost tender, about 10 minutes. Stir potatoes once or twice while cooking to assure even cooking; do not over cook. Drain liquid from potatoes. Rinse with cold water for a faster cool down. Chill potatoes in serving/storage container in freezer for 10 to 15 minutes; do not allow to freeze. Add remaining ingredients and mix gently. Cover and chill in refrigerator. Makes 8 servings.

This tangy potato salad makes a nutrient-rich lunch entree. Because it is an eggless potato salad, it is safe for picnics.

Hot German Potato Salad

A warm, tangy potato salad.

1 cup boiling water

¹/₂ teaspoon lite salt

5 medium potatoes, scrubbed, unpeeled, cut into 1-inch pieces

5 strips thin-sliced bacon

1 small onion, chopped

2 to 4 tablespoons cider vinegar or to taste

1 teaspoon sugar

¹/₂ teaspoon lite salt

black pepper to taste

Bring water and lite salt to a boil in one-quart saucepan. Add potatoes, cover with tight lid and simmer about 10 to 12 minutes until fork-tender; drain and set aside. Fry bacon in skillet until crisp; drain on paper towels. In skillet containing bacon drippings, combine potatoes, crumbled bacon and remaining ingredients. Cook over low heat 4 to 6 minutes until heated through, stirring to prevent sticking. Makes 4 servings.

A faster potato salad can be made by substituting instant potato flakes. Thinly sliced celery, pimento or prepared mustard may be added. Well-blotted bacon bits contain only 30 calories per tablespoon.

Nutrients per serving:

calories	256
protein	5 gm
carbohydrate	32 gm
total fat	12 gm
saturated fat	4 gm
monounsat'd fat	6 gm
cholesterol	10 mg
sodium	250 mg
potassium	846 mg
fiber	1 gm

% US-RDA

vitamin A	2
vitamin C	40
thiamin	14
riboflavin	6
vitamin B₆	5
folacin	5
iron	12
zinc	2
calcium	4

Hash Browns

A delicious, low-fat and quick potato for any meal.

4 teaspoons canola oil, unheated

4 (3 oz.) frozen hash brown potato patties or 12-ounces loose frozen hash browns

¹/₂ teaspoon paprika

¹/₂ teaspoon onion powder

¹/₄ teaspoon lite salt

black pepper to taste

Pour oil into unheated skillet. Do not preheat oil. Add frozen hash browns. Sprinkle on half the seasonings. Cook over medium heat. After oil begins to bubble around the edges of the potatoes, fry undisturbed 6 to 8 minutes. Turn, sprinkle on other half of the seasonings and fry for 3 to 4 more minutes to desired brownness. Makes 4 servings.

Read package label to be certain no oil or fat has been pre-added to the hash browns. When too small an amount of frying oil is used, potatoes are apt to stick. A nonstick or shiny smooth surface helps to prevent sticking. Caution: Ice crystals on food can cause spattering in hot oil. Remove ice crystals before adding hash browns to oil. If oil smokes, reduce the heat. If oil spatters, cover immediately and remove from heat. Be careful not to spatter or spill oil onto hot burner of range.

Nutrients per serving:

calories	*110*
protein	*2 gm*
carbohydrate	*16 gm*
total fat	*5 gm*
saturated fat	*1 gm*
monounsat'd fat	*3 gm*
cholesterol	*0 mg*
sodium	*75 mg*
potassium	*460 mg*
fiber	*0 gm*

% US-RDA

vitamin A	*3*
vitamin C	*20*
thiamin	*8*
riboflavin	*3*
vitamin B$_6$	*****
folacin	*****
iron	*4*
zinc	*****
calcium	*****

Baked Potato Wedges

Use this method for oven French fries.

4 medium potatoes

1¹/₂ tablespoons tub margarine

¹/₂ teaspoon lite salt

¹/₂ teaspoon garlic or onion powder

sprinkle of paprika

Preheat oven to 400°. Scrub potatoes, do not peel. Cut in quarters, lengthwise; blot to dry cut surfaces. Melt margarine in baking pan. Turn potato wedges in margarine to coat. With cut surfaces up, sprinkle with lite salt, garlic powder and paprika. Bake 30 to 40 minutes or until potatoes are lightly browned and tender. Makes 4 servings.

"What could be more versatile than the potato? It even comes in five basic types...and numerous varieties," says The Potato Board. "New" potatoes are not a variety but simply potatoes that come directly from the field and are available all year. The types of potato are the New Potato, Russet, Round Red, Long White and Round White.

Nutrients per serving:

calories	142
protein	2 gm
carbohydrate	20 gm
total fat	6 gm
saturated fat	1 gm
monounsat'd fat	3 gm
cholesterol	0 mg
sodium	200 mg
potassium	315 mg
fiber	2 gm

% US-RDA

vitamin A	8
vitamin C	20
thiamin	8
riboflavin	2
vitamin B_6	9
folacin	3
iron	5
zinc	***
calcium	***

Favorite Baked Sweet Potatoes

Sweet potatoes are delightfully enhanced with fruit and fruit toppings.

6 cups sliced, cooked sweet potatoes

1/4 cup orange juice

1/4 cup tub margarine, melted

1/2 cup brown sugar

1 cup crushed pineapple, drained

2 cups miniature marshmallows

Preheat oven to 375°. Lightly oil 9x13-inch baking dish. Arrange sweet potatoes in the dish. Pour orange juice over potatoes. Heat margarine, brown sugar and pineapple together. Spoon over sweet potatoes. Top with marshmallows. Bake 30 minutes or until marshmallows are lightly browned. Makes 8 servings.

The sweet potato and the yam are the two types of yellow colored potatoes. The sweet potato is rather dry with a pinky-yellow flesh and is extremely high in beta-carotene which is converted to vitamin A. This tuber is from the morning glory family and is grown in all but the northern states. The sweeter, softer and more moist yam is a vivid orange tuberous root and contains only a trace of beta-carotene. The yam originated in West Africa but is now cultivated in the United States and in tropical climates.

Nutrients per serving:

calories	266
protein	2 gm
carbohydrate	51 gm
total fat	6 gm
saturated fat	2 gm
monounsat'd fat	2 gm
cholesterol	0 mg
sodium	150 mg
potassium	350 mg
fiber	2 gm

% US-RDA

vitamin A	125
vitamin C	45
thiamin	6
riboflavin	5
vitamin B₆	9
folacin	10
iron	***
zinc	***
calcium	5

Flavorful Fruit

Fruit fulfills beautifully that end-of-the-meal craving for something sweet. In warmer countries, a typical dessert is a juicy peach, a plate of grapes or a tray of sliced apples and cheese. In northern countries, we relied on rich, calorie-laden desserts because the necessary ingredients of lard, shortening, sugar and flour were available year round. Change began with the era of air-freight and fast, refrigerated truck deliveries which brought us mountains of fresh fruit from all parts of the world.

More and more, we turn to the natural goodness of fruit as a choice for a low calorie, fat-free dessert that is low in sodium and rich in potassium and fiber. Fruit is the perfect dessert!

To bring out the best in fresh fruit:

- *Select the most flavorful fruits. Ask the supermarket produce manager or vendor for advice.*
- *Ripen fruits by placing them in a brown paper bag. Fold the top shut and place the bag in a warm place, such as the top of the refrigerator. Fruits that can be bag ripened are apricots, avocados, bananas, kiwi, melons, nectarines, peaches, pears and pineapples.*
- *Enhance the flavor of sliced fruit with a dash of cinnamon or ginger or a teaspoon of grated orange or lemon peel.*
- *Improve the flavor of tart fruits with a little powdered sugar or sugar substitute.*

Fruits get their sweetness from the natural sugar, fructose. When canned fruits are packed in their own juice, fructose adds 15 to 20 calories per serving above the calories of the raw fruit. These calories come from the extra juice added by the packer. Fruits in a light sugar-syrup pack add 20 to 30 calories per serving above those in the natural fruit, and fruits packed in heavy sugar-syrup add 35 to 45 calories per serving. Include two to four servings of fruit in your diet every day, whether it is fresh, canned or dried.

When eaten in the amounts shown below, each item of fruit provides 60 calories and 15 grams of carbohydrate. Because nutrient values vary for every fruit, figures are rounded.

	Serving	Sodium mgs	Potassium mgs	Fiber grams
Fresh and canned fruit:				
Apple, with skin	1 small	1	160	3
Applesauce, unsweetened	1/2 cup	2	90	1 1/2
Apricots, in natural juice	1/2	5	200	1 1/2
Apricots, medium, raw	4	1	400	1 1/2
Banana, 9 inch	1/2	1	330	1
Berries, except strawberries	3/4 cup	0	150	3
Cantaloupe, cubes	1 cup	14	490	1 1/2
Cherries, sweet, raw	12	0	180	2
Fruit cocktail, in natural jce	1/2 cup	4	120	1 1/2
Grapefruit, medium	1/2	0	160	1/2
Grapefruit, in natural juice	3/4 cup	12	300	1/2
Grapes, raw	15	2	175	1
Honeydew melon, cubes	1 cup	20	460	1 1/2
Kiwi	1 large	5	330	3
Mandarin orange, in nat. jce	3/4 cup	9	215	0
Mango, fresh	1/2	2	160	1
Nectarine, 1 1/2-inch diameter	1	0	280	2
Orange, 2 1/2-inch diameter	1	1	250	2 1/2
Papaya, cubes	1 cup	4	390	1
Peach, 2 3/4-inch diameter	1	1	340	1 1/2
Peaches, in natural juice	1/2 cup	5	160	1 1/2
Pear, fresh	1 small	1	130	4
Pears, in natural juice	1/2 cup	5	120	1 1/2
Pineapple, fresh	3/4 cup	1	160	2
Pineapple, in nat. juice	3/4 cup	2	140	2
Plum, raw, 2 1/8-inch dia.	2	0	220	1
Pomegranate	1/2	3	240	0
Raspberries, fresh	1 cup	0	185	3 1/2
Strawberries, fresh	1 1/4 cups	2	200	4
Tangerine, 2 1/2-inch dia.	2	2	260	1/2
Watermelon, cubes	1 1/4 cups	3	230	1/2

	Serving	Sodium mgs	Potassium mgs	Fiber grams
Dried fruit:				
Apple, sulfured	4 rings	22	115	1
Apricots, sulfured	7 halves	2	330	2½
Dates	2½ medium	2	135	1½
Figs	1½	2	200	2½
Prunes	3 medium	1	185	4½
Raisins	2 tbsp	2	150	1½
Fruit juices:				
Apple juice or cider	½ cup	3	150	0
Cranberry juice cocktail	⅓ cup	4	30	0
Dietetic cranberry juice	1 cup	9	60	0
Grape juice	⅓ cup	2	100	0
Grapefruit jce, unsweetened	½ cup	1	160	0
Orange juice	½ cup	1	250	0
Pineapple juice	½ cup	1	110	0
Prune juice	⅓ cup	4	230	1

Easy Applesauce
Aromatic with fresh apple flavor.

6 medium tart apples, cored, unpeeled

1/4 cup apple juice or water

sugar or sugar substitute to taste, if desired

Wash apples, remove cores but do not peel. Cut into thick slices. In two-quart saucepan, simmer slices in apple juice until just tender, about 5 minutes. Pour into blender. If blender container is glass, warm first. Puree to applesauce consistency; add sugar or sugar substitute to taste. Serve warm or chilled. Makes 4 servings.

Jonathan, Wine Sap, Rome Beauty and Granny Smith are tart apple varieties. Cooking briefly in apple juice preserves the fresh apple taste and fiber.

Add cinnamon flavored red hot candy for a spicy, sweet pink dessert.

Nutrients per serving:

calories	120
protein	0 gm
carbohydrate	30 gm
total fat	0 gm
saturated fat	0 gm
monounsat'd fat	0 gm
cholesterol	0 mg
sodium	2 mg
potassium	230 mg
fiber	4 gm

% US-RDA

vitamin A	2
vitamin C	16
thiamin	2
riboflavin	2
vitamin B_6	5
folacin	2
iron	3
zinc	***
calcium	***

Apricot Bread Pudding

Or any other fresh or canned fruit tastes good!

¹/₂ cup egg substitute or egg whites

1 cup ¹/₂% low-fat or skim milk

¹/₂ teaspoon vanilla

¹/₂ cup brown sugar

¹/₂ teaspoon cinnamon

5 slices wheat or white bread, torn into
   1-inch pieces

1 can (16 oz.) apricots, drained, chopped

sprinkle of nutmeg or ginger

Preheat oven to 350°. In skillet or Dutch oven, combine egg substitute, milk, vanilla, brown sugar and cinnamon. Mix well. Gently stir in torn bread and chopped apricots. Sprinkle top with nutmeg or ginger. Bake 20 to 25 minutes or until firm and knife comes out clean. Makes 5 servings.

An old-fashioned family dessert that includes foods from four food groups. A versatile recipe that provides a variety of desserts using just one pan for both mixing and baking.

Nutrients per serving:

calories	*272*
protein	*7 gm*
carbohydrate	*52 gm*
total fat	*4 gm*
saturated fat	*1 gm*
monounsat'd fat	*1 gm*
cholesterol	*2 mg*
sodium	*260 mg*
potassium	*330 mg*
fiber	*3 gm*

% US-RDA

vitamin A	*32*
vitamin C	*4*
thiamin	*13*
riboflavin	*13*
vitamin B₆	*17*
folacin	*10*
iron	*12*
zinc	*5*
calcium	*15*

Strawberry-Banana Gelatin

Young cooks quickly and successfully learn to make fruited gelatin desserts.

1 cup boiling water

1 package (3 oz.) strawberry gelatin powder

1 cup cold water

2 small bananas, sliced

Pour boiling water into serving bowl. Sprinkle gelatin on top and stir until completely dissolved. Add cold water and stir well. Gently stir in banana slices. Cover and refrigerate until firm. Makes 5 servings.

Add 1¹/₂ cups (¹/₂ pound) cooked or fresh fruit for two cups of gelatin-water mixture. Use peaches, pears, melon or apples in season, or a mixture of fresh, frozen, and drained canned fruits. Do not use fresh or frozen pineapple or kiwi; they contain an enzyme which prevents the gelatin from setting. Canned pineapple may be used.

Soft-set gelatin is ready to eat in 30 minutes. Pour ³/₄ cup boiling water into serving bowl. Sprinkle gelatin on top and stir until completely dissolved. Combine ¹/₂ cup cold water and ice cubes to make 1¹/₄ cups ice and water. Add to gelatin, stirring until slightly thickened. Remove any unmelted ice. Refrigerate uncovered for about 30 minutes until thickened.

Nutrients per serving:

calories	124
protein	2 gm
carbohydrate	29 gm
total fat	0 gm
saturated fat	0 gm
monounsat'd fat	0 gm
cholesterol	0 mg
sodium	50 mg
potassium	220 mg
fiber	1 gm

% US-RDA

vitamin A	***
vitamin C	8
thiamin	2
riboflavin	5
vitamin B₆	14
folacin	6
iron	***
zinc	***
calcium	***

Cherry-Apple Treat

A luscious, nonfat dessert or topping.

2 tablespoons cornstarch

1/2 cup sugar

1/2 teaspoon cinnamon

liquid drained from cherries

1 can (15 oz.) red sour pitted cherries, water packed

1/2 teaspoon almond extract (optional)

1 large unpeeled apple, diced, or 1 medium banana, sliced

In a two-quart saucepan, combine cornstarch, sugar and cinnamon; stir in liquid from cherries. Cook over medium heat until thick, stirring constantly. Add cherries and almond extract. Cool. (Puree in blender if it is to be used as a topping.) Add diced apple just before serving. Makes 5 dessert servings or 20 topping servings 2-tablespoons each.

An even quicker dessert is made by combining cherry fruit filling with sliced bananas. Fresh strawberries, drained fruit cocktail or drained pineapple tidbits may be substituted for banana. Nonfat Whipped Topping (see page 225) dresses up the treat.

Nutrients per serving:

calories *152*
protein .... *1 gm*
carbohydrate .... *37 gm*
total fat .... *0 gm*
saturated fat .... *0 gm*
monounsat'd fat .... *0 gm*
cholesterol .... *0 mg*
sodium .... *7 mg*
potassium .... *185 mg*
fiber .... *1 gm*

% US-RDA

vitamin A 18
vitamin C 7
thiamin 2
riboflavin 5
vitamin B$_6$ 13
folacin 6
iron 8
zinc .... ***
calcium 2

Spiced Fruit Compote

Avoid busy times — make a gingery fruit dessert days ahead.

1 can (20 oz.) juice-packed pineapple
   tidbits

10 each whole cloves

¹/₄ teaspoons ginger

1 cup dried, pitted prunes

1 cup orange juice

1 teaspoon fresh grated orange peel

2 large, seedless oranges, peeled and cut
   in bite sized chunks

2 medium apples, unpeeled, cored and
   thinly sliced

¹/₃ cup honey (more for sweeter flavor)

Nutrients per serving:

calories *128*
protein .... *1 gm*
carbohydrate .... *31 gm*
total fat .... *0 gm*
saturated fat .... *0 gm*
monounsat'd fat .... *0 gm*
cholesterol .... *0 mg*
sodium .... *2 mg*
potassium .... *250 mg*
fiber .... *2 gm*

% US-RDA

vitamin A 3
vitamin C 40
thiamin 7
riboflavin 3
vitamin B₆ 5
folacin 9
iron 3
zinc .... ***
calcium 3

Drain juice from pineapple tidbits into one-quart saucepan. Pour tidbits into a two-quart bowl. Add whole cloves and ginger to pineapple juice and simmer for 5 minutes. Remove cloves and pour over pineapple tidbits. Add prunes, orange juice, orange peel and orange chunks, sliced apple and honey. Gently mix together. Cover and refrigerate for 24 hours to allow flavors to mellow. Keeps 7 to 10 days in refrigerator. Makes 10 servings.

Honey, cloves and ginger help to preserve and develop the fruit flavors in a do-ahead dessert. Fruit compotes, kept warm and aromatic over a candle flame, are particularly tasty after a filling holiday or cold weather meal.

110

Any Season Fruit Salad

A quick dessert to enjoy now or later.

1 can (11 oz.) mandarin oranges, not
   drained

1 can (20 oz.) pineapple tidbits, not
   drained

1 cup miniature marshmallows

10 maraschino cherries, cut in half
   (optional)

1 to 2 cups of fresh fruits, chopped in
   bite-size pieces. (apples, apricots,
   grapefruit, melon, nectarines, oranges,
   peaches, plums or seedless grapes)

In a large serving bowl or storage container, gently mix together undrained canned fruit, marshmallows, maraschino cherries and fresh fruits. Cover and refrigerate until serving time. Keeps 24 to 48 hours and flavors blend and mellow. Makes 8 servings.

Any blend of fruit is a welcome, light and tasty way to complete your meal. An acidic fruit makes a tangy base. Remember to add bananas, kiwi and fresh berries just before serving to prevent them from becoming mushy.

Nutrients per serving:

calories	116
protein	1 gm
carbohydrate	28 gm
total fat	0 gm
saturated fat	0 gm
monounsat'd fat	0 gm
cholesterol	0 mg
sodium	5 mg
potassium	190 mg
fiber	2 gm

% US-RDA

vitamin A	2
vitamin C	47
thiamin	9
riboflavin	3
vitamin B_6	2
folacin	6
iron	5
zinc	***
calcium	2

Peach Crisp

Dressed up pie filling for a yummy dessert.

Crisp topping:

¼ cup tub margarine, softened

¼ cup brown sugar

½ cup oatmeal, uncooked quick or regular

½ cup all-purpose or whole wheat flour

1 teaspoon cinnamon

1 can (29 oz.) peach pie filling

1 can (11 oz.) mandarin orange sections, drained, or pineapple chunks, drained

Preheat oven to 400°. In a small mixing bowl, combine margarine, brown sugar, oatmeal, flour and cinnamon and mix until crumbly. In skillet or Dutch oven, mix pie filling with mandarin orange sections and heat until bubbly, stirring gently but constantly. Sprinkle on topping. Bake for 15 minutes to brown topping. Makes 6 servings.

Any pie filling may be used; add 1 to 2 cups of fresh, frozen, or drained canned fruit.
Serve warm or cold with a scoop of low-fat frozen yogurt or nonfat Whipped Topping (see page 225).

Nutrients per serving:

calories	298
protein	2 gm
carbohydrate	50 gm
total fat	10 gm
saturated fat	2 gm
monounsat'd fat	4 gm
cholesterol	0 mg
sodium	160 mg
potassium	270 mg
fiber	2 gm

% US-RDA

vitamin A	24
vitamin C	33
thiamin	10
riboflavin	5
vitamin B₆	4
folacin	10
iron	7
zinc	3
calcium	5

No-Cook Prunes
with Orange Juice

Great prune flavor and effortless to make.

1 package (24 oz.) prunes, dried, pitted

1 to 1¹/₂ cups boiling water

¹/₂ cup orange juice

Place dried prunes in storage bowl. Pour boiling water over prunes to just cover. Place lid loosely over container. When cool, add orange juice and stir. Cover and refrigerate for at least 6 hours. Makes 12 servings.

Prunes are a high *fiber, high iron fruit.*

The longer the prunes chill in the refrigerator, the more tender and plump they become in a rich, sweet juice.

Use this process to plump raisins or any dried fruit or fruit mix.

Nutrients per serving:

calories	*150*
protein	*1 gm*
carbohydrate	*36 gm*
total fat	*0 gm*
saturated fat	*0 gm*
monounsat'd fat	*0 gm*
cholesterol	*0 mg*
sodium	*3 mg*
potassium	*440 mg*
fiber	*4 gm*

% US-RDA

vitamin A	*20*
vitamin C	*10*
thiamin	*3*
riboflavin	*4*
vitamin B₆	*7*
folacin	*3*
iron	*9*
zinc	*****
calcium	*3*

Low-Fat Chocolate Prune Brownies

Delicious — and quick to fix.

1 box (21 ¹/₂ oz.) brownie mix (see note below)

1 egg, large, well beaten

¹/₃ cup finely mashed or pureed cooked prunes (see page 113)

¹/₄ to ¹/₂ cup water

Preheat oven to 350°. Oil bottom only of 9 x 13-inch pan. Pour dry brownie mix into mixing bowl. Add egg, prunes and water. Stir with spoon until just mixed, about 40 strokes. It may appear there is not enough water and prunes to dampen the mix, but continue mixing and stop when it is just dampened. Spread the thick mixture evenly over bottom of pan, smoothing to the sides and corners of pan. Bake until just barely done, about 25 to 30 minutes. The brownies will be moist, but not sticky when surface is touched. Do not continue baking unless you like a drier, cake-like brownie. Cool on rack. Cut with sharp, clean, wet knife. Cover to prevent drying. To develop flavors, allow to blend for 12 – 14 hours. Makes 24 2-inch squares.

Nutrients per serving:

calories	114
protein	2 gm
carbohydrate	22 gm
total fat	2 gm
saturated fat	1 gm
monounsat'd fat	1 gm
cholesterol	10 mg
sodium	110 mg
potassium	60 mg
fiber	2 gm

% US-RDA

vitamin A	***
vitamin C	***
thiamin	4
riboflavin	6
vitamin B_6	***
folacin	***
iron	10
zinc	3
calcium	***

To select a low-fat brownie mix, read the label and select one that contains 2 grams or less of fat, in the dry mix, for a 2-inch square brownie. Avoid those that contain chocolate chips, nuts, fudge syrups and toppings. Try different brands, as some make tastier brownies than others. The small amount of fat in the packaged mix provides the flavor and texture that only fat can give. To keep fat level low, do not frost.

Cooked, well-mashed or pureed prunes substitute particularly well for the vegetable oil called for in recipes for cocoa and chocolate baked items.

The Lowly Bean

The seemingly lowly bean is, in fact, a nutritional prince. It is low in fat and high in numerous elements such as fiber, complex carbohydrates, B vitamins, iron, zinc, calcium and potassium. Compare the nutritional analysis for a bean dish with any other to see how amazingly great they are. The bean family contains dozens of varieties. Cook them from scratch using dried beans, or use the canned varieties for quick-to-fix meals. Beans make a tasty side dish or an ingredient in soups, salads, casseroles or sandwich spreads.

Persons who don't normally eat many beans may experience flatulence, or gas. Dried beans and vegetables from the cabbage family such as broccoli and cauliflower may also cause this problem. Gas is produced by indigestible raffinose fibers which are fed upon by bacteria in the colon. Now, a gas preventing enzyme is available from your local pharmacy. It works in the stomach by digesting only raffinose fibers. Fortunately, other fibers remain indigestible, allowing people to benefit from them. Gas forming compounds may also be reduced by pouring the soaking water off beans. Some nutrients are lost, but it is better to be comfortable than to avoid the nutritious bean.

For the busy person, the supermarket provides a wide assortment of economical canned beans. These tend to be higher in sodium than the home-cooked variety, but are equally nutritious. For those who prefer to cook their own, a big pot of refrigerated beans will keep well for four or five days, or can be frozen for several months. Beans are easier to digest when they have been well cooked. To test, place a bean on your tongue and press it against the roof of your mouth. If it can be mashed, it is done.

For tasty beans remember:

- *Vinegar or lemon enhances the bean flavor. Add one or two teaspoons to one cup cooked beans and adjust to taste.*
- *Bay leaf, basil, sage or garlic improve bean flavor.*
- *Chopped fresh onion is a great addition.*

Crock Pot Beans

Presoaking is not necessary with crock pot cooking.

1 pound (3½ to 4 cups) dried small white beans

8 to 10 cups water

1 to 3 teaspoons lite salt

1 teaspoon garlic powder or other herbs as desired

1 to 2 medium onions, chopped

8 oz. lean ham, cut in ¾ inch cubes

1 teaspoon liquid smoke (optional)

Sort through beans to remove rocks and discolored beans. Rinse well. Combine all ingredients in crock pot. Set temperature setting at high until beans come to a boil, then cover and turn to low to cook 6 to 8 hours. Depending on the bean, more water may be needed. Makes ten 1-cup servings.

Nutritionally wonderful; low in fat but high in fiber, vitamins and minerals.

Cook a variety of beans together. Although there is a wide difference in cooking time among different beans, the long, slow cooking will cook the beans evenly.

Nutrients per serving:

calories	*323*
protein	*23 gm*
carbohydrate	*53 gm*
total fat	*3 gm*
saturated fat	*1 gm*
monounsat'd fat	*1 gm*
cholesterol	*11 mg*
sodium	*680 mg*
potassium	*1500 mg*
fiber	*9 gm*

% US-RDA

vitamin A	*****
vitamin C	*4*
thiamin	*59*
riboflavin	*13*
vitamin B₆	*20*
folacin	*140*
iron	*40*
zinc	*18*
calcium	*19*

Many Bean Soup

Colorful and delicious!

1 bag (12 oz.) mixed dried beans
   (2¹/₂ cups)

5 cups water

1 tablespoon lite salt

8 cups water

1 teaspoon lite salt

1 pound lean ham, cut in ¹/₃ inch cubes

1 can (28 oz.) tomatoes, chopped

1 large onion, chopped

1 tablespoon sugar

1 teaspoon garlic powder

black pepper to taste

Prepare in crock pot or four-quart cooking pot. Sort through beans to remove rock and discolored beans, then rinse. Cover beans with 5 cups of water and 1 tablespoon lite salt. Soak 3 hours or overnight. Drain and rinse. Add 8 cups of water and remaining ingredients to beans; cook 4 hours or until a bean mashes easily with tongue against the roof of mouth. Makes eight 1¹/₄ cup-servings.

For a spicier flavor, add any or all: pod of red pepper, 1 to 2 teaspoons chili powder or 1 small can chilies. Simmer another 30 to 60 minutes.

Nutrients per serving:

calories	380
protein	22 gm
carbohydrate	55 gm
total fat	8 gm
saturated fat	2 gm
monounsat'd fat	3 gm
cholesterol	30 mg
sodium	800 mg
potassium	1000 mg
fiber	9 gm

% US-RDA

vitamin A	10
vitamin C	20
thiamin	50
riboflavin	23
vitamin B₆	23
folacin	120
iron	40
zinc	18
calcium	19

Bean, Vegetable and Ham Soup

Super supper in 25 minutes!

1 can (15 oz.) white beans

1 can (15 oz.) tomatoes, chopped

1/4 medium onion, chopped

2 oz. low-fat ham chunks

1/4 small head cabbage, shredded

dash of any or all: black pepper, marjoram, garlic powder, thyme, parsley flakes, basil

1/4 teaspoon smoke flavor (optional)

Nutrients per serving:

calories 440
protein.................. 28 gm
carbohydrate........... 72 gm
total fat .... 4 gm
saturated fat............. 1 gm
monounsat'd fat......... 2 gm
cholesterol .... 20 mg
sodium .... 770 mg
potassium............ 1880 mg
fiber .... 14 gm

% US-RDA

vitamin A................. 28
vitamin C.................. 140
thiamin.................... 75
riboflavin 20
vitamin B₆................ 44
folacin.................... 90
iron....................... 53
zinc 24
calcium................... 35

In two-quart saucepan, mix all ingredients and herbs. Simmer 15 minutes or longer. Makes 2 servings.

Serve with chunks of bread, crackers or homemade low-fat muffins, fruit and a drink selected from the Low-Fat Milk Bar on pages 209-210.

Add carrots, celery, potatoes, left over vegetables and liquid poured from canned and cooked vegetables. As with most soups, flavor improves with longer cooking time. This soup, like most broth soups, can be cooked ahead, stored in refrigerator for up to three days, and then reheated.

Chili Beans and Tamales

A quick, spicy dinner.

1 can (15 oz.) chili beans or ranch-style
   beans

1 can (15 oz.) tamales

6 slices fresh tomato

2 oz. low-fat mozzarella cheese, shredded

1/4 head of lettuce, shredded

3 green onions, chopped

taco sauce to taste (optional)

Discard greasy layer from chili beans. Drain liquid off tamales. Pull wrapped tamales out of can and gently remove wrappers. Run warm water over each tamale to remove fat clumps. Spread 1 teaspoon vegetable oil evenly over skillet, place tamales in skillet and pour beans over tamales. Cover and simmer 10 minutes. To prevent sticking while heating, gently slide egg turner under tamales. Place tamales with beans on heated plates. Top with remaining ingredients. Makes 2 servings.

In winter, sliced whole canned tomatoes are tastier than fresh tomatoes.

This low-fat, nutrient rich, high-fiber meal would have 22 grams of fat per serving, but because greasy top layers and fat chunks are removed, there are only 10 grams of fat per serving.

Nutrients per serving:

calories	*517*
protein	*30 gm*
carbohydrate	*75 gm*
total fat	*10 gm*
saturated fat	*2 gm*
monounsat'd fat	*1 gm*
cholesterol	*12 mg*
sodium	*810 mg*
potassium	*525 mg*
fiber	*10 gm*

% US-RDA

vitamin A	45
vitamin C	37
thiamin	51
riboflavin	25
vitamin B_6	4
folacin	18
iron	28
zinc	6
calcium	35

Quick Baked Beans

*Use this basic recipe and include
your favorite beans and seasonings.*

1 can (15 oz.) pork and beans, not
   drained

1 can (15 oz.) barbecue or chili beans, not
   drained

1/2 cup onion, chopped

2 tablespoons brown sugar or molasses

1 teaspoon dry mustard or 2 teaspoons
   prepared mustard

1/4 cup catsup or tomato sauce

1/2 teaspoon liquid smoke (optional)

Nutrients per serving:

calories	303
protein	12 gm
carbohydrate	63 gm
total fat	3 gm
saturated fat	1 gm
monounsat'd fat	1 gm
cholesterol	8 mg
sodium	1100 mg
potassium	780 mg
fiber	15 gm

% US-RDA

vitamin A	15
vitamin C	14
thiamin	21
riboflavin	12
vitamin B$_6$	17
folacin	36
iron	18
zinc	22
calcium	18

Preheat oven to 350°. Discard greasy top layer and any fat chunks from canned beans. Place unoiled Dutch oven on burner over low heat, combine all ingredients, blend gently but well. Bake uncovered for 40 to 50 minutes. Makes 4 servings.

Pre-warming ingredients in Dutch oven cuts the baking time.
Mix ingredients together ahead of time and refrigerate until baking time.
Serve with a tossed green salad, bread or cornbread, a cold glass of milk and a serving of fruit to provide a nutritionally complete and balanced meal.

Nachos Special

For your guests, a nutritious, low-fat snack ready to serve in 25 minutes.

3/4 **pound lean ground beef**

1 **can (15 oz.) refried beans**

1 **teaspoon chili powder**

1/2 **teaspoon cumin**

1/8 **teaspoon oregano**

1/4 **small onion, finely chopped**

1/4 **pound low-fat mozzarella cheese, shredded**

2 **tomatoes, diced**

1/2 **head lettuce, shredded**

In heavy bottomed skillet, brown ground beef and drain and blot off fat. Set aside. In separate bowl, combine beans, herbs and onion; mix thoroughly and spread on medium platter or plate. Layer with ground beef, cheese, tomatoes and lettuce. Makes 8 snack-size servings.

Serve with low-fat, low salt tortilla chips and salsa.

Nutrients per serving:

calories	*190*
protein	*15 gm*
carbohydrate	*12 gm*
total fat	*9 gm*
saturated fat	*4 gm*
monounsat'd fat	*4 gm*
cholesterol	*36 mg*
sodium	*330 mg*
potassium	*410 mg*
fiber	*1 gm*

% US-RDA

vitamin A	*8*
vitamin C	*11*
thiamin	*6*
riboflavin	*13*
vitamin B$_6$	*9*
folacin	*8*
iron	*14*
zinc	*20*
calcium	*15*

Three Bean Salad

*A do-ahead salad can be put
together in 15 minutes.*

1 can (15 oz.) green beans, drained

1 can (15 oz.) white beans, drained

1 can (15 oz.) red beans, drained

1/2 green pepper, chopped

1 medium onion, sliced and separated
into rings

Vinaigrette dressing:

1/4 cup sugar

1 teaspoon dry mustard

1 teaspoon lite salt

1/4 teaspoon black pepper

1/3 cup canola or olive oil

1/2 cup vinegar

Place drained beans, green pepper and onion in large bowl. In a small bowl whisk together vinaigrette ingredients and pour over beans. Cover and refrigerate for 24 hours to blend flavors. Makes 12 servings.

Pinto beans, black-eyed peas, garbanzo beans (chick peas), green lima beans, butter beans or wax beans may be used. Refrigerated salad keeps well for a week. Great for picnics and buffet meals.

Nutrients per serving:

calories	*167*
protein	*6 gm*
carbohydrate	*21 gm*
total fat	*6 gm*
saturated fat	*1 gm*
monounsat'd fat	*4 gm*
cholesterol	*0 mg*
sodium	*305 mg*
potassium	*445 mg*
fiber	*5 gm*

% US-RDA

vitamin A	*3*
vitamin C	*20*
thiamin	*7*
riboflavin	*5*
vitamin B$_6$	*23*
folacin	*16*
iron	*14*
zinc	*5*
calcium	*5*

Any Bean Sandwich Spread

A tangy five-minute spread or dip.

1 can (15 oz.) drained beans

1/4 cup chili sauce or catsup or salsa

1/4 cup finely chopped onion

1/2 tablespoon vinegar or lemon juice

1 tablespoon chopped chives or dried
  parsley flakes (optional)

black pepper to taste

1/2 teaspoon lite salt

In a small deep bowl, mash ingredients together with a fork. Use immediately, or cover and refrigerate for use within 2 or 3 days. Makes 5 servings.

Use your creativity for a variety of sandwich or dip flavors. Garbanzo beans and soybeans do not mash easily. Try finely chopped celery, green peppers or grated carrots. Brighten the flavor with chili powder, cumin or hot pepper sauce.

Nutrients per serving:

calories *100*
protein . . . . *6 gm*
carbohydrate . . . . *19 gm*
total fat . . . . *1 gm*
saturated fat . . . . *0 gm*
monounsat'd fat . . . . *1 gm*
cholesterol . . . . *0 mg*
sodium . . . . *165 mg*
potassium . . . . *365 mg*
fiber . . . . *4 gm*

% US-RDA

vitamin A 4
vitamin C 5
thiamin 10
riboflavin 4
vitamin B$_6$ 24
folacin 14
iron 14
zinc 5
calcium 5

Basic Bean Burrito

A satisfying, fast, very low-fat meal.

2 tablespoons water

1 can (15 oz.) vegetarian refried beans

1/2 cup salsa or chopped green chilies

6 flour tortillas

2 medium tomatoes, chopped

4 green onions, chopped

1/2 small head of lettuce, shredded

1 cup low-fat yogurt

2 oz. low-fat mozzarella cheese, shredded

In heavy bottomed pan over medium heat, mix together water, refried beans and salsa. Stir while heating. Add water if needed to prevent sticking.

For each burrito:

Warm tortilla in pan with a thin film of canola oil; place on hot plate.

Mound 1/3 cup of hot bean mixture on tortilla.

Quickly top with tomato, green onion, lettuce, yogurt and cheese.

Fold tortilla over and eat while hot.

Makes 6 servings.

Like many Mexican dishes, this food is high in most nutrients and fiber. Because it is so low in fat, you can enjoy several of these filling treats.

Nutrients per serving:

calories	264
protein	12 gm
carbohydrate	45 gm
total fat	4 gm
saturated fat	2 gm
monounsat'd fat	1 gm
cholesterol	2 mg
sodium	595 mg
potassium	700 mg
fiber	4 gm

% US-RDA

vitamin A	16
vitamin C	38
thiamin	11
riboflavin	17
vitamin B_6	4
folacin	10
iron	24
zinc	12
calcium	21

Beef and Bean Stew

Delicious, cook ahead meal for a crowd.

1 pound lean trimmed round steak, cut in 1-inch
  cubes

1 tablespoon canola oil

1 can (28 oz.) tomatoes, chopped, not drained

2 cans (15 oz.) red or kidney beans, not drained

1/2 cup water or red wine

1 teaspoon sugar

1 teaspoon garlic powder or 2 minced garlic cloves

1/2 teaspoon basil

1/2 teaspoon thyme leaves

1/8 teaspoon black pepper

1 teaspoon lite salt

4 large potatoes, cubed

3 medium onions, cut in wedges

4 medium carrots, cut in 3-inch lengths

In heavy bottomed Dutch oven, brown meat in oil.
Add undrained tomatoes, beans, water, sugar, herbs,
black pepper and lite salt. Bring to a simmer for one
hour, or until meat is tender. Add potatoes, onions and
carrots. Continue cooking for 30 minutes. Longer
cooking improves the flavor. Makes 8 servings.

*Serve with hunks of herbed bread, a simple tossed salad
and fresh fruit or instant low-fat milk pudding.*

*Or, pour into large container to freeze for a future meal.
(Omit the potatoes until final heating, as frozen boiled
potatoes develop an unpleasant texture).*

Nutrients per serving:

calories	*257*
protein	*19 gm*
carbohydrate	*33 gm*
total fat	*5 gm*
saturated fat	*1 gm*
monounsat'd fat	*2 gm*
cholesterol	*32 mg*
sodium	*460 mg*
potassium	*1070 mg*
fiber	*6 gm*

% US-RDA

vitamin A	*215*
vitamin C	*48*
thiamin	*21*
riboflavin	*14*
vitamin B_6	*61*
folacin	*16*
iron	*22*
zinc	*17*
calcium	*8*

Faster Red Beans and Rice

Delightful and super nutritious.

1/3 cup canola or olive oil

1 large onion, chopped

1 medium green pepper, chopped

1 teaspoon garlic powder or 2 minced garlic cloves

1 bay leaf

1 can (15 oz.) tomatoes, chopped, not drained

3 cans (15 oz.) red or kidney beans, not drained

1/2 teaspoon oregano

1/2 teaspoon cumin

2 tablespoon vinegar

hot pepper sauce to taste

4 cups hot cooked rice

Nutrients per serving:

calories *460*
protein.................. *11 gm*
carbohydrate........... *70 gm*
total fat .... *15 gm*
saturated fat .... *2 gm*
monounsat'd fat........ *12 gm*
cholesterol.............. *0 mg*
sodium .... *440 mg*
potassium .... *590 mg*
fiber...................... *8 gm*

% US-RDA

vitamin A.................. *12*
vitamin C.................. *72*
thiamin *28*
riboflavin.................. *8*
vitamin B₆. *54*
folacin..................... *23*
iron........................ *30*
zinc *11*
calcium.................... *11*

In a heavy bottomed Dutch oven, heat oil, add onion, green pepper and garlic; cook for 4 minutes or until soft. Add bay leaf, undrained tomatoes and beans, oregano and cumin. Heat together for 30 minutes or longer. Stir to prevent sticking. While bean-vegetable mixture is cooking, prepare rice according to package directions. Remove bay leaf; add vinegar and hot pepper sauce. Serve immediately over freshly cooked hot rice. Makes 6 servings.

For a variation, serve over brown rice and topped with chopped onion and a dash of vinegar. A perfect meal when served with hot cornbread, cooked spinach, beet or turnip greens and a low-fat milk-based dessert. Speed the chopping chore by using a French knife.

Beneficial Tofu

It may look obscure — a small, white block in your grocery's produce section. But tofu has many virtues.

Tofu is a soybean product. The beans are first made into soy milk that is then curdled to form delicate white curds and pale yellow whey. The whey is drained and the curds are pressed into soft, white blocks. It is inexpensive, low in calories, fat and sodium, high in potassium and includes modest amounts of protein, calcium and other vitamins and minerals. As with all plant foods, tofu is cholesterol-free. And the small amount of oil that it does contain has almost no saturated fat.

Tofu's nutritional composition sounds as if it were custom-made for today's dietary recommendations. In fact, Oriental cultures have enjoyed tofu for more than 2,000 years. For generations, Oriental cultures were virtually free of cardiovascular trouble and other diseases induced by high-fat diets. As those cultures switched from their traditional diets to ours — high in fat and coupled with an inactive lifestyle — their rates for heart disease and cancer doubled and tripled.

Unless you plan to eat tofu immediately after purchase, cover it in fresh cold water daily. Changing the water allows tofu to keep in the refrigerator for a week to 10 days.

One of the most outstanding culinary qualities of tofu is its ability to assume the flavor of accompanying foods. Tofu may be used in main dishes, soups, salads, sauces, dips, sandwich spreads and desserts.

Macaroni-Tofu-Cheese Casserole

Speedy supper dish!

1 package (5¹/₂ to 7¹/₄ oz.) macaroni and cheese dinner

6 cups water

2 tablespoons tub margarine

¹/₂ cup ¹/₂% low-fat or skim milk

¹/₂ pound tofu cut in ¹/₃ inch cubes

In Dutch oven, cook macaroni according to package directions. Drain macaroni through collander. In same Dutch oven, melt margarine and blend in milk and cheese mix. Gently stir in tofu and heat. Add drained macaroni. Serve immediately or bake in 350° oven for 30 minutes. Herbed Breading added before baking (see page 12) makes an attractive topping. Makes 4 servings.

Save washing an extra pot by re-using the Dutch oven for the next step in recipe.
Serve with a bright green vegetable and/or tossed salad, a dinner roll and fruit dessert for an inexpensive, nutritious meal.

Nutrients per serving:

calories	431
protein	18 gm
carbohydrate	65 gm
total fat	11 gm
saturated fat	3 gm
monounsat'd fat	4 gm
cholesterol	3 mg
sodium	640 mg
potassium	465 mg
fiber	0 gm

% US-RDA

vitamin A	10
vitamin C	6
thiamin	34
riboflavin	19
vitamin B₆	15
folacin	18
iron	16
zinc	9
calcium	24

Spanish Rice with Tofu

*Use this recipe or the ten minute
instant recipe shown below.*

2 tablespoons canola oil

1 cup uncooked rice

1 medium onion, chopped

1 medium green pepper, chopped

1 can (15 oz.) tomatoes, chopped, but not
   drained

1 teaspoon lite salt

1/2 pound tofu, cut in 1/3-inch cubes

1 cup water

garlic powder to taste

black pepper to taste

In heavy bottomed Dutch oven, stir oil and rice
together and heat until rice starts to brown. Add onion
and green pepper and cook until vegetables are softened.
Add undrained tomatoes, lite salt, tofu, water, garlic
powder and pepper. Bring to a boil, reduce to a simmer
and cover with a tight fitting lid. Cook about 20 minutes,
or until rice is tender. Makes 4 servings.

Instant method: Prepare 3 cups cooked instant rice.
Heat 2 tablespoons canola oil in skillet. Add rice, 1 cup
picante sauce, 1 teaspoon lite salt and 1/2 pound tofu, cut
in cubes. Heat through and serve.

Nutrients per serving:

calories	*437*
protein	*15 gm*
carbohydrate	*65 gm*
total fat	*13 gm*
saturated fat	*1 gm*
monounsat'd fat	*8 gm*
cholesterol	*0 mg*
sodium	*700 mg*
potassium	*1200 mg*
fiber	*3 gm*

% US-RDA

vitamin A	*16*
vitamin C	*57*
thiamin	*39*
riboflavin	*9*
vitamin B_6	*18*
folacin	*16*
iron	*12*
zinc	*7*
calcium	*21*

Scrambled Vegetables and Tofu

Light, tasty, fast and easy.

2 tablespoons canola oil

1/2 small onion, chopped

1/2 stalk celery, chopped

1 cup snow peas or peas, fresh or frozen

1/4 medium green pepper, chopped

1/2 pound tofu, crumbled

1 can (4 oz.) mushrooms, drained

2 tablespoons light soy sauce

1/2 cup egg substitute

Nutrients per serving:

calories	350
protein	24 gm
carbohydrate	23 gm
total fat	18 gm
saturated fat	3 gm
monounsat'd fat	11 gm
cholesterol	0 mg
sodium	880 mg
potassium	950 mg
fiber	7 gm

% US-RDA

vitamin A	19
vitamin C	78
thiamin	31
riboflavin	27
vitamin B_6	19
folacin	45
iron	93
zinc	18
calcium	34

In heavy bottomed Dutch oven, heat oil and keep very hot while adding vegetables. Add vegetables slowly enough to crisply stir-fry; do not steam. Stir in tofu, mushrooms and soy sauce. Heat 4 minutes. Pour egg substitute over mixture. Do not stir but allow to congeal. Serve with rice, noodles or toast. Makes 2 servings.

Tofu is a complete protein, which means it contains all amino acids needed for body growth and repair. In 1/4-pound (about 1/2 cup) there are 9 grams protein, 5 grams fat (much of which is mono-unsaturated), 3 grams carbohydrate, 130 milligrams calcium and almost no sodium.

Cheese-Tofu Stuffed Shells

Tofu is great protein and very economical.

4 ounces uncooked jumbo macaroni
  shells

2 cups spaghetti sauce

1 pound tofu, mashed

1/2 pound low-fat mozzarella cheese,
  shredded

1/4 cup dried or chopped fresh parsley

2 tablespoons onion powder

1/2 teaspoon garlic powder

1/2 teaspoon basil

1/4 cup grated Parmesan cheese

Preheat oven to 350°. Cook shells in boiling water according to package directions; drain and set aside. Spread unheated spaghetti sauce on bottom of 9x9-inch baking pan. Mix together remaining ingredients, except Parmesan cheese, and stuff into shells. Place shells down into sauce. Sprinkle on Parmesan cheese and bake until sauce is bubbly, about 35 minutes. Makes 4 servings.

To extend this recipe to six servings (which decreases fat and calories per serving) defrost and squeeze dry a 10-ounce package frozen chopped spinach. Mix uncooked spinach into tofu-cheese mixture before stuffing shells. Zucchini, yellow squash or other fresh or canned and drained vegetable may be substituted.

Nutrients per serving:

calories	428
protein	20 gm
carbohydrate	42 gm
total fat	20 gm
saturated fat	6 gm
monounsat'd fat	10 gm
cholesterol	48 mg
sodium	1100 mg
potassium	665 mg
fiber	2 gm

% US-RDA

vitamin A	48
vitamin C	36
thiamin	20
riboflavin	55
vitamin B6	4
folacin	16
iron	21
zinc	10
calcium	92

Fried Rice with Tofu

Another quick-to-the-table meal
for hungry diners.

2 tablespoons canola oil, divided

1/2 pound tofu, cut in 1/3-inch cubes

3 tablespoons light soy sauce, divided

1 medium green pepper, cut into strips

1 large onion, chopped

2 stalks celery, thinly sliced

2 cups cooked rice

2 large eggs, slightly beaten

chopped green onion, chives or parsley

In heavy bottomed skillet, heat 1 tablespoon oil until very hot; stir-fry tofu cubes with 2 tablespoons soy sauce for 1 minute. Remove tofu. Add remaining tablespoon oil and heat until very hot. Stir-fry green pepper, onion and celery 3 to 4 minutes. Add crumbled rice and heat. Add eggs, cooked tofu cubes and 1 tablespoon soy sauce; heat until eggs congeal. Garnish with chopped onion, chives or parsley. Makes 2 servings.

Even tastier when prepared with freshly cooked or left over brown rice. By using your French knife, the vegetables are ready in half the time. Egg substitute or egg whites may be substituted for whole eggs.

Nutrients per serving:

calories	532
protein	27 gm
carbohydrate	61 gm
total fat	20 gm
saturated fat	3 gm
monounsat'd fat	14 gm
cholesterol	220 mg
sodium	1200 mg
potassium	680 mg
fiber	5 gm

% US-RDA

vitamin A	10
vitamin C	75
thiamin	42
riboflavin	20
vitamin B$_6$	33
folacin	40
iron	105
zinc	18
calcium	36

From The Stream,
Lake and Ocean

Broadening our culinary horizons to include bounties from the sea is a smart and scrumptious thing to do. When fish began moving from the water to the America's dinner table, we were treated with a healthy and versatile main-dish alternative. Today, the term "seafood" is meant to include edible finfish or shellfish from either salt or fresh water sources.

Eating finfish is so healthy, in fact, that it is associated with a reduced risk of coronary heart disease. Some studies show that incorporating fish into your diet twice a week will lower your risk of having a heart attack. This stems from the fact that most fish is low in fat and that the Omega-3 polyunsaturated fatty acids found in fish are less likely to raise your blood cholesterol level than the saturated fats that would likely have been consumed with other main dishes.

Just about everything at the fish counter is good for you. Freshly caught salt or fresh water fish are equally low in sodium, with 20 to 25 milligrams per ounce. Most seafoods are naturally lean, with a four ounce portion of low-fat fish or shellfish providing less than 100 calories. The color and flavor are indicators of the fat content, which also determines the most desirable cooking method.

- **Low-fat fish** (fat content lower than 2.5 percent). Generally mild in flavor with a tender, flaky, white or pale flesh. Because of a tendency to dry out during cooking, low-fat fish benefit from poaching and other moist-heat cooking methods. Dry heat methods such as baking or broiling can be used if the fish is basted with margarine, or a sauce is used to keep it moist. Mild seasonings include parsley, white pepper, tarragon, marjoram, chives, basil and dill weed.

    Examples: cod, halibut, pollock, rockfish, grouper, shark, flounder, sole, red snapper, sea bass, haddock and whiting.

- **Medium-fat fish** (fat content between 2.5 percent and 5 percent). Adapt well to almost all cooking methods. In addition to the milder herbs, this slightly stronger flavor calls for such herbs as garlic, black pepper, tarragon, oregano, bay leaf or Italian seasonings.

    Examples: catfish, yellowfin tuna, rainbow trout, swordfish, bluefish and walleye.
- **High-fat fish** (fat content between 5 percent and 13 percent). Generally have a firm meat-like texture, more pronounced flavor and a deeper color than low-fat fish. Grilling, baking and other dry heat methods are ideal for fatty fish; poaching and microwaving also give good results. The stronger flavored fish benefit from the herbs shown above and also, thyme, rosemary and red pepper.

    Examples: salmon, mackerel, tuna, orange roughy, sardines, herring, anchovies, shad and trout.

Remember to take advantage of whatever fresh fish is available and avoid prebreaded and precooked seafoods as they are much higher in saturated fat and sodium.

Shellfish, such as crab, lobster, scallops, clams, oysters, shrimp and crayfish, contain some cholesterol but are extremely low in fat — only one to two percent. At one time those on low cholesterol diets were cautioned to avoid them. Fortunately, newer analytical methods show crab and clams contain 15 milligrams of cholesterol per ounce, on up to 50 milligrams per ounce in shrimp. If you enjoy eating lobster and shrimp, you can feel comfortable eating these very low-fat treats.

Fish lends itself well to quick cooking methods which means it fits nicely into fast-to-cook meal plans. Featured are basic recipes for poaching, broiling, baking , grilling and low-fat pan frying. The microwave oven is handy for defrosting or preparing fish, but follow the manufacturer's instructions. Canned water-packed tuna and salmon, well drained of the salty broth, are delicious in our recipes for patties, fast main dishes, salads and sandwiches.

Poached Fish with Sauce

Perfect when you want a light, fast meal.

¹/₄ cup boiling water

¹/₂ teaspoon chicken flavor bouillon granules

1 tablespoon lemon juice

2 tablespoons tub margarine

¹/₂ small onion, chopped

¹/₄ cup thinly sliced celery

1 pound fish fillets, fresh or defrosted

sprinkle of garlic powder, dill weed, basil, marjoram or black pepper

2 teaspoons all-purpose flour in ¹/₄ cup water

In a small saucepan, dissolve bouillon granules in ¹/₄ cup boiling water; add lemon juice. Melt margarine in skillet, add onion and celery and cook over low heat until soft. Place fish over celery and onions; add bouillon-lemon juice mixture and sprinkle with herbs. Bring liquid to a boil, cover, then reduce to a simmer. Cook fish until it flakes easily, about 5 to 8 minutes; remove to heated plate. Whip flour into ¹/₄ cup cool water, mix into fish liquid in skillet, simmer and stir constantly until thickened. Pour sauce over fish; serve immediately. Makes 4 servings.

While this sounds complicated, once you've made it you'll see how easy it is. Poached fish has a mild flavor and benefits from the delicate sauce.

Nutrients per serving:

calories	197
protein	23 gm
carbohydrate	3 gm
total fat	10 gm
saturated fat	1 gm
monounsat'd fat	3 gm
cholesterol	42 mg
sodium	335 mg
potassium	200 mg
fiber	0 gm

% US-RDA

vitamin A	6
vitamin C	2
thiamin	7
riboflavin	6
vitamin B₆	***
folacin	***
iron	5
zinc	2
calcium	***

Broiled Fish

So easy, so quick, so low in saturated fat!

1 pound fillets or steaks, fresh or defrosted

1 tablespoon canola oil

sprinkle of paprika, garlic powder, dill weed, basil, marjoram, lemon juice, black pepper and lite salt to taste

Line broiler pan with foil, do not oil. Preheat oven and broiler pan to 500°. Pat fillets dry, rub all surfaces with oil and place on foil. Sprinkle lightly with paprika, herbs, lemon juice and lite salt. With oven door open several inches, broil until fish is nicely browned and tender, about 5 to 8 minutes. Do not try to turn fish. Serve immediately. Makes 4 servings.

An unoiled, shallow, heatproof dish or iron skillet may be lined with foil and used instead of the lined broiler pan.

Salmon, orange roughy and other higher fat fish broil nicely. Remember, even these so called higher fat fish contain fish oils which may do good things for your heart and blood vessels. And, they are generally lower in fat than the red meats. So, even high fat fish is a great addition to your diet.

Nutrients per serving:

calories	*206*
protein	*29 gm*
carbohydrate	*0 gm*
total fat	*10 gm*
saturated fat	*0 gm*
monounsat'd fat	*4 gm*
cholesterol	*56 mg*
sodium	*185 mg*
potassium	*300 mg*
fiber	*0 gm*

% US-RDA

vitamin A	*****
vitamin C	*2*
thiamin	*6*
riboflavin	*6*
vitamin B$_6$	*****
folacin	*****
iron	*6*
zinc	*2*
calcium	*4*

Baked Fish

*With your choice of four simple
seasonings for baking or broiling.*

1 pound fillets, fresh or defrosted

1 tablespoon canola oil

1 tablespoon lemon juice

**sprinkles of garlic powder, parsley,
chives, dill weed, paprika, marjoram,
black pepper and lite salt to taste**

Preheat oven to 425°. Rinse and pat dry fillets. Rub all
surfaces with oil. Arrange fillets in single layer in 9x13-
inch glass or nonstick baking dish. Sprinkle with lemon
juice, black pepper, herbs and lite salt. Bake 8 to 10
minutes. Makes 4 servings.

*Seasonings to use before baking or broiling (omit oil and
herbs listed above):*

- *1 tablespoon melted tub margarine, 2 tablespoons sliced
  almonds and 1 teaspoon dried parsley flakes. Combine
  and spread over fillets.*

- *2 teaspoons melted tub margarine and 2 teaspoons soy
  sauce; combine and brush over fillets.*

- *2 tablespoons lemon juice, 1 tablespoon Dijon mustard, 1
  tablespoon melted margarine and 1/4 teaspoon black
  pepper; combine and spread over fillets.*

Nutrients per serving:

calories	*206*
protein	*29 gm*
carbohydrate	*0 gm*
total fat	*10 gm*
saturated fat	*0 gm*
monounsat'd fat	*4 gm*
cholesterol	*56 mg*
sodium	*185 mg*
potassium	*300 mg*
fiber	*0 gm*

% US-RDA

vitamin A	***
vitamin C	*2*
thiamin	*6*
riboflavin	*6*
vitamin B$_6$	***
folacin	***
iron	*6*
zinc	*2*
calcium	*4*

Creole Catfish Fillets

Easy baked fish with spicy sauce
made in the same dish.

1 teaspoon canola oil

1 pound fillets, fresh or defrosted

1 can (10$^{1}/_{2}$ oz.) zesty tomato soup

$^{1}/_{2}$ cup chopped green pepper

$^{1}/_{4}$ cup dried onion flakes

2 tablespoons lemon juice

Preheat oven to 425°. Spread oil in 9x13-inch glass or nonstick baking dish. Arrange fish in single layer. Spoon soup evenly over fillets. Sprinkle green pepper, onion flakes and lemon juice over soup. Bake 8 to 10 minutes. Makes 4 servings.

Always keep fresh fish in the coldest part of the refrigerator. For the best flavor, use the next meal after buying. Your nose will tell you if the fish is not fresh. The fresher the fish, the milder the odor.

Nutrients per serving:

calories	231
protein	24 gm
carbohydrate	18 gm
total fat	7 gm
saturated fat	2 gm
monounsat'd fat	3 gm
cholesterol	43 mg
sodium	695 mg
potassium	595 mg
fiber	1 gm

% US-RDA

vitamin A	13
vitamin C	108
thiamin	9
riboflavin	8
vitamin B$_6$	24
folacin	6
iron	16
zinc	11
calcium	5

Vegetable Baked Orange Roughy

With a colorful, nutritious sauce.

2 tablespoons tub margarine

2 to 3 cups chopped vegetables: any, some or all of these: green onions, onions, celery, thinly sliced carrots, mushrooms, tomatoes, green and red peppers, summer squashes

1 pound orange roughy, or other fish fillets

1 tablespoon canola oil

sprinkle of paprika, black pepper, marjoram, basil and lite salt

lemon juice

Preheat oven to 425°. In skillet, melt margarine, add vegetables and cook until slightly tender. Pat fish dry; rub all surfaces with oil and place over vegetables. Sprinkle fish with paprika, pepper, herbs and lite salt. Bake for 10 to 12 minutes. Serve fish on heated plates; sprinkle with lemon juice and top with vegetables. Makes 4 servings.

When baking fish, follow the 10-minute rule. Measure the thickest part of the fish. Allow 10 minutes per inch with a minimum of 5 minutes. If fish is stuffed or rolled, measure it after stuffing or rolling. Bake stuffed fish at 450°.

Nutrients per serving:

calories	247
protein	24 gm
carbohydrate	4 gm
total fat	15 gm
saturated fat	2 gm
monounsat'd fat	8 gm
cholesterol	42 mg
sodium	130 mg
potassium	620 mg
fiber	1 gm

% US-RDA

vitamin A	38
vitamin C	81
thiamin	4
riboflavin	4
vitamin B$_6$	3
folacin	5
iron	11
zinc	4
calcium	2

Baked Sole with Onion Sauce

Ideal method for low-fat fish fillets.

2 tablespoons tub margarine

1 pound fish fillets, fresh or defrosted

6 to 8 green onions, chopped, or 1 small onion, finely chopped

2 tablespoons lemon juice

For white sauce:

2 tablespoons tub margarine

3 tablespoons all-purpose flour or crystallized flour

1½ cups ½% low-fat or skim milk

lite salt to taste

black or white pepper to taste

Preheat oven to 425°. Melt margarine in oven in 9x13-inch glass or nonstick baking dish. Dip, then rub all fish surfaces with melted margarine. Top with chopped onion and sprinkle with lemon juice. Place in oven; bake 8 to 10 minutes.

While fish is baking, make white sauce. In small saucepan, melt margarine; stir in flour. Slowly blend in milk. Cook, stirring constantly, until mixture boils. Reduce heat, continue stirring gently until raw flour taste is gone. Remove fish from oven and pour drippings from onion-lemon-fish dish into white sauce and blend together. Add lite salt and pepper to taste. Serve fish on heated plates topped with the delicate sauce. Makes 4 servings.

Served with quick oven-steamed rice, oven-baked vegetable, a heated roll and a baked fruit dessert, it is a complete oven-baked meal.

Flounder with Mushroom Sauce

A gourmet treat.

1 tablespoon tub margarine

1 pound flounder fillets

1 tablespoon lemon juice

For white sauce:

2 tablespoons tub margarine

1/2 pound fresh mushrooms, sliced, or 1 can (8 oz.) mushrooms, drained

4 tablespoons all-purpose flour or crystallized flour

2 cups 1/2% low-fat or skim milk

lite salt to taste

black or white pepper to taste

Preheat oven to 425°. In skillet, melt margarine, coat all fish surfaces with margarine. Roll the fillets and place back in skillet. Sprinkle with lemon juice; bake until opaque, about 12 to 15 minutes. While fish is baking, make sauce. In small sauce pan, melt margarine, add sliced mushrooms and cook 1 to 2 minutes. Blend in flour, then milk, stirring constantly until thickened and raw flour taste is gone. Season sauce with lite salt and pepper to taste. Serve fish topped with mushroom sauce. Makes 4 servings.

Like any other living thing, fish has its seasons. The size of the catch depends upon reproductive cycles, migratory patterns, weather conditions and water temperature. All these factors determine the quality of fresh fish. These same factors also influence the price; when a particular kind of seafood is abundant, the price tends to be lower than when it is scarce.

Nutrients per serving:

calories	312
protein	28 gm
carbohydrate	12 gm
total fat	16 gm
saturated fat	3 gm
monounsat'd fat	5 gm
cholesterol	42 mg
sodium	490 mg
potassium	660 mg
fiber	1 gm

% US-RDA

vitamin A	15
vitamin C	7
thiamin	12
riboflavin	21
vitamin B_6	33
folacin	10
iron	10
zinc	2
calcium	23

Charcoal Grilled Fish Steaks

Well suited to thick cuts of fish, whole fish and fish steaks.

2 tablespoons canola oil

2 pounds fish steak, fresh or defrosted

**oil based marinade or sauces, such as
    Basic Seafood Marinade (see page 21),
    your own or a commercial recipe**

When coals are ready, lightly brush grill with oil. Pat fish dry and rub all surfaces with oil. For fish 1-inch thick or less, place grill 2 to 4 inches above the coals; for thicker pieces, 5 to 6 inches above. Placing fish in a hinged wire basket designed for fish grilling makes handling and turning easier. Baste frequently with the marinade or your own dressing. Follow the 10-minute rule as a guide to cooking time (see page 139). Makes 4 servings.

Match the flavor of the fish with the sauce. Marinades and sauces should enhance the flavor of fish, not mask it. Use our basic recipe and then experiment with herbs of your liking. When a marinade has been used, omit rubbing the fish surfaces with oil. Use the same marinade to keep the fish moist by basting during grilling.

Nutrients per serving:

calories	232
protein	31 gm
carbohydrate	0 gm
total fat	12 gm
saturated fat	2 gm
monounsat'd fat	6 gm
cholesterol	55 mg
sodium	200 mg
potassium	300 mg
fiber	20 gm

% US-RDA

vitamin A	***
vitamin C	2
thiamin	6
riboflavin	6
vitamin B$_6$	***
folacin	***
iron	7
zinc	4
calcium	***

Pan Fried Trout

Fast, low-fat frying for small,
whole fish or fillets.

2 pounds brook trout, fresh or defrosted

1/4 cup egg substitute or egg white

**1/2 cup cornmeal or flour seasoned with
lite salt, black pepper, paprika and
onion powder; or use Herbed Breading
(see page 12)**

2 to 3 tablespoons canola oil

Dip the fish into egg substitute, then into cornmeal or
other breading just before frying. Heat the oil in a skillet
large enough to hold the fish comfortably. Allow oil to
become very hot, but not smoking hot, then slip fish into
skillet. If the fish is less than 1-inch thick, it need not be
turned over. Trout or fillet will cook in 5 to 10 minutes.
Makes 4 servings.

*Our Herbed Breading is an instant, tasty, fat-free coating
to use when frying or baking.*

*The secret to successful pan frying in a small amount of
oil, is to use a very smooth or nonstick pan and to keep the oil
hot at all times. To avoid crowding the fish and cooling the oil,
you may find it best to use two skillets. Slide egg turner under
fish during cooking to prevent sticking.*

Nutrients per serving:

calories 206
protein .... 25 gm
carbohydrate .... 4 gm
total fat .... 10 gm
saturated fat .... 0 gm
monounsat'd fat .... 7 gm
cholesterol .... 20 mg
sodium .... 200 mg
potassium .... 300 mg
fiber .... 1 gm

% US-RDA

vitamin A 5
vitamin C .... ***
thiamin 11
riboflavin 5
vitamin B$_6$ .... ***
folacin .... ***
iron 10
zinc 2
calcium 2

Salmon (or Tuna) Patties

When the family wants to eat right now, enjoy this.

1 can (15½ oz.) pink salmon, water-packed, drained

½ cup plain low-fat yogurt or ⅓ cup skim milk

2 egg whites or ¼ cup egg substitute

⅓ cup crushed cornflakes or ¼ cup bread crumbs

2 tablespoons dried onion flakes or chopped green onion

1 tablespoon canola oil

Combine all ingredients, except oil; form into 4 thin patties. Heat oil in large skillet and brown patties over medium heat 4 to 6 minutes on each side or until golden brown. Makes 4 servings.

Atlantic salmon comes to our markets mainly fresh and pink, while Pacific salmon reaches us in many varieties and comes fresh, canned or smoked. These varieties include King or Chinook, pink or white fleshed, the red fleshed Sockeye salmon and the pinkish silver Coho. We enjoy these fresh or canned. If you have chosen fresh fish, use it immediately to capture the wonderful flavor.

Nutrients per serving:

calories	220
protein	28 gm
carbohydrate	11 gm
total fat	7 gm
saturated fat	1 gm
monounsat'd fat	4 gm
cholesterol	39 mg
sodium	275 mg
potassium	390 mg
fiber	0 gm

% US-RDA

vitamin A	6
vitamin C	7
thiamin	8
riboflavin	16
vitamin B_6	8
folacin	14
iron	7
zinc	2
calcium	9

Tuna Noodle Casserole

The familiar meal-in-one family favorite.

4 ounces uncooked egg noodles

1 can (10½ oz.) cream of celery or
   chicken soup

½ cup ½% low-fat or skim milk

1 cup raw or cooked peas or peas and
   carrots

2 tablespoons pimento (optional)

2 cans (6 oz. each) water-packed flaked
   tuna, drained

1 tablespoon tub margarine

2 tablespoons dry bread crumbs

Preheat oven to 375°. Cook egg noodles following package directions, but reduce cooking time by one-third. In two-quart casserole dish or Dutch oven, combine soup, milk, peas, partially cooked noodles, pimento and tuna. In a small saucepan, melt margarine, stir in bread crumbs and blend well. Sprinkle over noodle mixture. Bake for 25 minutes. Makes 4 servings.

Either water-packed or oil-packed tuna may be used. With thorough draining, the salty, oily brine is removed leaving, per serving, ½ teaspoon fish oil in the water-packed fish and 1 to 2 teaspoons of oil in the oil-packed fish. One teaspoon of oil provides 40 calories.

Nutrients per serving:

calories	390
protein	31 gm
carbohydrate	44 gm
total fat	11 gm
saturated fat	2 gm
monounsat'd fat	4 gm
cholesterol	58 mg
sodium	900 mg
potassium	535 mg
fiber	4 gm

% US-RDA

vitamin A	17
vitamin C	18
thiamin	20
riboflavin	16
vitamin B_6	42
folacin	20
iron	28
zinc	4
calcium	21

Salmon Salad

*Makes a delicious sandwich
spread or main dish salad.*

**1 can (15¹/₂ oz.) salmon, water-packed,
drained, flaked**

**1 small onion finely chopped, or 8 green
onions, chopped**

2 stalks celery, finely chopped

¹/₄ cup pickle relish

¹/₂ cup salad dressing

dash of red pepper or hot pepper sauce

Drain salmon well, then flake. Add onion, celery,
pickle relish and salad dressing. Mix gently and
thoroughly. Cover; refrigerate to chill and blend flavors.
Because it contains no egg or fresh fish, it remains tasty
and fresh up to 48 hours. Makes 4 servings.

*For a main dish salad, cut green onion and celery into
¹/₃ inch pieces. Add a garnish of green pepper slices,
cucumbers wedges, tomato quarters or summer squash rings
and a lemon wedge. Salmon bones are rich in calcium, don't
remove them!*

*In place of salmon, use 2 cans (6 oz.) water-packed chunk
or solid tuna, drained and flaked, or ³/₄ pound surimi, or ³/₄
pound cooked shrimp, crab or scallops.*

Nutrients per serving:

calories	*185*
protein	*18 gm*
carbohydrate	*11 gm*
total fat	*7 gm*
saturated fat	*2 gm*
monounsat'd fat	*3 gm*
cholesterol	*13 mg*
sodium	*600 mg*
potassium	*410 mg*
fiber	*1 gm*

% US-RDA

vitamin A	*15*
vitamin C	*12*
thiamin	*4*
riboflavin	*15*
vitamin B₆	*12*
folacin	*8*
iron	*13*
zinc	*6*
calcium	*8*

Fluffy Tuna Casserole

A moist and flavorful dish.

1 tablespoon tub margarine

1/2 small onion, chopped

2 tablespoons all-purpose flour or
crystallized flour

1 cup 1/2% low-fat or skim milk

1 can (6 oz.) water-packed tuna, drained,
chunked

3 slices whole wheat or white bread torn
into 1-inch pieces

1 egg, beaten until frothy

black pepper to taste

sprinkle of paprika

Preheat oven to 375°. In skillet or Dutch oven, melt margarine over low heat; cook onions until soft. Add flour and blend in. Slowly and gently stir in milk and continue stirring to prevent sticking. Simmer until sauce has thickened. Add tuna, bread, egg and black pepper; gently mix together. Sprinkle paprika on surface and place skillet in oven for 25 minutes. Makes 4 servings.

When salty foods like tuna or salmon are used, the sodium per serving can be reduced by extending the recipe with fresh or frozen vegetables. Add 4 ounces of vegetable for each additional serving. For example, by adding 8 ounces of peas, the recipe yields 2 additional servings, each containing 270 milligrams of sodium rather than 350 milligrams. Other vegetables may be added, such as green beans, carrots, summer squash, green pepper or mixed vegetables.

Nutrients per serving:

calories	177
protein	16 gm
carbohydrate	17 gm
total fat	5 gm
saturated fat	1 gm
monounsat'd fat	3 gm
cholesterol	92 mg
sodium	350 mg
potassium	270 mg
fiber	3 gm

% US-RDA

vitamin A	6
vitamin C	2
thiamin	8
riboflavin	6
vitamin B6	34
folacin	12
iron	14
zinc	4
calcium	9

Spanish Surimi

You'll think it is real crabmeat!

1 pkg (8 oz.) surimi, deli or defrosted, in
   bite-sized pieces

1 tablespoon lemon juice

3 tablespoons canola oil

1 medium green pepper, chopped

1 medium onion, chopped

½ teaspoon garlic powder

1 can (15 oz.) whole tomatoes, drained,
   chopped

1 teaspoon basil

¼ teaspoon oregano (optional)

black pepper to taste

Nutrients per serving:

calories	182
protein	11 gm
carbohydrate	12 gm
total fat	10 gm
saturated fat	2 gm
monounsat'd fat	7 gm
cholesterol	18 mg
sodium	235 mg
potassium	370 mg
fiber	2 gm

% US-RDA

vitamin A	14
vitamin C	81
thiamin	6
riboflavin	3
vitamin B_6	10
folacin	6
iron	8
zinc	2
calcium	5

Preheat oven to 375°. Place surimi in bowl and sprinkle with lemon juice. In skillet, heat oil. Add green pepper, onion and garlic; cook together until soft, about 3 to 5 minutes. Gently mix in tomatoes, surimi and seasonings. Bake 30 minutes. Makes 4 servings.

The word "surimi" is derived from the Japanese term for restructured food. It is made from Alaskan pollock, a mild, white fleshed fish, because of its gelling qualities, light color and good texture. Flavorings are added to make it taste like shellfish.

Surimi, which is always precooked, has other names such as mock crab, imitation crabmeat, seatails, sealegs or imitation lobster. Keep frozen surimi handy for seafood salads or quick meals.

Crab Louis Salad

Main dish salad, good made with crabmeat or surimi.

8 oz. crabmeat, in bite-sized pieces

1 tablespoon lemon juice

1/2 cup salad dressing

1/2 cup chili sauce

6 to 8 green onions, chopped

2 stalks celery, thinly sliced in crescents

1 medium green pepper, chopped

12 bright green lettuce leaves

1/2 to 1 pound fresh vegetables in season
   such as cucumber slices, tomato
   wedges, summer squash rings, cooked
   asparagus spears, broccoli or
   cauliflower florets

4 to 8 lemon wedges

Place crabmeat in bowl and sprinkle with lemon juice. Combine salad dressing and chili sauce, pour over crabmeat. Stir in green onions, celery and green pepper. Cover and chill for at least 1 hour before assembling salad. To make salad, cover salad plate with bed of lettuce leaves, mound crab salad on leaves. Garnish with fresh vegetables and lemon wedges. Makes 4 servings.

Shellfish such as crab, shrimp and scallops are flavorful, low-fat alternatives to cheese in chilled pasta salads. For a quick do-ahead salad, combine cooked rotini pasta, shellfish in bite-sized pieces, fresh vegetables and Italian salad dressing. Allow 1 hour or more for flavor blending.

Nutrients per serving:

calories	262
protein	12 gm
carbohydrate	31 gm
total fat	10 gm
saturated fat	1 gm
monounsat'd fat	6 gm
cholesterol	33 mg
sodium	720 mg
potassium	515 mg
fiber	2 gm

% US-RDA

vitamin A	42
vitamin C	100
thiamin	8
riboflavin	7
vitamin B_6	6
folacin	22
iron	10
zinc	2
calcium	7

How to Reduce Sodium in Recipes

As you read food labels, you will notice many low-fat, packaged and canned foods are quite high in sodium. When using these processed foods, the salt and sodium per serving can be reduced by extending them with fresh and unprocessed vegetables, fruit, poultry, fish, meat, pasta and grains.

The Food and Drug Administration requires the sodium content, in milligrams per serving, be included on the "Nutrition Facts" label. Compare like products, and select the one with the least sodium.

While this has nothing to do with recipes, be aware that many over the counter products such as antacids, alkalizers, laxatives and sedatives may contain sodium; reading the label is essential.

- *Omit salt or cut in half, and continue reducing this amount over time.*
- *Omit baking powder and baking soda. Substitute 1¼ teaspoons of low sodium baking powder for each teaspoon of regular baking powder.*
- *Use low sodium bouillon granules or cubes in place of the regular ones.*
- *Use reduced or low sodium canned soups in place of regular canned soups.*
- *Use fresh, frozen or no-salt added canned vegetables.*
- *Use fresh or no-salt added canned tomatoes, tomato and vegetable juices.*
- *Use fresh, frozen or no-added-salt canned fish, shrimp, chicken, and other meats.*
- *Cook your own dried beans without salt.*
- *Use low sodium margarine.*
- *Omit or cut in half the bacon, ham, cheese or Parmesan cheese.*
- *Omit steak sauces and regular catsup.*
- *Run warm water over salt containing foods in a sieve to remove some sodium.*

Poultry Internationale

Worldwide, poultry has found a solid niche in everyday cuisine, for it can be transformed into a spectacular dinner, or dressed down for a casual meal. The most abundant bird, the chicken, is found in dishes ranging from the family stew pot, Chinese stir-fry and Texas barbecue to East Indian curry, South American chili con pollo and Italian cacciatore. Turkey, once a holiday treat, is now a common food in many kitchens. Thanks to scientific poultry raising and processing methods, we can now enjoy an abundance of low-fat chicken and turkey products.

Skinless and with all visible fat removed, the breast, legs and thighs are low in total fat. The small remaining amount of fat is high in the more desirable unsaturated fats, and the percent of saturated fat is lower than that in beef or pork. Roasted breast of tender young broilers or turkey is only three to five percent fat, while the cooked dark meat is seven to nine percent fat.

When using a quick-cooking method, coatings and sauces are needed to preserve the moistness and flavor. Such preparation methods fit very well with the needs of many families today, and they also assure retention of poultry's good amounts of thiamin, riboflavin, vitamin B_6, iron and zinc.

An important thing to remember is that chicken does not have to be the main attraction to taste good. Use chicken to complement salads, casseroles, sandwiches or soup dishes and you will boost your meal in both savoriness and nutrition. Instead of using canned chicken, you can prepare your own flavor-rich broth and cooked chicken pieces with our recipe (see page 158). Keep them in the freezer for faster meals at lower cost.

On the following pages we have included a variety of recipes that can be adapted to your family's preferences. We hope you will enjoy these American and international favorites.

Lemon Baked Chicken

Your choice of two lemon-flavored sauces.

3 tablespoons tub margarine

1¹/₂ tablespoons lemon juice

1¹/₂ pounds chicken thighs and legs, skinless (see note below)

¹/₂ teaspoon lite salt

¹/₄ teaspoon marjoram or tarragon leaves

¹/₂ teaspoon paprika

black pepper, as desired

Preheat oven to 350°. In oven, melt margarine in 9x13-inch glass baking dish. Remove dish from oven; mix lemon juice into margarine. Rinse and dry chicken pieces thoroughly. Roll pieces in margarine-lemon mixture and arrange in one layer in baking dish. Sprinkle with seasonings. To marinate, cover and chill one hour. Cover with foil and bake for 30 minutes. Uncover, bake 10 to 15 minutes or until browned and tender. Makes 4 servings.

Two pounds of legs and thighs from a medium chicken weigh about 1¹/₂ pounds after skin and fat are removed. After cooking, a combination of one leg and one thigh yields 3 ounces of edible chicken. One-half breast from a medium chicken yields 3 ounces of cooked, edible meat.

Another tasty sauce to use before and during baking is made with ¹/₄ cup honey, ¹/₄ cup light soy sauce, ¹/₄ cup catsup and ¹/₄ cup lemon juice. Omit margarine, lite salt, herbs and spices from recipe above. To enhance flavors, cover and marinate chicken in refrigerator for one hour.

Nutrients per serving:

calories	259
protein	31 gm
carbohydrate	0 gm
total fat	15 gm
saturated fat	2 gm
monounsat'd fat	7 gm
cholesterol	91 mg
sodium	265 mg
potassium	360 mg
fiber	0 gm

% US-RDA

vitamin A	9
vitamin C	2
thiamin	6
riboflavin	17
vitamin B_6	24
folacin	4
iron	11
zinc	20
calcium	2

Quick Chick Casserole

All-in-one meal ready in 35 minutes.

1 tablespoon margarine

12 ounces skinless, boneless chicken or turkey breast cut into 1/2-inch strips

2 cups broccoli cuts

3/4 cup carrots, thinly sliced

1 can (101/2 oz.) cream of mushroom, broccoli or chicken soup

1 cup 1/2% low-fat or skim milk

sprinkle of black pepper

11/2 cups uncooked instant rice

In large skillet, melt margarine. Add chicken strips slowly; stir frequently. Add broccoli and carrots and stir until tender-crisp. Add soup, milk and pepper. Stir constantly, to prevent sticking, while bringing to a boil. Stir in rice, cover, remove from heat. Let stand 5 minutes. Fluff with fork before serving. Makes 4 servings.

This basic recipe invites substituting. Instead of chicken, use lean ground turkey, beef or pork. Substitute vegetables such as peas, green beans, celery, onion or defrosted California vegetable mix. For the soup, use any canned, low-fat cream or tomato soup. Refer to Low-Fat Soup chart on page 250.

Nutrients per serving:

calories	387
protein	28 gm
carbohydrate	35 gm
total fat	15 gm
saturated fat	4 gm
monounsat'd fat	4 gm
cholesterol	45 mg
sodium	960 mg
potassium	575 mg
fiber	4 gm

% US-RDA

vitamin A	290
vitamin C	86
thiamin	20
riboflavin	20
vitamin B_6	30
folacin	28
iron	13
zinc	16
calcium	19

Parmesan Breaded Chicken

While chicken bakes, cook up spaghetti and sauce for a speedy dinner.

1 tablespoon canola oil

1/2 cup Herbed Breading (see page 12) or crushed cornflakes with garlic powder and black pepper

1/4 cup parmesan cheese

4 halves skinless, boneless chicken breast or 1 pound turkey breast cut into 4 pieces

1/2 cup egg substitute or skim milk

Nutrients per serving:

calories	*271*
protein	*32 gm*
carbohydrate	*11 gm*
total fat	*10 gm*
saturated fat	*3 gm*
monounsat'd fat	*4 gm*
cholesterol	*77 mg*
sodium	*380 mg*
potassium	*270 mg*
fiber	*0 gm*

% US-RDA

vitamin A	*13*
vitamin C	*11*
thiamin	*15*
riboflavin	*26*
vitamin B$_6$	*41*
folacin	*24*
iron	*12*
zinc	*7*
calcium	*13*

Preheat oven to 350°. In skillet, heat oil over medium heat. In pie pan, stir breading and parmesan cheese together. Rinse and dry chicken pieces thoroughly. Dip chicken in egg substitute, coat with breading and immediately place in skillet. Place skillet in oven 15 to 20 minutes or until brown and tender. Makes 4 servings.

Spaghetti and sauce topped with this Parmesan Breaded Chicken, a tossed green salad with herb-and-vinegar dressing (see page 24), a large dinner roll and a fruit or instant milk pudding completes your Italian dinner.

When skinless, boneless chicken or turkey breast is on sale, buy several pounds. Carefully rinse, divide into meal size portions and seal in air tight containers. Date and freeze immediately. Use within 4 weeks.

Chicken Hobo Dinner

*A fun meal for children, baked in
the oven or over a campfire!*

4 medium potatoes, thin skinned, peeled
  or unpeeled, sliced

4 medium carrots, sliced

4 halves skinless, boneless chicken breast

2 stalks celery, sliced

1 medium green pepper, diced

4 teaspoons dried onion flakes or 1 small
  onion, chopped

1/2 teaspoon lite salt

herbs and spices to taste

1 can (15 oz.) tomatoes

Preheat oven to 375°. Oil the inside of four 13-ounce coffee cans. Into each can, slice one potato and one carrot; place one-half chicken breast on top. In a bowl, mix together celery, green pepper, onion flakes, lite salt, herbs and spices; sprinkle one-fourth of mixture over chicken in each can. Divide one-fourth of tomatoes and juice into each can. Cover with aluminum foil; place cans on baking sheet. Bake immediately, do not hold over in can (see note below). Bake for one hour or until chicken and vegetables are tender. Makes 4 servings.

In the true hobo fashion, you may use whatever is on hand, such as chunks of lean ham or beef, little raw meat balls, cabbage, corn, cooked beans, raw apples and tomato or mushroom soup.

The acidic tomato juice may dissolve small amounts of the can lining and give an off flavor. So, it is wise to prepare, bake and serve immediately.

Nutrients per serving:

calories	*356*
protein	*32 gm*
carbohydrate	*39 gm*
total fat	*8 gm*
saturated fat	*2 gm*
monounsat'd fat	*3 gm*
cholesterol	*76 mg*
sodium	*375 mg*
potassium	*1200 mg*
fiber	*4 gm*

% US-RDA

vitamin A	*250*
vitamin C	*120*
thiamin	*23*
riboflavin	*14*
vitamin B$_6$	*41*
folacin	*8*
iron	*21*
zinc	*9*
calcium	*11*

Chicken Paprika
with Noodles

Another easy, fast, nutritious dish.

6 oz. uncooked noodles (2¹/₂ cups)

2 tablespoons tub margarine

**4 halves skinless, boneless chicken breast or 1
pound turkey breast, cut into 1-inch cubes**

1 can (4 oz.) mushrooms, drained

1 small onion, chopped

**¹/₂ cup chicken broth or 1 teaspoon chicken
bouillon granules dissolved in ¹/₂ cup water**

1 teaspoon paprika

¹/₂ teaspoon dill weed

dash of black pepper

1 tablespoon dried or fresh chopped parsley

**1¹/₂ tablespoons cornstarch mixed with 3
tablespoons water**

1 cup low-fat plain yogurt at room temperature

Have noodles ready to serve when chicken paprika is
done; follow package instructions for preparing noodles.
In Dutch oven, melt margarine over medium heat. Slowly
add chicken cubes and cook 5 minutes, while stirring. Add
mushrooms and onion; cook until onion is soft. Add broth,
paprika, dill weed, pepper and parsley; cover, simmer for
10 to 12 minutes. Restir cornstarch to mix thoroughly, add
to chicken mixture. Continue cooking and stirring until
mixture thickens. Remove from heat; stir in yogurt. Serve
immediately over hot noodles. Makes 4 servings.

*Other quick-to-fix starches to use in place of noodles include
other pastas, rice, instant mashed potato, lima beans or corn.*

Nutrients per serving:

calories	427
protein	36 gm
carbohydrate	37 gm
total fat	15 gm
saturated fat	3 gm
monounsat'd fat	5 gm
cholesterol	85 mg
sodium	350 mg
potassium	450 mg
fiber	4 gm

% US-RDA

vitamin A	11
vitamin C	3
thiamin	18
riboflavin	20
vitamin B₆	38
folacin	16
iron	15
zinc	11
calcium	18

Chicken-Rice Pilaf

Special treat for rice lovers.

4 tablespoons tub margarine

4 halves skinless, boneless chicken breast,
   cut into 1/2-inch strips

1 teaspoon garlic powder

1 1/2 cups uncooked rice, brown or white

1 can (8 oz.) mushroom pieces, not
   drained

1 medium onion, chopped

3 1/2 cups chicken broth or 3 1/2 cups water
   with 3 teaspoons chicken flavor
   bouillon granules

1/2 teaspoon basil

4 tablespoons Parmesan cheese

In large skillet, melt 2 tablespoons margarine over medium heat. Slowly add chicken strips; sprinkle on garlic powder, continue stirring until strips are well browned. Remove from skillet. Melt other 2 tablespoons margarine in skillet, add rice and stir constantly until rice is lightly browned. Add mushrooms, onions, broth and basil. Bring to a boil; cover, reduce heat and simmer for 15 minutes or until rice is tender. Gently stir in chicken strips and heat for 5 minutes or until heated through. Top each serving with Parmesan cheese and serve immediately. Makes 4 servings.

Cracked whole-wheat or other grains are also tasty in pilaf.

Nutrients per serving:

calories	*516*
protein	*35 gm*
carbohydrate	*58 gm*
total fat	*16 gm*
saturated fat	*4 gm*
monounsat'd fat	*6 gm*
cholesterol	*78 mg*
sodium	*850 mg*
potassium	*325 mg*
fiber	*2 gm*

% US-RDA

vitamin A	*17*
vitamin C	*6*
thiamin	*25*
riboflavin	*10*
vitamin B_6	*37*
folacin	*8*
iron	*31*
zinc	*9*
calcium	*18*

Barbara's Savory Chicken Chunks and Broth

For delicious broth and precooked chicken. Eat some now, freeze some.

8 cups water

3 medium carrots, sliced

1 medium onion, diced

3 stalks celery with leaves, in 1/4 inch slices

1 tablespoon sage

1 tablespoon thyme

1 teaspoon black pepper

1 tablespoon lite salt

3 1/2 pound package chicken legs and thighs with skin on.

In large cooking pot, combine all ingredients; cover. Simmer for 1 hour; stir once or twice to assure even cooking of chicken pieces. Strain off fat; drain off chicken broth. Discard vegetables as they were added to improve flavor. Cool chicken pieces; remove and discard skin, fat and bones. Makes 6 cups broth and 1 1/2 pounds chicken chunks.

Use a big cooking pot and double the recipe. Cook 1 1/2 hours and stir every 30 minutes to assure even cooking of chicken. Do not cook longer, as chicken becomes stringy. Use in chicken dishes or freeze chicken in meal size portions. Freeze broth separately in 1 or 2 cup containers. When using precooked (room temperature) chicken in a simmered dish, add and heat about 5 to 7 minutes immediately before serving.

Nutrients listed at left are for 3 ounces of cooked chicken chunks.

Nutrients per serving:

calories	*184*
protein	*27 gm*
carbohydrate	*1 gm*
total fat	*8 gm*
saturated fat	*2 gm*
monounsat'd fat	*4 gm*
cholesterol	*85 mg*
sodium	*470 mg*
potassium	*795 mg*
fiber	*0 gm*

% US-RDA

vitamin A	*10*
vitamin C	*****
thiamin	*6*
riboflavin	*14*
vitamin B_6	*23*
folacin	*6*
iron	*9*
zinc	*19*
calcium	*3*

Chicken and Noodles

Forever a family favorite.

5 cups water

5 teaspoons chicken flavor bouillon
   granules (or omit water and granules
   and use 5 cups chicken broth)

1 pound chicken breast, whole, with bone
   in and skin on

1 small onion, chopped

1 medium carrot, sliced

1 stalk celery, sliced

2 tablespoons dried or fresh chopped
   parsley (optional)

1 package (12 oz.) frozen noodles

In Dutch oven, bring water to a boil; add bouillon granules, chicken breast, onion, carrot, celery and parsley. When water is boiling vigorously, add frozen noodles, a few at a time, to maintain boiling. Lower to a simmer and cook uncovered for 30 minutes, or to desired tenderness, stirring occasionally. Add more water if needed, to prevent sticking. Turn breast to assure even cooking and remove to plate after 20 minutes of simmering. Cool, remove skin and bones; cut into cubes. Add cubes back to broth and simmer 5 minutes to blend flavors. Makes 5 servings.

Avoid long simmering of chicken pieces which over cooks it, creating shreds. Frozen noodles require longer cooking and careful stirring to prevent sticking, but give a rich, chewy, flavorful taste. If dried noodles are substituted, less cooking time is required. Add the dried noodles to the broth and cook only the length of time specified on the package.

Nutrients per serving:

calories *323*
protein . . . . *27 gm*
carbohydrate . . . . *38 gm*
total fat . . . . *7 gm*
saturated fat . . . . *1 gm*
monounsat'd fat . . . . *3 gm*
cholesterol . . . . *85 mg*
sodium . . . . *700 mg*
potassium . . . . *425 mg*
fiber . . . . *4 gm*

% US-RDA

vitamin A *100*
vitamin C *12*
thiamin *18*
riboflavin *15*
vitamin B₆ *24*
folacin *12*
iron *33*
zinc *6*
calcium *10*

Honey-Mustard Chicken

Handy to make with a low-fat soup.

4 cups hot cooked rice

1 tablespoon canola oil

4 halves boneless, skinless chicken breast

1 can (10½ oz.) cream of chicken soup

¼ cup ½% low-fat or skim milk

1 tablespoon honey

1 tablespoon spicy brown mustard

Have rice ready to serve when chicken is done. Heat oil in skillet over medium high heat. Add chicken and cook until browned on each side. Move chicken to side of pan; stir in soup, milk, honey and mustard. Move chicken into soup mixture. Reduce heat to low. Cover and simmer, about 10 minutes, or until chicken is tender. Serve over hot rice. Makes 4 servings.

Canned soups are high in salt and sodium but are a mainstay for the busy cook. Choosing the reduced salt soups is wise.

Because many canned soups are also high in fat, selecting soups from the Low-Fat Soup chart on page 250 will lower the fat in the dish.

Nutrients per serving:

calories	525
protein	35 gm
carbohydrate	67 gm
total fat	13 gm
saturated fat	3 gm
monounsat'd fat	6 gm
cholesterol	85 mg
sodium	640 mg
potassium	425 mg
fiber	1 gm

% US-RDA

vitamin A	8
vitamin C	***
thiamin	27
riboflavin	15
vitamin B6	38
folacin	6
iron	30
zinc	8
calcium	16

Fried Chicken Cutlets

Here is how to low-fat fry, two ways.

4 halves skinless, boneless chicken breast

2 tablespoons all-purpose flour

1/2 teaspoon lite salt

1/2 teaspoon garlic powder

dash of black pepper

3 tablespoons canola oil

1 small onion, sliced

**1/2 cup chicken broth, or 1/2 cup water
   with 1/2 teaspoon chicken bouillon
   granules**

**3 tablespoons dried or fresh chopped
   parsley**

3 tablespoons lemon juice

Place chicken between two sheets of waxed paper; pound to 1/4-inch thick cutlets. Mix flour, lite salt, garlic powder and pepper; pound mixture into cutlets. In large skillet, bring 1 1/2 tablespoons oil to medium high heat. Add cutlets so pieces do not touch. Fry about 4 minutes on each side, or until lightly browned. Remove cutlets to warm dish. Heat remaining 1 1/2 tablespoons of oil; add onion, broth, parsley and lemon juice. Return cutlets and stir until glazed and little liquid remains in pan. Makes 4 servings.

Because chicken breast can taste quite dry, the herbed liquid and oil keep it moist and develop the richer chicken flavor. If you prefer to simply low-fat fry, use 3 tablespoons of oil. Remember to keep the fat hot and spread evenly over bottom while gradually adding the cutlets. Chicken can be breaded with crushed wheat flakes or corn flakes, instant mashed potato flakes or Herbed Breading mix (see page 12).

Nutrients per serving:

calories	*245*
protein	*27 gm*
carbohydrate	*5 gm*
total fat	*13 gm*
saturated fat	*1 gm*
monounsat'd fat	*7 gm*
cholesterol	*72 mg*
sodium	*270 mg*
potassium	*425 mg*
fiber	*1 gm*

% US-RDA

vitamin A	*8*
vitamin C	*18*
thiamin	*7*
riboflavin	*7*
vitamin B$_6$	*32*
folacin	*12*
iron	*10*
zinc	*6*
calcium	*4*

Tangy Chicken Dinner

Delicious! You will never know it was made with buttermilk.

1½ cups chicken broth or 1½ teaspoons chicken bouillon granules in 1½ cups water

½ teaspoon marjoram

½ teaspoon thyme

2 pounds skinless chicken breast, legs and thighs

6 medium potatoes, peeled and quartered, or 2 pounds whole new potatoes

2 medium onions, sliced

3 medium carrots, cut lengthwise

1 cup low-fat buttermilk

3 tablespoons all-purpose flour or crystallized flour

In Dutch oven, combine broth, marjoram and thyme. Place chicken pieces bone side up in broth and simmer 15 minutes. Add more water, if needed. Turn chicken pieces over, place potatoes, onions and carrots over chicken. Simmer 30 minutes or until chicken and vegetables are tender. Heat oven to 200°. Remove chicken and vegetables to platter and place in warm oven. To remaining broth, add buttermilk. Blend in flour; gently stir and simmer for 5 minutes. Serve gravy over chicken and vegetables. Makes 6 servings.

This recipe is well suited to chicken pieces from larger, older fowl. Mature chickens are less tender, but more flavorful. Because older chickens have accumulated more fat, remove all visible fat. Trimming out fat is easier when the chicken is very cold and fat is firm.

Nutrients per serving:

calories	296
protein	27 gm
carbohydrate	29 gm
total fat	8 gm
saturated fat	2 gm
monounsat'd fat	3 gm
cholesterol	85 mg
sodium	300 mg
potassium	850 mg
fiber	2 gm

% US-RDA

vitamin A	140
vitamin C	46
thiamin	16
riboflavin	16
vitamin B₆	33
folacin	10
iron	14
zinc	17
calcium	10

Roasted Turkey Breast

Versatile as hot or cold slices and as cubes for casseroles.

4 to 5 pound turkey breast, skin-on

2 tablespoons canola oil

¹/₂ teaspoon garlic powder

¹/₂ teaspoon onion powder

¹/₂ teaspoon thyme or other herbs listed below

dash of black pepper

Preheat oven to 350°. Rinse turkey and dry well. Leave skin on but trim excess; remove fat chunks. Rub oil over all surfaces. Sprinkle herbs over all surfaces. Place bone-side down on rack in shallow roasting pan. Insert thermometer into thickest part. Bake uncovered 30 minutes, cover and bake 1¹/₂ to 2 hours or until internal temperature is 170°. Remove skin before serving. Makes 10 to 12 servings.

Oven barbecue: Remove skin and coat breast with a thick bottled sauce. Bake 45 minutes. Turn breast side down in sauce. Continue turning and coating every 30 to 40 minutes until internal temperature is 170°.

Herbs and spices for seasoning poultry are basil, dill weed, ginger, nutmeg, oregano, marjoram, thyme, celery seed, chives, bay leaf, garlic powder, onion powder, black pepper, dry mustard, parsley, paprika, rosemary, sage, tarragon and poultry seasoning.

Nutrients per serving:

calories	*117*
protein	*27 gm*
carbohydrate	*0 gm*
total fat	*1 gm*
saturated fat	*0 gm*
monounsat'd fat	*0 gm*
cholesterol	*75 mg*
sodium	*50 mg*
potassium	*265 mg*
fiber	*0 gm*

% US-RDA

vitamin A	*****
vitamin C	*****
thiamin	*3*
riboflavin	*7*
vitamin B₆	*29*
folacin	*****
iron	*9*
zinc	*10*
calcium	*****

Turkey Chili and Beans

A do-ahead meal that is even better after reheating.

1 tablespoon canola oil

3/4 pound lean ground turkey

1 large onion, chopped

1½ teaspoon garlic powder

1½ teaspoon cumin powder

1½ teaspoon chili powder

1 can (15 oz.) tomato sauce

1 can (15 oz.) tomatoes, chopped, not drained

3 cans (15 oz.) ranch beans, not drained

1 teaspoon lite salt

1 cup water

Nutrients per serving:

calories	250
protein	19 gm
carbohydrate	30 gm
total fat	6 gm
saturated fat	1 gm
monounsat'd fat	2 gm
cholesterol	28 mg
sodium	1115 mg
potassium	1185 mg
fiber	2 gm

% US-RDA

vitamin A	22
vitamin C	44
thiamin	10
riboflavin	12
vitamin B$_6$	11
folacin	4
iron	26
zinc	23
calcium	12

In a heavy bottomed three-quart dutch oven, heat oil, add turkey and stir until it loses pink color. Add onion, garlic, cumin and chili powder. Stir gently until onion is soft. Add tomato sauce and tomatoes. Discard fat layer from top of ranch beans; add beans, lite salt and water. Simmer for 2 hours over low heat, stirring frequently to prevent sticking. Makes 10 servings.

A heavy Dutch oven cooks chili in the oven with less sticking. Preheat oven to 325°. Combine ingredients and heat together, as shown above. Place cover on Dutch oven and bake 2 to 3 hours. Stir at end of each hour to prevent sticking.

Freeze remaining chili for future meals. One cup of canned commercial chili contains 20 to 30 grams (4 to 6 teaspoons) of fat, while this recipe has only 6 grams (1¼ teaspoons).

Sweet-Sour Turkey

Ready for the table in 35 minutes.

4 cups hot cooked rice, brown or white

**1 package (8 oz.) frozen snow peas or cut
    green beans**

⅓ cup brown sugar, firmly packed

3 tablespoons cornstarch

2 tablespoons cider vinegar

2 tablespoons tub margarine

**1 can (20 oz.) pineapple tidbits in natural
    juice**

2 cups cooked turkey or chicken, cubed

1 medium green pepper, in strips

2 medium tomatoes, cut in eighths

Have rice ready to serve when sweet-sour turkey is done. Cook snow peas until tender-crisp, drain and set aside. In medium saucepan, combine brown sugar and cornstarch. Stir in vinegar and margarine, add juice drained from pineapple and stir to blend. Cook until sauce boils and thickens, stirring constantly. Gently stir in snow peas, pineapple tidbits, turkey and green pepper. Gently stir over medium heat until thoroughly heated, about 5 to 7 minutes. Add tomato pieces just before serving over hot rice. Makes 4 servings.

Don't worry if you have no leftover cooked turkey or chicken to cut up and use in recipes. Poach the chicken in a skillet with one cup boiling water. Simmer bone-in raw chicken for 18 to 20 minutes, or boneless raw chicken for 12 to 14 minutes until chicken is tender and no longer pink. Cool and cut into cubes.

Nutrients per serving:

calories	586
protein	33 gm
carbohydrate	91 gm
total fat	10 gm
saturated fat	2 gm
monounsat'd fat	4 gm
cholesterol	73 mg
sodium	155 mg
potassium	645 mg
fiber	3 gm

% US-RDA

vitamin A	21
vitamin C	72
thiamin	37
riboflavin	13
vitamin B_6	40
folacin	16
iron	36
zinc	9
calcium	10

165

Turkey Sausage and Potatoes

A 30 minute skillet meal for your hungry family.

1 pound turkey sausage, 20% or less fat

5 medium potatoes, thinly sliced, peeled or unpeeled

¼ cup water

2 cups frozen or canned peas, drained

¼ cup water

½ teaspoon lite salt

black pepper to taste

Nutrients per serving:

calories	340
protein	34 gm
carbohydrate	33 gm
total fat	8 gm
saturated fat	2 gm
monounsat'd fat	2 gm
cholesterol	85 mg
sodium	540 mg
potassium	950 mg
fiber	4 gm

% US-RDA

vitamin A	10
vitamin C	36
thiamin	26
riboflavin	20
vitamin B_6	45
folacin	32
iron	26
zinc	37
calcium	7

In heavy bottomed skillet, brown finely crumbled turkey sausage. Pour off excess fat and blot with paper towels to remove as much fat as possible. Add potatoes and water; stir gently to mix sausage and potatoes. Cover and steam over low heat for 10 minutes. Add more water if needed to prevent sticking. Add peas, lite salt and pepper; stir to mix. Cover and steam 5 minutes. Makes 4 servings.

For vegetable variety, use corn, green beans, lima beans, carrots or summer squash.

Because lean turkey sausage contains half the fat of lean pork sausage, it makes a tasty low-fat breakfast meat. Bake or broil on a rack to allow fat to drip away. Blot surfaces of cooked patty to remove more fat.

166

Beef: Battling
The Bum Steer?

Nutritionally speaking, beef and other red meats have received a bum steer. In an attempt to cut down fat and cholesterol intake, many Americans erased red meats from their grocery lists and thought their dietary problems were solved.

Not so. Lean meats, which are now readily available, are an excellent source of high-quality protein, iron, zinc and vitamins B_1 (thiamin), B_2 (riboflavin), B_6 and B_{12}. Fresh meats are also naturally low in sodium, providing only about 60 milligrams for every three ounce serving. The lean cuts of beef, lamb, pork and veal also compare favorably with poultry and fish in cholesterol content. A three ounce serving yields 75 milligrams of cholesterol, only 25 percent of the 300 milligram recommended daily allowance. One serving of lean meat daily can boost your nutrient intake and tantalize your palate.

Despite all the elements in its favor, red meat still has a bad reputation. But it is not the meat that should be avoided, it is the fat in the meat. Fats in the diet, particularly the saturated fat in red meats, are used by the liver to produce cholesterol in the blood. That is why the fat in the diet is more likely to raise blood cholesterol than is the amount of cholesterol eaten in foods. Remember to watch the total amount of dietary fat eaten and not just the cholesterol content of selected foods. Fats are high in calories, too. Omitting one tablespoon of fat per day from your diet translates into not eating eleven pounds of fat per year!

In choosing meats, select those that appear to be all muscle with no white streaks or marbling of fat. Ground beef should be dark red with little fat showing. The leanest cuts are top round, top loin, round tip, eye of round, sirloin and tenderloin. These meats are not as expensive as they appear because there is less fat to be wasted and are entirely edible.

Be aware that the percentage of fat listed on a package is by weight. If the lean ground beef is 10 percent fat, that is 10 percent of the meat's weight. The other 90 percent of the weight is the natural water and protein in the meat. Muscle meats contain no carbohydrate. In three ounces of 10 percent fat meat, there are 24 grams of protein (96 protein calories) and nine grams of fat (81 fat calories) for a total of 177 calories. By dividing the fat calories by total calories, we find 46 percent of the calories in lean meat are from fat.

In a typical low-fat meal we enjoy a three ounce serving of lean meat, potatoes seasoned with margarine, vegetables, bread, a simple dessert and low-fat milk. The 800 total calorie meal contains about 25 grams of fat (225 fat calories). This translates to 28 percent of calories from fat, an ideal meal in terms of fat, nutrients and satisfaction.

Lean red meats, in moderate amounts, may be included in a low-fat diet even though they are higher in saturated fat than poultry and fish. The reason, as we saw in the simple meal above, is dilution. Because we also eat many low-fat and nonfat foods during a typical day, the amount of saturated fat and the total fat in the diet is kept at acceptable levels.

The following hints will help you prepare meats in a healthier, low-fat manner. The recipes on following pages promise to do the same.

- *Before cooking, always remove all visible fat. It is easier to remove chilled fat, so place meat in the freezer for 20 minutes prior to trimming fat.*

- *Roasting on a rack, broiling or pan frying in a few teaspoons of oil are recommended cooking methods.*

- *When browning ground beef, begin cooking meat in two tablespoons of water to prevent sticking. Don't use oil. As the fat cooks out, the meat browns in its own fat. Drain off fat and blot meat with paper towels.*

- *Keep your daily limit of red meat to three ounces, cooked. A four ounce raw portion yields three ounces of cooked meat.*

Basic Meat Loaf
or Meat Balls

Mini-meat loaves bake in half the time.

1 pound lean ground beef

¹/₂ small onion, finely chopped or grated

**10 (2x2-inch) crackers, crushed, or ³/₄ cup
    uncooked oatmeal**

2 egg whites or ¹/₄ cup egg substitute

1 teaspoon lite salt

black pepper and other herbs, if desired

Preheat oven to 325°. Combine all ingredients and
blend well. For mini-meat loaves, shape into 5 loaves.
Leave 1 inch between loaves, place on rack in shallow
baking pan and bake for 30 minutes. Or shape into 25
walnut-sized balls and bake on rack for 20 minutes. Or
shape into 1 loaf and bake on rack for 60 minutes.
Makes 5 or 6 servings.

*Reduce fat and sodium per serving, while increasing
vitamins, fiber and the number of servings to eight, by adding
2 grated carrots and 2 unpeeled grated potatoes. Placing a
rack in the bottom of the pan is important for this allows the
fat to drip out of the meat, reducing the total fat.*

*After the meat has begun to brown, top with ¹/₂ cup catsup
or ¹/₂ to 1 can (10¹/₂ oz.) of tomato, golden mushroom, or other
low-fat soups. Refer to Low-Fat Soup chart (see page 250).*

Nutrients per serving:

calories	*200*
protein	*18 gm*
carbohydrate	*5 gm*
total fat	*12 gm*
saturated fat	*5 gm*
monounsat'd fat	*5 gm*
cholesterol	*75 mg*
sodium	*310 mg*
potassium	*570 mg*
fiber	*0 gm*

% US-RDA

vitamin A	*****
vitamin C	*2*
thiamin	*28*
riboflavin	*18*
vitamin B₆	*15*
folacin	*6*
iron	*14*
zinc	*26*
calcium	*****

169

Clara May's Ground Beef Hash

Yummy, economical and fast.

2 tablespoons water

3/4 pound lean ground beef

1 medium onion, chopped

5 medium potatoes, peeled, cubed

2 teaspoons beef flavor bouillon granules

dash black pepper or use other herbs (see below)

1/2 to 1 cup water

Place water in heated skillet. Add crumbled ground beef. As fat cooks out, meat browns in its own fat. Drain and blot off fat. Add onion, potatoes, beef granules and pepper. Heat together, stirring gently. Add water to desired consistency; cover, simmer until potatoes are done, about 10 to 12 minutes. Makes 4 servings.

Flavor improves if prepared ahead and re-warmed. Cubed roast beef and de-fatted drippings are tasty alternatives.

Herbs and spices for seasoning beef are black pepper, thyme, oregano, marjoram, bay leaf, garlic powder, onion powder, chili powder, parsley, cumin, ground red pepper, rosemary, dry mustard, ginger and curry.

Nutrients per serving:

calories	280
protein	24 gm
carbohydrate	28 gm
total fat	8 gm
saturated fat	3 gm
monounsat'd fat	4 gm
cholesterol	60 mg
sodium	320 mg
potassium	890 mg
fiber	1 gm

% US-RDA

vitamin A	***
vitamin C	53
thiamin	15
riboflavin	14
vitamin B₆	16
folacin	6
iron	21
zinc	32
calcium	3

Beef-Macaroni Skillet

Four generous servings ready in 30 minutes.

2 teaspoons canola oil

1 pound lean ground beef or turkey

1 medium onion, chopped

$1/2$ teaspoon garlic powder

1 cup catsup or 1 can (10$1/2$ oz.) tomato
   soup

2 to 3 cups water, more if needed

$1/2$ teaspoon lite salt

dash of black pepper and other herbs, if
   desired

1$1/2$ cups uncooked elbow macaroni

In large skillet or Dutch oven, heat oil over medium heat. Add crumbled ground beef, onion and garlic powder; cook together until beef loses pink color. Pour off excess fat and blot with paper towel. Add remaining ingredients except macaroni and bring to boil. Add macaroni and simmer until macaroni is done. Stir gently and frequently; add water as needed to prevent sticking. Makes 4 servings.

If you prefer baking, which allows more time for flavors to develop and blend, preheat oven to 350°. After all ingredients have been heated together, cover and place in oven. Check after 15 minutes, stir in more water if needed to prevent sticking. Bake 20 to 30 minutes more, or until macaroni is done.

Nutrients per serving:

calories	*434*
protein	*33 gm*
carbohydrate	*44 gm*
total fat	*14 gm*
saturated fat	*4 gm*
monounsat'd fat	*5 gm*
cholesterol	*85 mg*
sodium	*840 mg*
potassium	*950 mg*
fiber	*2 gm*

% US-RDA

vitamin A	*17*
vitamin C	*19*
thiamin	*20*
riboflavin	*18*
vitamin B_6	*27*
folacin	*16*
iron	*27*
zinc	*26*
calcium	*5*

Sloppy Joes

Easily put together, loved by children of any age.

1 teaspoon canola oil

1 pound lean ground beef or turkey (see note below)

1 medium green pepper, chopped

1 small onion, chopped

1 cup catsup

1/4 cup water

2 teaspoons beef flavor bouillon granules

2 teaspoons sugar

1 teaspoon prepared mustard

6 hamburger buns, split and toasted

Nutrients per serving:

calories	224
protein	20 gm
carbohydrate	18 gm
total fat	8 gm
saturated fat	3 gm
monounsat'd fat	4 gm
cholesterol	75 mg
sodium	700 mg
potassium	420 mg
fiber	1 gm

% US-RDA

vitamin A	13
vitamin C	38
thiamin	9
riboflavin	12
vitamin B$_6$	18
folacin	8
iron	17
zinc	29
calcium	3

In skillet, heat oil. Add crumbled ground beef, green pepper and onion. Cook until beef loses its red color. Pour off excess fat and blot with paper towel. Add remaining ingredients, except buns, and bring to boil. Reduce heat, cover and simmer for 15 to 20 minutes. Stir frequently to prevent sticking. Serve over toasted buns. Makes 6 servings.

Lean ground turkey often appears as an off-white color in meat patties or meat loaf. Many cooks prefer to use it in dishes like this one, when color is darkened by other ingredients.

172

Hamburger Soup

Another all-in-one meal.

1 pound lean ground beef or turkey

1 small head cabbage, cut in ½-inch
    wedges

2 cans (15 oz.) red kidney beans, not
    drained

1 package (16 oz.) frozen mixed
    vegetables

2 teaspoons lite salt

2 tablespoons dried parsley flakes

1 teaspoon garlic powder

other herbs, if desired

2 cans (15 oz.) tomatoes, peeled and
    chopped, but not drained

water or tomato juice to cover

In a large Dutch oven or slow cooker, crumble beef
and cook until it loses its red color. Pour off excess fat
and blot with paper towel. Add remaining ingredients,
adding enough water or tomato juice to cover other
ingredients. Cook until vegetables are tender. Makes 10
servings.

*Instead of frozen vegetables, use fresh, canned or leftover
ones. Also use the liquid drained and saved from vegetables
and potatoes.*

Nutrients per serving:

calories	221
protein	19 gm
carbohydrate	25 gm
total fat	5 gm
saturated fat	2 gm
monounsat'd fat	2 gm
cholesterol	34 mg
sodium	650 mg
potassium	940 mg
fiber	7 gm

% US-RDA

vitamin A	54
vitamin C	60
thiamin	10
riboflavin	12
vitamin B₆	41
folacin	24
iron	32
zinc	25
calcium	11

Tangy Beef Barbecue

This fast meal is sure to be a real kid pleaser.

1¼ pounds lean beefsteak

1 tablespoon canola oil

1 large onion, sliced

²/₃ cup catsup

3 tablespoons brown sugar

1½ tablespoon cider vinegar

2 teaspoons dry mustard

¼ cup water to thin, if needed

hot pepper sauce, if desired

4 hamburger buns, split and toasted

Nutrients per serving:

calories	*361*
protein	*28 gm*
carbohydrate	*42 gm*
total fat	*9 gm*
saturated fat	*2 gm*
monounsat'd fat	*5 gm*
cholesterol	*75 mg*
sodium	*600 mg*
potassium	*650 mg*
fiber	*1 gm*

% US-RDA

vitamin A	*10*
vitamin C	*13*
thiamin	*18*
riboflavin	*21*
vitamin B₆	*36*
folacin	*15*
iron	*24*
zinc	*21*
calcium	*4*

On cutting board, remove all visible fat from steak. Cut into ⅛-inch thick strips. In skillet, heat oil over medium high heat. Sear strips in hot oil. Add remaining ingredients, except buns. Simmer about 15 minutes, stirring to prevent sticking; add water, if needed. One tablespoon cornstarch may be dissolved in ¼ cup cold water and added to thicken barbecue sauce. Serve over toasted buns. Makes 4 servings.

For an even faster meal, brown the beef strips or lean ground beef and sliced onions in hot oil in skillet, pour bottled barbecue sauce over strips and heat together.

Skillet Sauerbraten

Speedy method for this German favorite.

**3 cups cooked mashed potatoes or
noodles**

16 gingersnaps

1¼ pounds lean beefsteak

2 tablespoons canola oil

1 can (10½ oz.) onion soup, undiluted

⅔ cup water

⅓ cup cider vinegar

Have hot mashed potatoes or noodles ready to serve
when sauerbraten is cooked. Using a rolling pin, finely
crush cookies in plastic bag. On cutting board, remove
all visible fat from steak (see note below); cut into ⅛-inch
thick strips. Place strips into bag with gingersnap
crumbs and shake until evenly coated. In skillet, heat oil
over medium high heat; cook beef until lightly browned.
Add soup, water and vinegar; cook until tender, about 20
minutes. Add remaining crumbs from bag, stir to blend;
simmer 1 minute. Serve over hot mashed potatoes or
noodles. Makes 4 servings.

*One and one-fourth pounds of raw beefsteak, trimmed of
all visible fat, yields 1 pound of lean meat. Before cooking,
this is 4 four-ounce portions of beefsteak. After cooking, it
becomes 4 three-ounce servings. So, even with a delightful meal,
we have stayed within our guideline of three ounces of cooked
red meat per day!*

Nutrients per serving:

calories	433
protein	29 gm
carbohydrate	41 gm
total fat	17 gm
saturated fat	4 gm
monounsat'd fat	8 gm
cholesterol	75 mg
sodium	1130 mg
potassium	1010 mg
fiber	1 gm

% US-RDA

vitamin A	3
vitamin C	9
thiamin	14
riboflavin	19
vitamin B_6	32
folacin	10
iron	27
zinc	22
calcium	9

Green Pepper Steak

Fast and colorful meal for guests or family.

3 cups hot cooked rice, brown or white

1¹/₄ pounds lean beefsteak

2 tablespoons canola oil

1 teaspoon garlic powder

1 medium onion, chopped

1 cup water

1 teaspoon beef bouillon granules

2 medium green peppers, cut into strips

2 medium tomatoes, cut into eighths

2 tablespoons cornstarch in ¹/₄ cup water

Nutrients per serving:

calories	438
protein	32 gm
carbohydrate	55 gm
total fat	10 gm
saturated fat	2 gm
monounsat'd fat	6 gm
cholesterol	75 mg
sodium	710 mg
potassium	875 mg
fiber	5 gm

% US-RDA

vitamin A	21
vitamin C	100
thiamin	25
riboflavin	19
vitamin B_6	44
folacin	16
iron	29
zinc	23
calcium	5

Have hot cooked rice ready to serve when pepper steak is done. On cutting board, remove all visible fat from steak; cut into ¹/₈-inch thick strips. In skillet, heat oil over medium high heat. Slowly add strips to skillet, sprinkle with garlic powder and sear strips. Add onions and cook one minute. Add 1 cup water and bouillon granules; simmer until beef is tender, about 10 to 15 minutes. Add green pepper and tomatoes. Whip together water and cornstarch and add to beef and vegetables. Simmer, stirring constantly, until mixture thickens. Serve immediately over hot rice. Makes 4 servings.

To complete the meal, add a deep green romaine lettuce salad with herb-and-oil dressing, a dinner roll and Apricot Velvet for dessert (see page 226).

London Broil

Marinades elevate meats from
mundane to marvelous!

1¼ pounds lean flank or round steak

¼ cup canola oil

½ cup vinegar

1 teaspoon garlic powder

¼ teaspoon black pepper

2 teaspoons dry mustard

1 teaspoon thyme

1 teaspoon basil

1 teaspoon dried parsley flakes

¼ cup dried onion flakes

dash of hot sauce or cayenne pepper

Place steak on cutting board and remove all visible fat. With a long, sharp knife, make angled ¼-inch deep cuts in a diamond pattern on both sides. In glass dish, combine oil, vinegar and herbs. Pour marinade over steak and gently work into cuts. Turn and repeat. Cover and refrigerate 6 to 24 hours. Turn several times. Grill, broil or pan broil. Makes 4 servings.

To remove the mystery from marinades, refer to All About Marinades (see page 20).

Nutrients per serving:

calories	188
protein	26 gm
carbohydrate	2 gm
total fat	8 gm
saturated fat	2 gm
monounsat'd fat	4 gm
cholesterol	75 mg
sodium	60 mg
potassium	475 mg
fiber	0 gm

% US-RDA

vitamin A	4
vitamin C	***
thiamin	9
riboflavin	16
vitamin B₆	33
folacin	6
iron	23
zinc	22
calcium	3

Beef Stew Bourbonnais

Our family's favorite for 30 years.

1 tablespoon canola oil

1 pound lean 1-inch beef cubes, all fat removed

1 teaspoon garlic powder

1 medium onion, chopped

1 can (10¹/₂ oz.) tomato soup, undiluted

³/₄ cup beef bouillon or dry red wine

¹/₄ teaspoon basil

¹/₄ teaspoon black pepper

¹/₄ teaspoon thyme

¹/₂ cup catsup

¹/₄ cup water

6 medium carrots, cut into 2-inch lengths

4 stalks celery, cut into 1-inch pieces

6 medium potatoes, peeled, quartered

Nutrients per serving:

calories	421
protein	31 gm
carbohydrate	54 gm
total fat	9 gm
saturated fat	2 gm
monounsat'd fat	4 gm
cholesterol	50 mg
sodium	950 mg
potassium	1680 mg
fiber	4 gm

% US-RDA

vitamin A	250
vitamin C	110
thiamin	35
riboflavin	27
vitamin B₆	45
folacin	16
iron	33
zinc	24
calcium	7

In Dutch oven, heat oil; slowly add and brown beef cubes. Add garlic and onion and cook until onion is transparent. Add tomato soup, bouillon, basil, pepper, thyme, catsup and water. Simmer together for 30 minutes. Stir well. Arrange carrots, celery, with potatoes on top. Cover; simmer or bake in 350° oven for 1¹/₂ to 2 hours. To prevent sticking, add water and stir, if needed. Stir vegetables, sauce and meat together before serving. Makes 6 servings.

Double this recipe except for carrots, celery and potatoes. Freeze half the recipe for later use. Cooked carrots potatoes and celery should not be frozen because they develop a mushy texture and an "off" flavor.

Cooking Today's Low-Fat Pork

Using yesterday's cooking methods for today's pork will probably result in a dry, tough product. The new, cleaner and leaner pork calls for cooking in moist heat at lower temperatures. In the past, it was imperative that pork be cooked to a well done state to destroy tiny parasites, trichinae, found in pork muscle. Today, producers raise a healthier product which provides safe meat, improved flavor and decreased fat content.

In the 1950s there were 475 cases of trichinosis per year, and most were attributed to undercooked pork. In 1986 there was only one case linked to pork consumption. When roasted pork is cooked to 155° (faintly pink and juicy) and removed from the heat source, the heat continues to penetrate and the internal temperature rises 10° to 15°, yielding a white colored, moist meat. The trichinae, very seldom present, are killed at 137°.

When preparing pork:

- *Select lean cuts. Fresh, lean ham leg with leg bone in can be roasted, but is good for making pork slices for cubing, stewing and braising. Loin produces loin chops and tenderloin, which are very lean meats for grilling and moist baking.*

- *Enhance the delicate, mild flavor of pork by adding herbs such as garlic, rosemary, ginger, pepper and fennel seed.*

- *Cook pork, and all meats, only after trimming off all visible fat. If roasting, cook pork until the internal temperature is 155°. Because the internal temperature will continue to rise, let meat stand for 10 minutes before slicing.*

- *Grill thin slices, but lower the temperature to the point that sear marks are barely made.*

- *When cooked pork is white and still moist, the meat has reached the very safe and desirable temperature of 155° to 160°. Long cooking at a high temperature results in a dry, less tender meat.*

Herbed Roast Pork

Keys to moist and tasty pork are herbs and lower heat.

3 to 5 pound pork leg or roast, bone in

¹/₂ teaspoon garlic powder

¹/₄ teaspoon ginger

¹/₂ teaspoon rosemary

¹/₂ teaspoon pepper

Preheat oven to 325°. Trim all visible fat from roast; wash and dry roast thoroughly. Sprinkle roast with herbs and rub into all surfaces. Roast in shallow pan, on rack, for 45 minutes to 2 hours until meat thermometer registers 155°. Let roast stand for 5 to 10 minutes before slicing. Makes 2 to 3 servings per pound of bone-in roast.

Changes in animal breeding practices have resulted in a 37 percent increase in the amount of meat on the leaner hog. Unfortunately, many people were misinformed and led to believe that pork is high in cholesterol. The truth is that a cooked 3-ounce serving of pork contains only 85 milligrams of cholesterol. This is similar to the amounts of cholesterol found in fish, poultry and beef. Remember that fat, particularly saturated fat, is more likely to raise your blood cholesterol than cholesterol eaten in your food.

Nutrients per serving:

calories	194
protein	26 gm
carbohydrate	0 gm
total fat	10 gm
saturated fat	4 gm
monounsat'd fat	5 gm
cholesterol	85 mg
sodium	65 mg
potassium	350 mg
fiber	0 gm

% US-RDA

vitamin A	***
vitamin C	***
thiamin	54
riboflavin	19
vitamin B₆	16
folacin	3
iron	7
zinc	18
calcium	***

Granny Smith's Pork

Tender pork and tasty apples — delicious!

2 tablespoons canola oil

1 pound boneless pork leg or steak cut
  into 1/2-inch cubes

4 apples, tart or Granny Smiths,
  unpeeled, cut into 1/2-inch slices

1 cup chicken flavor bouillon or white
  wine

3 tablespoons cornstarch

1/2 cup brown sugar

1/4 cup cider vinegar

2 tablespoons worcestershire sauce

1/2 teaspoon lite salt

1/4 teaspoon black pepper

Remove all visible fat from pork. In large skillet, heat oil over medium heat. Add pork and brown on all sides. Add apple slices; cook 3 minutes, stirring occasionally. Add 1/2 cup bouillon, reduce heat; cover, simmer for 10 minutes. Stir remaining bouillon and cornstarch together; add brown sugar, vinegar, worcestershire sauce, lite salt and pepper. Stir into pork-apple mixture. Cook over medium heat, stirring constantly until sauce thickens. Serve over hot rice or noodles. Makes 4 servings.

Pork leg, also called a fresh ham, might be hard to find. Ask your butcher to order a very lean one. The butt end can be cut into 1/3-inch pork slices. The shank end can be used for roast pork or for cubing.

Nutrients per serving:

calories	448
protein	26 gm
carbohydrate	50 gm
total fat	16 gm
saturated fat	4 gm
monounsat'd fat	10 gm
cholesterol	85 mg
sodium	450 mg
potassium	725 mg
fiber	3 gm

% US-RDA

vitamin A	2
vitamin C	31
thiamin	55
riboflavin	16
vitamin B_6	26
folacin	***
iron	18
zinc	14
calcium	5

Cranberry-Orange Pork Chops

Used together or alone, cranberry and orange flavors compliment pork.

4 lean pork chops, 6 to 7 ounces each, bone in

1/4 teaspoon marjoram

1/4 teaspoon black pepper

1 can (8 oz.) whole cranberry sauce

1/3 cup orange marmalade

2 tablespoons water

1 teaspoon chicken flavor bouillon granules

1 teaspoon lemon juice

1/2 teaspoon ginger

1/4 teaspoon garlic powder

1 tablespoon canola oil

Nutrients per serving:

calories	391
protein	26 gm
carbohydrate	38 gm
total fat	15 gm
saturated fat	4 gm
monounsat'd fat	8 gm
cholesterol	85 mg
sodium	300 mg
potassium	360 mg
fiber	1 gm

% US-RDA

vitamin A	***
vitamin C	3
thiamin	54
riboflavin	15
vitamin B₆	24
folacin	2
iron	9
zinc	14
calcium	***

Trim all visible fat from chops. Sprinkle on marjoram and pepper and rub into both sides. While herbs are seasoning the chops, prepare sauce. In small sauce pan over low heat, heat together cranberry sauce, marmalade, water, bouillon granules, lemon juice, ginger and garlic powder. In large skillet, heat oil. Slip chops into hot oil and cook 10 to 15 minutes until done, turning once. Drain off excess fat and blot with paper towel. Pour sauce over chops and heat together for 5 minutes. Makes 4 servings.

Instead of the above sauce, use 3/4 cup bottled barbecue sauce, your own recipe or use our Tangy Beef Barbecue sauce (see page 174). Brown and cook chops as above; add sauce and heat together for 5 minutes.

Pork and Rice Casserole

White meat of chicken or turkey can be substitued in most pork recipes.

1 pound boneless pork steak, cut in strips

3 tablespoons tub margarine

1½ cup uncooked rice, brown or white

1 medium onion, chopped

2 stalks celery, sliced

1 can (10½ oz.) cream of chicken soup

1 can (10½ oz.) cream of celery soup

10½ ounces water

1 can (4 oz.) mushrooms, pieces and stems

½ teaspoon each basil, thyme and parsley

Preheat oven to 400°. Trim all visible fat from pork and cut in ¼-inch strips. In Dutch oven, melt margarine over medium heat. Add pork strips and cook 5 to 7 minutes until pink color is gone. Remove pork from Dutch oven and blot off excess fat; set aside. In same Dutch oven, add uncooked rice, onion and celery. Stir constantly over medium heat for 5 minutes. Stir in soups, water, mushrooms and herbs. Bring to boil while stirring constantly to prevent sticking. Place pork strips over rice mixture. Bake uncovered 30 to 40 minutes or until rice is tender. Makes 6 servings.

For a golden brown top, sprinkle with paprika 10 minutes before removing from oven.

Nutrients per serving:

calories	*392*
protein	*21 gm*
carbohydrate	*32 gm*
total fat	*20 gm*
saturated fat	*7 gm*
monounsat'd fat	*8 gm*
cholesterol	*51 mg*
sodium	*950 mg*
potassium	*600 mg*
fiber	*2 gm*

% US-RDA

vitamin A	*12*
vitamin C	*8*
thiamin	*43*
riboflavin	*23*
vitamin B_6	*17*
folacin	*8*
iron	*15*
zinc	*11*
calcium	*21*

Plum-Braised Pork Strips

Fruit sauces are a delightful alternative to gravies.

4 lean butterfly pork chops

1 tablespoon canola oil

2 apples, tart, unpeeled, in 1/2-inch wedges

1/2 cup water

1/2 cup red plum jam

1 tablespoon cornstarch

1 teaspoon chicken flavor bouillon

1/4 teaspoon black pepper

Trim all visible fat from pork chops; cut into 1/4-inch thick slices. In large skillet, heat oil. Add pork strips; cook and stir 3 minutes. Add apple wedges and cook 3 minutes, stirring occasionally. In small bowl, mix water, jam, cornstarch, bouillon granules and pepper. Pour over apples and pork strips. Simmer 10 minutes or until pork is tender. Stir to prevent sticking. Makes 4 servings.

Make a plum sauce from syrup-packed canned plums. Drain juice from 16 oz. can of plums and save juice for use in a fruit punch. Pit and chop plums into small saucepan. Add 1/2 teaspoon garlic powder, 2 tablespoons brown sugar, 1 tablespoon lemon juice, 1/4 teaspoon cinnamon and 1/4 teaspoon ginger. Simmer, stirring constantly, for 5 minutes. Use in place of plum jam and water in recipe.

Pork Chops and Julienne Vegetables

Yummy vegetable sauce.

4 lean pork chops, 6 to 7 ounces each, with
    bone in

1/4 teaspoon ginger or garlic powder

1/4 teaspoon marjoram

1/4 teaspoon black pepper

1 tablespoon canola oil

2 medium carrots, cut julienne

2 stalks celery, cut julienne

1 medium onion, cut into thin slices

2 teaspoons chicken flavor bouillon granules

1 cup water

2 tablespoons cornstarch in 1/4 cup water

Trim all visible fat from pork chops. Combine and rub herbs into both sides of chops. In large skillet, heat oil. Slip chops into hot oil, cooking 4 minutes on each side. Top with carrots, celery and onion. Dissolve bouillon granules in water; add to vegetables and pork. Cover and simmer 15 minutes. Remove chops. Add cornstarch-water mixture to vegetables and broth in skillet. Cook over medium heat, stirring constantly until sauce thickens. Return pork chops to sauce and heat together for 5 minutes. Makes 4 servings.

Different cuts of lean, quick-cooking pork can be interchanged in these recipes. Alternates include pork tenderloin, pork chops, or pork leg slices or cubes. Avoid the shoulder cuts which are high in fat. Skinless chicken breast can also be used in most pork recipes.

Nutrients per serving:

calories	275
protein	28 gm
carbohydrate	7 gm
total fat	15 gm
saturated fat	4 gm
monounsat'd fat	8 gm
cholesterol	85 mg
sodium	315 mg
potassium	555 mg
fiber	2 gm

% US-RDA

vitamin A	210
vitamin C	13
thiamin	58
riboflavin	16
vitamin B₆	29
folacin	6
iron	9
zinc	15
calcium	4

Pork Tenderloin ala Orange

Another quick-to-cook pork dish.

1¼ pound pork tenderloin or chops cut
  into ¼-inch thick strips

2 teaspoons dry mustard

⅛ teaspoon black pepper

1 orange

½ cup orange juice

½ cup water

¼ cup honey

1 teaspoon chicken bouillon granules

1 tablespoon cornstarch

1 tablespoon canola oil

Nutrients per serving:

calories	323
protein	26 gm
carbohydrate	21 gm
total fat	15 gm
saturated fat	4 gm
monounsat'd fat	8 gm
cholesterol	85 mg
sodium	200 mg
potassium	390 mg
fiber	0 gm

% US-RDA

vitamin A	***
vitamin C	15
thiamin	55
riboflavin	14
vitamin B₆	24
folacin	8
iron	7
zinc	14
calcium	***

Trim all visible fat from meat; cut into ¼-inch thick slices. Sprinkle on mustard and pepper and rub into slices. Grate peel from orange; squeeze juice into 2 cup measure, adding enough orange juice or water to make ½ cup. Add grated orange peel, water, honey, bouillon granules, and cornstarch; mix well. In large skillet, heat oil over medium heat. Add pork and cook 8 minutes or until lightly browned. Pour orange-honey mixture over pork. Cook over medium heat 5 minutes or until sauce thickens, stirring constantly to prevent sticking. Makes 4 servings.

For a more delicate flavor, use tangerines and tangerine juice in place of oranges. Instead of grating, remove peel from one tangerine; cut peel into ½-inch pieces. Simmer peel for just 5 minutes in ½ cup water. Remove peel and use liquid in place of water and grated orange peel in recipe above. Fresh tangerine sections make a lovely garnish.

Pork Lo Mein

Chinese stir-fry over thin spaghetti.

8 ounces uncooked thin spaghetti

1/2 pound pork tenderloin or butterfly pork chops

1/2 teaspoon garlic powder

3 tablespoons canola oil

1/2 teaspoon ginger

2 medium carrots, thinly sliced

4 stalks celery or bok choy thinly sliced on diagonal

1 medium green pepper cut into strips

10 green onions, cut on diagonal

1 can (16 oz.) mushroom pieces and stems, drained

3/4 cup mushroom liquid

2 tablespoons cornstarch

2 tablespoons light soy sauce

Have spaghetti ready to serve when stir-fry is done. Trim all visible fat from tenderloin. Cut into 1/8 inch thin slices; rub garlic powder into slices. Cut all vegetables, leave in separated mounds. In large, heavy bottomed skillet or wok, bring 1 1/2 tablespoons oil and ginger to high heat. Immediately add pork slices to oil, stirring and searing until almost done, about 8 minutes. Remove pork or move to side of pan. Add 1 1/2 tablespoons oil, bring to high heat. Add vegetables in the order shown above, stirring until tender-crisp. Add water to mushroom liquid to make 3/4 cup. Mix in cornstarch and soy sauce; pour over meat and vegetables. Cook, stirring constantly, until mixture thickens. Serve over hot spaghetti. Makes 4 servings.

Use fresh vegetables in season. See page 88 for more stir-fry information.

Nutrients per serving:

calories	*467*
protein	*22 gm*
carbohydrate	*52 gm*
total fat	*19 gm*
saturated fat	*3 gm*
monounsat'd fat	*12 gm*
cholesterol	*40 mg*
sodium	*490 mg*
potassium	*625 mg*
fiber	*7 gm*

% US-RDA

vitamin A	*230*
vitamin C	*66*
thiamin	*47*
riboflavin	*19*
vitamin B$_6$	*24*
folacin	*24*
iron	*27*
zinc	*20*
calcium	*7*

187

Creamed Ham on Toast

It is easy to make this creamy, low-fat sauce.

2 tablespoons tub margarine

1/2 medium green pepper, chopped

1 small onion or 5 green onions, chopped

4 tablespoons all-purpose flour or
   crystallized flour

2 cups 1/2% low-fat or skim milk

1 1/2 cups cooked lean ham, in 1/3-inch
   cubes

1 cup frozen peas, defrosted

1 tablespoon pimento (optional)

black pepper to taste

4 slices whole wheat or white toast

Nutrients per serving:

calories	270
protein	16 gm
carbohydrate	29 gm
total fat	10 gm
saturated fat	3 gm
monounsat'd fat	4 gm
cholesterol	40 mg
sodium	850 mg
potassium	440 mg
fiber	2 gm

% US-RDA

vitamin A	23
vitamin C	41
thiamin	52
riboflavin	17
vitamin B_6	42
folacin	18
iron	14
zinc	9
calcium	23

In skillet, melt margarine over low heat. Add green pepper and onion; cook until soft. Blend in flour until smooth. Over low heat, stir in milk to remove lumps. Simmer, stirring constantly, until raw flour taste is gone. Add ham, peas, pimento and pepper. Heat together 5 minutes or until bubbly and hot. Serve over toast. Makes 4 servings.

Substitute any cooked meat and any vegetable to your liking.

Ham and Rice Primavera

Happy days are here again;
another all-in-one meal.

2 tablespoons tub margarine

1 cup uncooked rice, brown or white

1½ cups lean ham, cut into ⅓-inch cubes

1 medium onion, chopped

2 stalks celery, sliced in crescents

1 can (4 oz.) pieces and stems mushrooms,
   with liquid

½ cup frozen peas, defrosted

1 medium carrot, sliced

4 cups water

1 teaspoon chicken flavor bouillon granules

½ teaspoon basil

½ teaspoon garlic powder

¼ teaspoon oregano

⅓ cup Parmesan cheese

Nutrients per serving:

calories	488
protein	19 gm
carbohydrate	76 gm
total fat	11 gm
saturated fat	2 gm
monounsat'd fat	5 gm
cholesterol	23 mg
sodium	800 mg
potassium	500 mg
fiber	4 gm

% US-RDA

vitamin A	80
vitamin C	17
thiamin	27
riboflavin	7
vitamin B_6	12
folacin	6
iron	19
zinc	5
calcium	10

In Dutch oven, melt margarine. Add rice, ham, onion and celery. Heat and stir together for 5 minutes. Add mushrooms and liquid, peas, carrots, water, bouillon and herbs. Bring to a boil; reduce heat to simmer. Cover and simmer 25 to 35 minutes until rice is tender. Or cover and bake in 350° oven for 45 minutes. Serve topped with Parmesan cheese. Makes 4 servings.

Blending of flavors occurs with all foods, even when refrigerated. Prepare this meal the day before and reheat in 350° oven for a quick dinner.

Bacon-Lettuce-Tomato Sandwich

Plump, vine-ripened tomatoes make a perfect BLT.

1 pound lean bacon, thin or thick sliced

8 teaspoons salad dressing

8 slices whole wheat or white bread

4 leaves lettuce

3 medium tomatoes, sliced

Lay bacon slices on cold skillet or griddle. Cook on a low heat, about 275 to 300°. Check constantly and turn several times to assure even browning on both sides. Tilt skillet or griddle to drain fat as it cooks out of bacon. This prevents the fat from reabsorbing into cooked bacon. When brown and crisp, remove to triple thickness of paper towels. Blot well. Use fresh paper toweling continuously to assure as much fat as possible is removed from bacon strips.

To prepare sandwiches, use 1 teaspoon of salad dressing on each slice of bread. Place lettuce leaf, tomato slices and 1/4 of bacon slices on bread slice. Top with slice of bread. Makes 4 servings.

Because bacon is a high-fat food, it should be cooked to remove as much fat as possible and used only once, or possibly twice per week.

Nutrients per serving:

calories	332
protein	15 gm
carbohydrate	32 gm
total fat	16 gm
saturated fat	5 gm
monounsat'd fat	7 gm
cholesterol	27 mg
sodium	870 mg
potassium	400 mg
fiber	7 gm

% US-RDA

vitamin A	18
vitamin C	37
thiamin	26
riboflavin	15
vitamin B_6	13
folacin	22
iron	19
zinc	13
calcium	8

The Unique Egg

A bit of culinary wisdom: No single food is good or bad. Moderation and variety make for delightful eating experiences. With that in mind, let us talk about the egg.

Many people, concerned about their blood cholesterol levels, have cut eggs from their diet. While watching dietary intake of cholesterol is wise, it is important to know that eggs have a special place in the well balanced diet.

Keep in mind that it is fat, particularly saturated fat, which is used by the liver to produce cholesterol in the blood. Cutting the saturated fat in the diet is usually more effective for lowering your blood cholesterol than reducing your cholesterol intake.

In terms of high quality protein, egg whites are second only to mother's milk. Whole eggs are an excellent source for vitamin B_2 (riboflavin) and folacin, and a good source for vitamins A, B_6 and D, as well as the minerals, zinc and iron. All of these nutritional benefits come with a relatively small price tag. One egg has only one teaspoon (5 grams) of fat and 75 calories. Recent research has revealed there are only 210 milligrams of cholesterol per egg, rather than 275 milligrams as was once believed. With moderation in mind, three or four nutrient rich egg yolks may be included in your diet each week. The egg white is fat and cholesterol-free and may be used generously. When using egg whites as a substitute for the whole egg, for each egg, substitute two egg whites and, if fat is needed in the recipe, add one teaspoon canola oil.

Packaged egg substitutes may be purchased refrigerated or frozen, and are a popular item for persons counting cholesterol. The substitutes allow even the strictest of dieters to enjoy scrambled "eggs" anytime. These products adapt easily in recipes for yeast breads, muffins, cakes, cookies, casseroles, puddings and sauces. Egg substitutes have the added benefit of being pasteurized, making them a safe alternative for recipes requiring uncooked eggs, such as eggnog. If you prefer to make your own egg substitute, for each one egg-sized serving, use two egg whites, one teaspoon canola oil, $^1/_2$ teaspoon instant nonfat dry milk and a tiny drop of yellow food color. To control color, dip clean tip of an ice pick or baked potato nail into food color and stir color into egg white. If color is not deep enough, rinse off tip to avoid contaminating food color and dip again into food color.

The unused egg yolks can be whipped into a variety of skin and hair beauty treatments that offer a lasting, natural glow.

- *Shampoo: For short hair, use one or two egg yolks plus one or two tablespoons water. For long hair, use two or three egg yolks plus ¼ cup water. Blend yolks and water using a fork. Massage into scalp and through the hair for five minutes. Cover hair with shower cap and let set for 20 to 30 minutes. Rinse. No other shampoo is necessary.*

- *Facial: Blend one or two egg yolks, one teaspoon honey and one teaspoon vegetable oil. Blend until thick enough to smooth on face without running off. Apply mask to a clean, rinsed face avoiding eye area. Leave on 20 minutes. Lie down the entire time with head a little lower than the body. Rinse off with warm water.*

By using the recipes in this book, you will find it is easy to enjoy a diet low in dietary cholesterol without completely eliminating the nourishing egg.

The nutritional analysis for one large egg:

Nutrients per serving:		% US-RDA	
calories	75	vitamin A	6
protein	6 gm	vitamin C	***
carbohydrate	0 gm	thiamin	2
total fat	5 gm	riboflavin	15
saturated fat	1 gm	vitamin B₆	4
monounsat'd fat	2 gm	folacin	12
cholesterol	210 mg	iron	5
sodium	60 mg	zinc	4
potassium	60 mg	calcium	3
fiber	0 gm		

Scrambled Egg Treat

For a quick and easy breakfast, lunch or supper.

³/₄ cup egg substitute

1 egg

¹/₄ cup ¹/₂% low-fat or skim milk

¹/₂ teaspoon lite salt

dash of black pepper

2 tablespoons tub margarine

In small bowl, pour egg substitute, egg, milk, lite salt and pepper. Beat lightly with fork until uniform in color. In very smooth or nonstick skillet, melt margarine over medium heat until bubbly; tilt pan to coat. Add egg mixture. Reduce heat to low. Add fillers from the list below. stir occasionally from outside edge to center, allowing uncooked egg mixture to flow to bottom of skillet. Cook until egg mixture is set, but still moist. Makes 2 servings.

Using part whole egg will bring out the eggy flavor which some people miss when only egg substitute is used.

For a more filling dish, add one or more of the following: chopped chives, parsley or pimento, hot pepper sauce, mushrooms, fresh chopped tomato or green pepper; cooked and diced lean ham, potato, vegetable or rice.

Nutrients per serving:

calories	*216*
protein	*16 gm*
carbohydrate	*2 gm*
total fat	*16 gm*
saturated fat	*4 gm*
monounsat'd fat	*8 gm*
cholesterol	*108 mg*
sodium	*540 mg*
potassium	*700 mg*
fiber	*0 gm*

% US-RDA

vitamin A	*52*
vitamin C	*****
thiamin	*8*
riboflavin	*24*
vitamin B₆	*10*
folacin	*8*
iron	*16*
zinc	*10*
calcium	*12*

Don's Basic Omelet

Father's treat for guests or family.

³/₄ **cup egg substitute**

2 eggs

¹/₄ **cup ¹/₂% low-fat or skim milk**

¹/₂ **teaspoon lite salt**

dash of black pepper

2 tablespoons tub margarine

In small bowl, pour egg substitute, eggs, milk, lite salt and pepper. Whip vigorously until frothy. In very smooth or nonstick skillet or omelet pan, melt margarine over medium heat until bubbly. Tilt pan to coat. Add egg mixture. Add omelet fillings of your choice from the list below. Cook without stirring until bottom is slightly browned. Using spatula, fold half the circle over on top of the other half, leaving a half moon shape. Reduce heat, cook until center is done and outside is a golden brown. Serve on warmed plate. Makes 2 servings.

Omelet fillings: chopped green onions, sliced mushrooms, cooked and cubed potatoes, cooked vegetables, cooked lean ham, cottage cheese, diced tomato, shredded low-fat mozzarella cheese, jelly or marmalade, sweetened fresh or frozen berries.

Nutrients per serving:

calories 264
protein .... 18 gm
carbohydrate .... 3 gm
total fat .... 20 gm
saturated fat .... 5 gm
monounsat'd fat .... 9 gm
cholesterol .... 215 mg
sodium .... 590 mg
potassium .... 650 mg
fiber .... 0 gm

% US-RDA

vitamin A 55
vitamin C .... ***
thiamin 9
riboflavin 34
vitamin B₆ 5
folacin 12
iron 17
zinc 12
calcium 14

Egg, Ham 'n Cheese Muffin

Kids of any age like this
English muffin sandwich.

1/2 cup egg substitute

1 egg

2 tablespoons all-purpose flour

dash of black pepper

2 tablespoons tub margarine

4 slices lean boiled ham or Canadian bacon

4 English muffins, split

2 ounces low-fat mozzarella cheese

In small bowl, combine egg substitute, egg, flour and pepper; beat lightly with fork until uniform in color. On nonstick griddle, melt margarine over medium heat; spread over surface and heat until bubbly. Sizzle ham slices on one end of griddle; turn when brown. Place half of split muffin over ham slice. For each sandwich, slowly pour 2 tablespoons egg mixture to form a 3-inch circle, allow to congeal slightly; then add more egg mixture on top, making a 4-inch circle. Turn egg when top surface is set but still moist; top with cheese and other half of muffin. Heat 2 minutes and combine with ham and muffin-half. Serve on warm plate. Makes 4 servings.

Unless the ingredients are low-fat products, this sandwich can be high in fat. Served with a tossed salad, low-fat dressing and a drink from the Low-Fat Milk Bar (see page 209), the total fat for the meal is reduced to about 1/3 of the total daily fat allowance.

Nutrients per serving:

calories	318
protein	18 gm
carbohydrate	30 gm
total fat	14 gm
saturated fat	5 gm
monounsat'd fat	6 gm
cholesterol	75 mg
sodium	870 mg
potassium	525 mg
fiber	0 gm

% US-RDA

vitamin A	21
vitamin C	11
thiamin	35
riboflavin	27
vitamin B_6	6
folacin	14
iron	18
zinc	12
calcium	26

Egg Salad

A yummy spread for 5 sandwiches.

3 raw eggs

¹/₄ cup finely chopped celery

¹/₃ cup salad dressing

¹/₄ teaspoon lite salt

dash of black pepper

Place cold eggs in enough cold water to cover. Bring water to a simmer, then allow to simmer for 12 to 14 minutes, but no longer. Immediately pour off hot water, run cold water over eggs for a fast cool down. Peel eggs and grate or finely chop into a small bowl. Gently stir in salad dressing, celery, lite salt and pepper. Makes filling for 5 sandwiches.

Eggs peel more easily if refrigerated overnight after cooking.

For each additional egg in the pot, increase the simmering time by 1 minute. When used for deviled eggs, stir eggs gently every 2 minutes during simmering to keep yolk in center of egg. Over cooking and not cooling immediately causes a green coating to form on the yolk. The above method assures an attractive hard-cooked egg.

Add ¹/₄ cup finely mashed cottage cheese or tofu to make filling for 6 sandwiches and further reduce fat and cholesterol.

Nutrients per serving:

calories	86
protein	5 gm
carbohydrate	3 gm
total fat	6 gm
saturated fat	2 gm
monounsat'd fat	2 gm
cholesterol	136 mg
sodium	265 mg
potassium	155 mg
fiber	0 gm

% US-RDA

vitamin A	5
vitamin C	***
thiamin	2
riboflavin	12
vitamin B₆	3
folacin	6
iron	4
zinc	2
calcium	4

Mexican Scramble

*Four fast, rib sticking servings
for hungry diners.*

1 tablespoon tub margarine

10 green onions, chopped

1 medium green pepper, chopped

1 medium tomato, chopped

1/2 can (12 oz.) whole kernel corn, drained

1 can (15 oz.) pinto beans, drained

2 whole eggs, well beaten

1/2 cup egg substitute, or 4 egg whites

1/2 cup low-fat cheddar cheese, grated

1/2 cup salsa

1/2 teaspoon lite salt

dash of black pepper

In a very smooth or nonstick skillet, melt margarine over medium heat until bubbly. Tilt pan to coat. Add onions and green pepper, stir and cook 3 to 4 minutes. Add tomato, drained corn and beans, stir until hot. Beat egg and egg substitute together; add cheese, lite salt and pepper. Pour over vegetable-bean mixture. Reduce heat to low; stir occasionally from outside edge to center, allowing uncooked egg to flow to bottom of skillet. Cook until eggs are set but still moist. Serve on heated plates with salsa. Makes 4 servings.

Egg substitute tends to break down and stick if vigorously stirred while cooking. By using a very smooth or nonstick pan and stirring gently and occasionally, these problems are minimized.

Nutrients per serving:

calories	373
protein	22 gm
carbohydrate	42 gm
total fat	13 gm
saturated fat	5 gm
monounsat'd fat	5 gm
cholesterol	125 mg
sodium	675 mg
potassium	685 mg
fiber	6 gm

% US-RDA

vitamin A	67
vitamin C	75
thiamin	32
riboflavin	34
vitamin B_6	9
folacin	18
iron	34
zinc	10
calcium	26

197

Denver Egg Special

Easy, all-in-one nutritious meal.

3 patties (3 oz. each) nonfat hash brown potatoes, defrosted

1 tablespoon canola oil

1 tablespoon tub margarine

4 ounces lean ham, in 1/2-inch cubes

1/2 medium onion, chopped

1 medium green pepper, chopped

1 cup egg substitute

1/4 teaspoon lite salt

black pepper to taste

Nutrients per serving:

calories	*202*
protein	*14 gm*
carbohydrate	*14 gm*
total fat	*10 gm*
saturated fat	*2 gm*
monounsat'd fat	*6 gm*
cholesterol	*14 mg*
sodium	*600 mg*
potassium	*615 mg*
fiber	*1 gm*

% US-RDA

vitamin A	*30*
vitamin C	*50*
thiamin	*28*
riboflavin	*16*
vitamin B6	*20*
folacin	*6*
iron	*13*
zinc	*10*
calcium	*5*

Pour oil into a very smooth or nonstick unheated skillet. Do not preheat oil. Add hash browns; heat over medium heat. After oil begins to bubble around edges, fry undisturbed for 5 minutes; turn, fry for 3 minutes. Remove from skillet. Melt margarine in same skillet, add ham and cook 4 minutes. Stir in onion and green pepper; cook 3 minutes. Add back pre-fried potatoes, stir and heat together 4 minutes. Pour on egg substitute, sprinkle with lite salt and pepper. Stir occasionally from outside edge to center allowing uncooked egg to flow to bottom of skillet. Cook until egg substitute is set but still moist. Makes 4 servings.

For baked Denver Egg Special: Preheat oven to 350°. Remove from burner after adding egg substitute, lite salt and pepper. Gently mix egg substitute into vegetable-ham mixture. Sprinkle top with paprika. Bake for 12 to 15 minutes.

Using Low-Fat Dairy Foods

R emember how Mom said drinking milk would make us grow up big and strong? Well, she was right. Milk and other dairy products are rich in calcium and important nutrients needed to develop sturdy bones. But, it isn't just an important beverage for children. Teenagers and adults, too, need a daily dose of calcium.

Growing strong bones depends upon eating plenty of calcium from birth through age 35. During this time of life you are building a "bone bank" for the future. But, your need for calcium continues throughout life to replenish gradual bone loss. Durable bones depend on factors other than calcium. Your physician or registered dietitian will be glad to share this information. Another bonus from generous calcium intake may be a decrease in the likelihood of developing high blood pressure or colon cancer.

Many people are concerned about the fat in dairy products, such as milk. By switching to nonfat and low-fat dairy products, you can cut the fat without jeopardizing your calcium needs. Changing from two eight-ounce glasses of whole milk containing four teaspoons of butterfat (the fat found in dairy products), to $1/2$ percent low-fat or skim milk containing only one teaspoon of butterfat, you avoid eating three teaspoons of saturated butterfat per day — or 11 pounds in one year!

Three servings of dairy foods will supply about 900 milligrams of calcium. A serving is one cup (eight ounces) of low-fat milk or yogurt, one to two ounces of low-fat hard cheeses, or $1/2$ cup (four ounces) of low-fat cottage cheese. To compare the amount of fat, calcium and cholesterol in various dairy products, refer to the chart on page 261.

Each cup of dried cooked beans supplies 150 milligrams of calcium; broccoli and dark green, leafy vegetables, about 50 to 150 milligrams per half cup. The calcium percentage, based on the US-RDA of 800 milligrams, is shown in all our recipes. Calcium from tablets is not as effective as calcium from dairy products because it lacks the nutrients which help your body to properly absorb the calcium.

Many people do not drink milk. But, milk is just as nutritious in soups, puddings, sauces and yogurt. We have included a variety of low-fat dairy-food recipes in this section.

Guidelines for selecting and using dairy products:

- *Choose skim milk, or low-fat milk containing one percent or less fat.*

- *Select skim or low-butterfat hard cheeses, containing less than six grams of fat per ounce.*

- *Substitute low-fat buttermilk or plain low-fat yogurt for sour cream.*

- *Use evaporated skim milk instead of cream or regular evaporated milk.*

- *Make your own whipped topping from instant nonfat dry milk (see page 225).*

- *Sprinkle instant nonfat dry milk in soups and puddings, hot cereal, stews and meatloaf.*

- *Make your own low-fat flavored yogurt from vanilla low-fat or nonfat yogurt and fresh or canned fruits or jam.*

- *Use sherbets and low-fat frozen yogurt to replace ice cream. Low-fat yogurts will surprise you; many people prefer them to ice cream. Nutrition-wise, one cup of frozen yogurt is equivalent to 1/2 cup of milk and has much less fat than regular ice cream.*

The National Research Council recommends the intake of calcium:

Stage	Age	RDA (mg)
Infants	Birth to six months	400
	Six months to one year	600
Children	One to 10 years	800
Adolescents/		
young adults	11 to 25 years	1200
Adults	25 years and older	800
Pregnant/breast-		
feeding women	All ages	1200

Easy Potato Soup

Filling, almost instant soup!

2 tablespoons tub margarine

1 stalk celery, thinly sliced

1/4 cup dried onion flakes

2 cups 1/2% low-fat or skim milk

2 teaspoons dried parsley flakes

**2 teaspoons chicken flavor bouillon
   granules**

black pepper to taste

3/4 cup mashed potato flakes, uncooked

In large sauce pan, melt margarine. Add celery; cook until soft. Add remaining ingredients. Heat gently, stirring frequently; do not boil. Makes 2 large servings.

Make corn chowder by adding one can of corn. Or make fish chowder by adding 1/2 pound fresh or defrosted fish chunks.

Nutrients per serving:

calories	324
protein	12 gm
carbohydrate	42 gm
total fat	12 gm
saturated fat	3 gm
monounsat'd fat	5 gm
cholesterol	7 mg
sodium	750 mg
potassium	1000 mg
fiber	2 gm

% US-RDA

vitamin A	29
vitamin C	27
thiamin	11
riboflavin	20
vitamin B_6	50
folacin	12
iron	28
zinc	7
calcium	38

Cheese and Potato Casserole

*Stove top heating cuts baking time
to 40 minutes.*

2 tablespoons tub margarine

1/2 medium onion, chopped

2 tablespoons dried parsley flakes

1 can (10 1/2 oz.) mushroom soup

1/2 cup 1/2% low-fat or skim milk

6 medium potatoes, peeled, thinly sliced

**4 ounces low-fat cheddar or mozzarella
cheese, cut into 1/4-inch cubes**

Preheat oven to 350°. In Dutch oven, melt margarine.
Add onion and parsley flakes; cook until onion is soft.
Add soup and milk; stir until well mixed. Stir in potatoes
and cheese and bring to a boil. Place in oven and bake
40 minutes or until potatoes are tender. Makes 5
servings.

*A glance at the nutritional analysis shows this dish to be a
winner. High in carbohydrate and moderate in fat, it provides
a generous amount of many vitamins and minerals. Round out
this main dish with a bright green vegetable, a slice of herbed
bread (see page 46) and a fruit cobbler for a satisfying meal.*

Nutrients per serving:

calories	268
protein	8 gm
carbohydrate	32 gm
total fat	12 gm
saturated fat	3 gm
monounsat'd fat	4 gm
cholesterol	9 mg
sodium	650 mg
potassium	735 mg
fiber	1 gm

% US-RDA

vitamin A	10
vitamin C	53
thiamin	12
riboflavin	9
vitamin B$_6$	9
folacin	2
iron	13
zinc	4
calcium	20

Cheddar Cheese — Pimento Spread

Makes 10 quick-to-fix, moist and tasty sandwiches.

¹/₂ pound low-fat cheddar cheese

¹/₂ pound tofu or 2% low-fat cottage cheese

2 tablespoons canned pimentos, or more for a stronger flavor

¹/₃ cup salad dressing

¹/₂ cup celery, finely chopped (optional)

¹/₂ cup green pepper, finely chopped (optional)

¹/₄ teaspoon black pepper (optional)

Grind or grate and blend all ingredients very thoroughly together. Keep refrigerated in closed container. Best if used within 4 days. Makes 10 servings.

Spread may be used cold or in grilled cheese sandwiches. No salad dressing or mayonnaise is needed on the sandwich bread.

By using tofu, the fat is cut by one third when compared to regular pimento-cheese spread; sodium and cholesterol are cut by one-half. The flavor is milder than the usual tangy cheese-pimento spread. A dash of red pepper or hot sauce adds lively taste.

Nutrients per serving:

calories	*138*
protein	*10 gm*
carbohydrate	*2 gm*
total fat	*10 gm*
saturated fat	*5 gm*
monounsat'd fat	*3 gm*
cholesterol	*27 mg*
sodium	*200 mg*
potassium	*85 mg*
fiber	*0 gm*

% US-RDA

vitamin A	*8*
vitamin C	*5*
thiamin	*3*
riboflavin	*7*
vitamin B₆	*3*
folacin	*6*
iron	*17*
zinc	*7*
calcium	*27*

Vegetable-Cottage Cheese Salad

Simple and tasty, anytime.

1 container (24 oz.) 2% low-fat cottage cheese

1 stalk celery, finely chopped

1/2 medium green pepper, finely chopped

1 tablespoon dried or fresh parsley flakes

6 radishes, thinly sliced

2 green onions, chopped

1 carrot, finely chopped or grated

black pepper to taste

herbs if desired: dill weed, chives or basil

8 large, deep green lettuce leaves

2 medium tomatoes, quartered

1 cucumber or zucchini squash, unpeeled, sliced

Nutrients per serving:

calories	196
protein	25 gm
carbohydrate	15 gm
total fat	4 gm
saturated fat	2 gm
monounsat'd fat	1 gm
cholesterol	14 mg
sodium	725 mg
potassium	600 mg
fiber	3 gm

% US-RDA

vitamin A	140
vitamin C	70
thiamin	10
riboflavin	24
vitamin B$_6$	15
folacin	26
iron	17
zinc	7
calcium	20

Gently combine all ingredients except lettuce, tomatoes and cucumber. Chill together for 1 to 2 hours. Place lettuce leaves on salad plate. Mound 1/4 of vegetable-cottage cheese mixture on lettuce. Garnish with tomato wedges and cucumber slices. Makes 4 large luncheon salads or 8 side-dish salads.

Versatile 2% low-fat cottage cheese, at 100 calories per 1/2 cup, is equally good with all in-season fresh fruits, or with off-season canned fruits. With vegetables or fruits, low-fat cottage cheese is a nutritional winner.

Classic Cocoa and Cocoa Syrup

Make your own low-fat cocoa syrup for hot cocoa, or buy a low-fat chocolate syrup.

1 cup cocoa powder

2 cups sugar

1/2 teaspoon lite salt

1¹/₃ cups hot water

Stir together cocoa, sugar and lite salt in one-quart saucepan. Add hot water and blend thoroughly. Bring to a boil over medium heat. Stirring constantly, boil 4 minutes. Pour into storage jar, cap and refrigerate. Makes 2 cups of syrup.

To make hot cocoa, add 2 to 3 tablespoons of this syrup for each 7-ounce cup of milk; stir and heat but do not boil. Add ¹/₄ teaspoon vanilla for each cup. Beat with rotary beater until foamy. Top with marshmallows and a sprinkle of cinnamon, if desired.

A 2¹/₄-tablespoon serving of fudge-type chocolate syrup contains 1 teaspoon of fat. However, a thin-type chocolate syrup similar to this recipe may be purchased in a squeeze bottle and is actually a cocoa syrup which contains almost no fat. Compare the labels to select the low-fat syrup.

The nutritional analysis at the right is for one 8-ounce serving of hot cocoa.

Nutrients per serving:

calories	*170*
protein	*7 gm*
carbohydrate	*32 gm*
total fat	*1.5 gm*
saturated fat	*1 gm*
monounsat'd fat	*0 gm*
cholesterol	*6 mg*
sodium	*125 mg*
potassium	*430 mg*
fiber	*0 gm*

% US-RDA

vitamin A	8
vitamin C	3
thiamin	6
riboflavin	21
vitamin B₆	5
folacin	6
iron	5
zinc	7
calcium	31

Peach Melba Pudding

Shaker method is fun for children.

4 peach halves, fresh or canned, drained

2 cups ½% low-fat or skim milk

1 package (3.4 oz.) vanilla instant pudding

4 teaspoons raspberry jam or jelly

Place a peach half in each of 4 sauce dishes. Pour 2 cups milk into 4-cup measure; add pudding mix. Using whip, gently beat for 1 to 2 minutes, or until well blended. Immediately pour over peaches and let stand for 5 minutes. Cover and chill. Just before serving, top with 1 teaspoon of jam or jelly, if desired. Makes 4 servings.

Shaker method: Pour cold milk into leakproof one-quart container. Add pudding mix and blend into milk. Cover tightly; shake vigorously for at least 45 seconds. Pour at once into sauce dishes. Pudding will be soft-set and ready to eat in 5 minutes.

Create an endless variety of low-fat puddings by changing the pudding, fruits and jams. Enjoy a great taste while getting your calcium.

For a creamy light dessert, blend 1 or 2 cups Whipped Topping (see page 225) into the pudding before it firms up.

Nutrients per serving:

calories	173
protein	4 gm
carbohydrate	37 gm
total fat	1 gm
saturated fat	1 gm
monounsat'd fat	0 gm
cholesterol	5 mg
sodium	220 mg
potassium	290 mg
fiber	0 gm

% US-RDA

vitamin A	10
vitamin C	7
thiamin	4
riboflavin	13
vitamin B$_6$	4
folacin	4
iron	***
zinc	4
calcium	19

Clara May's Pistachio Sauce

Sauce in five minutes.

**1 package (3.6 oz.) instant pistachio
 pudding mix**

2/3 cup light corn syrup

3/4 cup evaporated skim milk, undiluted

In a small mixing bowl, combine all ingredients; mix thoroughly. Cover and chill. Serve over low-fat frozen yogurt, angel food cake or fruit. Makes 1 1/2 cups or six 1/4-cup servings.

This sauce is almost fat-free and is another way to add the important nutrients from milk.

Use instant lemon, vanilla, french vanilla and chocolate puddings for delicious made-with-milk toppings.

For a less sweet sauce, combine pudding mix with 1 cup 1/2% low-fat or skim milk and omit corn syrup.

Nutrients per serving:

calories	168
protein	2 gm
carbohydrate	40 gm
total fat	0 gm
saturated fat	0 gm
monounsat'd fat	0 gm
cholesterol	0 mg
sodium	165 mg
potassium	110 mg
fiber	0 gm

% US-RDA

vitamin A	2
vitamin C	***
thiamin	***
riboflavin	6
vitamin B$_6$	***
folacin	***
iron	8
zinc	2
calcium	13

Tapioca Pudding

A delicious dessert from the olden days.

¹/₃ cup sugar

3 tablespoons quick-cooking tapioca

2³/₄ cups ¹/₂% low-fat or skim milk

1 egg, well beaten, or ¹/₃ cup egg
   substitute

1 teaspoon vanilla

In two-quart saucepan, combine sugar, tapioca, milk and egg. Let stand 5 minutes. Cook, stirring gently and constantly over medium heat, until mixture comes to a full boil. Remove from heat; stir in vanilla. Pudding thickens as it cools. Cool 20 minutes, stir. Serve warm or chilled. Makes 5 servings.

A fluffy tapioca cream, which takes longer to make, may be made by separating the egg yolk from the white. Instructions are given on the quick-cooking tapioca package.

Before granular, quick-cooking tapioca, there were tapioca pearls. These cooked into clear globules, giving rise to the boarding house name, "fish eyes and glue".

Nutrients per serving:

calories	*167*
protein	*7 gm*
carbohydrate	*28 gm*
total fat	*3 gm*
saturated fat	*1 gm*
monounsat'd fat	*1 gm*
cholesterol	*42 mg*
sodium	*85 mg*
potassium	*230 mg*
fiber	*0 gm*

% US-RDA

vitamin A	*7*
vitamin C	*2*
thiamin	*6*
riboflavin	*17*
vitamin B₆	*5*
folacin	*6*
iron	*4*
zinc	*5*
calcium	*22*

The Low-Fat Milk Bar

Fruit + milk = a milk drink.
Add low-fat frozen yogurt = a milkshake.

(See blending instructions following)

Apricot milk punch:	1 cup $1/2$ percent low-fat or skim milk, 1 cup canned apricots and liquid, 1 tablespoon sugar.
Banana-chocolate drink:	1 cup $1/2$ percent low-fat or skim milk, 1 banana cut in pieces, $1/4$ cup chocolate syrup
Frosty orange drink:	1 cup orange juice, 3 tablespoons instant nonfat dry milk, 1 tablespoon sugar.
Jam 'n milk treat:	1 cup $1/2$ percent low-fat or skim milk, 2 tablespoons fruit jam.
Maple drink:	1 cup $1/2$ percent low-fat or skim milk, 2 or 3 tablespoons maple syrup.
Milk fruit shrub:	1 cup $1/2$ percent low-fat or skim milk, $1/2$ cup fresh berries or fresh fruit, 2 tablespoons sugar, 3 tablespoons orange juice.
Peanut butter smoothie: *(21 grams of fat, but mostly monounsaturated)*	1 cup $1/2$ percent low-fat or skim milk, 3 tablespoons peanut butter, 2 tablespoons honey or sugar.
Peppermint milk:	1 cup $1/2$ percent low-fat or skim milk, $1/4$ cup crushed peppermint candy.
Strawberry milk:	1 cup $1/2$ percent low-fat or skim milk, $1/2$ 10-ounce package frozen strawberries (partially defrosted), 1 tablespoon sugar.

Pour liquids into blender container first. This allows the other more solid ingredients to float and dissolve for better blending. Chill filled container in freezer 15 to 25 minutes. Set timer as a reminder! Remove and blend 15 to 45 seconds. Serve icy cold in tall glasses.

Cold foods have less flavor than the same foods at warm temperatures. You may wish to add flavorings such as additional honey or sugar, malted milk, cinnamon, nutmeg or vanilla, maple, lemon, almond or rum extract.

For a luscious milkshake, add one or two scoops of low-fat frozen yogurt to the chilled mixture before blending for 30 to 60 seconds.

No fresh milk on hand? Substitute 2/3 cup water and 6 tablespoons instant nonfat dry milk for 1 cup milk. For a higher nutrient and calcium drink, use 2/3 cup water and 1/2 cup instant nonfat dry milk.

Nutrient analyses on these drinks will vary considerably depending upon the ingredients. The basic ingredient is 1/2 percent low-fat milk. The nutrients in one cup (8 ounces) are:

Nutrients per serving:		% US-RDA	
calories	90	vitamin A	10
protein	8 gm	vitamin C	4
carbohydrate	12 gm	thiamin	6
total fat	1 gm	riboflavin	20
saturated fat	0.3 gm	vitamin B_6	6
monounsat'd fat	0 gm	folacin	6
cholesterol	4 mg	iron	***
sodium	125 mg	zinc	7
potassium	406 mg	calcium	38
fiber	0 gm		

Low-Fat Yogurt — Plain or Fancy

Yogurt is one of the most versatile of foods. Yogurt is the product of cultured milk, made under super clean conditions and strict temperature controls to assure only the desired bacteria are growing. During the warm culturing time, the microorganisms turn the pre-pasteurized milk from a liquid to a soft custard-like consistency.

Regular yogurt is made from whole milk containing 3½ percent butterfat. Low-fat yogurt is produced from 1½ percent butterfat milk and nonfat yogurt is made from skim milk containing less than one-half percent butterfat. Usually, nonfat dry milk has been added to the liquid milk; this adds firmness to the set and boosts the calcium and other nutrients above that of milk. After culturing, some yogurts are heated to destroy the bacteria, while others are kept at cold temperatures to keep the active culture alive. These healthy bacteria help maintain a normal balance in the intestine, and research has found these good bacteria protect against some digestive illnesses.

A few industrious cooks love to make their own fresh, economical yogurt. The majority of cooks, however, prefer to purchase their yogurt, So when buying yogurt, check the label to determine:

- *The percent of fat. Choose one or two percent low-fat or nonfat yogurt.*
- *If an active culture is present. Active cultured yogurt is preferred because these bacteria may promote a healthy digestive tract.*
- *The foods and flavorings that have been added. Sugar and sweeteners are in vanilla yogurt and fruits and jams are in fruit yogurt.*
- *The calories, fats and nutrients in an eight-ounce serving.*
- *The "use before" date.*

Using tangy, low-fat yogurt is an easy and tasty way to add

flavor and interest to many foods and at the same time, increase nutritional value.

- *Enhance plain yogurt with finely chopped chives, green onions, parsley or herbs and serve with breads, potatoes, rice, vegetables, salads, poultry and meats.*
- *Make your own fruit and yogurt combinations by using ideas from the Low-Fat Milk Bar on page 209 and substitute low-fat or nonfat yogurt. You may prefer the taste and cost of making your own combinations.*
- *Combine honey and yogurt and use as a topping on tart fresh fruits. Use a dollop of vanilla yogurt as a topping on sweet foods.*
- *Use yogurt when making salad dressings or toppings for baked potatoes. For ideas, check the recipes on pages 27 to 30.*
- *Use yogurt as a substitute for sour cream in hot food recipes. Add the yogurt last and don't allow to boil and separate.*

Take the time to get acquainted with versatile yogurt. You will be glad you did!

The analysis for eight ounces of one and one-half percent low-fat yogurt is:

Nutrients per serving:		% US-RDA	
calories	140	vitamin A	2
protein	11 gm	vitamin C	***
carbohydrate	15 gm	thiamin	6
total fat	4 gm	riboflavin	30
saturated fat	2 gm	vitamin B_6	7
monounsat'd fat	1 gm	folacin	12
cholesterol	15 mg	iron	***
sodium	120 mg	zinc	12
potassium	570 mg	calcium	40
fiber	0 gm		

Sweet Surprises with Sugar, Honey and Desserts

It may come as a surprise to you, but sugar is not a "bad" food. Mother Nature added sugar to ripe fruits and even gave babies an enjoyment of sweet flavors. Each year the average American consumes 43 pounds of sugar and sweeteners, which translates to four tablespoons per day. Granulated white sugar (sucrose), made from sugar cane or sugar beets, is a common staple in the home. With just 46 calories per tablespoon, it contains only half the calories of a tablespoon of fat or oil.

Sweet treats are very much a part of our diet. We mark special occasions such as birthdays and anniversaries with frosted cakes and sugary desserts. These celebrations need not change. Between these celebrations, we must not allow sweets to crowd out nutrient rich foods in our daily diet.

In the past, sugar has been blamed for causing heart disease, diabetes, hypoglycemia and hyperactivity in children. Yet, hundreds of research studies have shown that sugar has no direct connection to these diseases. The only disease firmly linked to sugar is dental cavities.

Many weight-conscious adults have switched to artificial sweeteners in an attempt to satisfy their sweet craving without adding calories. But artificial sweeteners do not replace the desire for sugar because they can't send the brain the correct message to satisfy the craving for sweets. That is why a person who uses artificial sweeteners may find the desire for something sweet is even greater than that of the average person who uses sugar. Research has also shown that the use of artificial sweeteners does not promote weight loss.

Sugar facts:

- *Some people prefer to replace granulated sugar with natural sweeteners such as honey and brown sugar. While there are differences in taste and texture, the body does not recognize them and treats all natural sweeteners in the same way. All are rapidly absorbed and converted to glucose to satisfy quick energy needs. All three contribute simple sugar and only negligible amounts of fat, protein, vitamins and minerals to the diet.*

- *Brown sugar is a mixture of granulated sugar and molasses. The darker the brown sugar, the more molasses it contains. Brown sugar can easily be substituted for granulated sugar and will impart a slightly darker color and a subtle molasses flavor.*

- *Honey is made ... ...ctose and glucose and is treasured for its special sweetness, flavor and smoothness.*

- *Besides eating the sugars that are added to foods, we eat many simple sugars that occur naturally in our diets, such as in fruits.*

- *Simple sugars such as white sugar, brown sugar, honey and the naturally occurring sugars in fruit are made up of short strings of sugar molecules. Simple sugars should make up about 10 to 15 percent of your caloric need. The complex carbohydrates are made up of long strings of sugar molecules. These are the starches found in grains and vegetables and should contribute 30 to 40 percent of your total daily calories. Simple and complex carbohydrates should total 40 to 55 percent of your energy needs.*

As always, moderation is the key. Sweet foods should be enjoyed as long as they don't interfere with eating more wholesome foods. The following dessert recipes follow our simple, moderate approach to eating: they are low in saturated fat, moderate in calories and sugar and easy to make. Above all, they are bound to satisfy your sweet tooth.

Crispy Rice Bars

Easy, fast and low-fat.

¹/₄ cup tub margarine

**1 package (10 oz.) marshmallows, about
40 regular or 4 cups miniature**

6 cups crispy rice cereal

Oil a 9x13x2-inch pan. Melt margarine in three-quart saucepan over low heat. Add marshmallows and stir until completely melted. Remove from heat. Add crispy rice cereal; stir until well coated. Using large spoon, scoop into oiled pan. To spread evenly, press with back of large, clean wet spoon. When cool, cut into 24 bars, 2x2-inches. Makes 12 servings.

For peanut butter-rice bars, melt ¹/₄ cup of chunky peanut butter and blend with margarine; follow recipe as shown above. This adds about 1¹/₂ grams of fat per bar. The 2-bar serving has 3 additional grams of fat, mostly the desirable monounsaturated fat, and has 200 calories rather than 173.

Nutrients per serving:

calories	173
protein	1 gm
carbohydrate	31 gm
total fat	5 gm
saturated fat	1 gm
monounsat'd fat	2 gm
cholesterol	0 mg
sodium	220 mg
potassium	20 mg
fiber	0 gm

% US-RDA

vitamin A	15
vitamin C	5
thiamin	12
riboflavin	14
vitamin B₆	11
folacin	22
iron	10
zinc	***
calcium	***

Peanut Butter Cookies

Low in saturated fat, rich in monounsaturated oil.

1/2 **cup tub margarine**

1/2 **cup peanut butter, creamy or chunky (see below)**

1/2 **cup sugar**

1/2 **cup brown sugar, firmly packed**

1 **egg**

11/4 **cups all-purpose flour**

1 **teaspoon baking soda**

1/4 **teaspoon lite salt**

Nutrients per 3 cookies:

calories	*254*
protein	*4 gm*
carbohydrate	*28 gm*
total fat	*14 gm*
saturated fat	*2 gm*
monounsat'd fat	*8 gm*
cholesterol	*27 mg*
sodium	*270 mg*
potassium	*145 mg*
fiber	*1 gm*

% US-RDA

vitamin A	*6*
vitamin C	*****
thiamin	*6*
riboflavin	*6*
vitamin B6	*3*
folacin	*3*
iron	*9*
zinc	*3*
calcium	*3*

In mixing bowl, blend margarine, peanut butter, sugars and egg. Thoroughly mix in remaining ingredients. Chill dough for at least one hour. Preheat oven to 375°. Roll dough into walnut-sized balls; place 3 inches apart on lightly oiled baking sheet. Flatten with fork dipped in flour; crisscross fork lines. Bake 10 to 12 minutes, or until set but not hard. Cool on rack 5 minutes; remove from baking pan. Makes thirty-six 21/2-inch cookies.

Peanut butter cookies are richer in desirable monounsaturated oil and nutrients than other cookies. They are not low-fat, but may be used in moderation with low-fat menus. Use of nonhydrogenated peanut butter is not necessary as there is very little hydrogenated oil in commercial peanut butter.

Sugar Cookies or Bars

The bar method cuts preparation time.

2½ cups Quick Mix (see page 47)

1 cup sugar

½ cup canola oil

½ cup ½% low-fat or skim milk

1 egg, slightly beaten

1 teaspoon vanilla, lemon or other extract

¼ cup sugar for top sprinkle

Preheat oven to 375°. Stir together Quick Mix and sugar. Add oil, milk, egg and vanilla; blend well.

For cookies: Lightly oil baking sheets; drop by teaspoonfuls onto sheet. Bake 10 to 12 minutes until lightly browned. Cool on rack for 5 minutes; remove from baking sheets. Makes 36 cookies.

For bars: Lightly oil 12x18x½-inch jellyroll pan. Press mixture evenly into pan. Sprinkle with sugar and roll smooth with rolling pin. Bake 12 to 15 minutes or until lightly browned. Remove from oven; make 5 cuts each way (6 rows) and place on rack to cool for 10 minutes. Remove from baking pan. Makes 36 bars.

Lower fat cookies and bars are less crisp and benefit from flavorful additions such as ½ teaspoon cinnamon in sugar sprinkle, raisins, tiny gumdrops or grated lemon or orange peel.

Nutrients per 3 cookies:

calories	262
protein	3 gm
carbohydrate	40 gm
total fat	10 gm
saturated fat	1 gm
monounsat'd fat	6 gm
cholesterol	27 mg
sodium	290 mg
potassium	25 mg
fiber	1 gm

% US-RDA

vitamin A	***
vitamin C	***
thiamin	11
riboflavin	7
vitamin B$_6$	3
folacin	2
iron	5
zinc	***
calcium	10

Molasses Cookies or Bars

The high-iron cookie!

2¹/₂ cups Quick Mix (see page 47)

¹/₃ cup sugar

¹/₂ teaspoon cinnamon

¹/₂ teaspoon ginger

¹/₄ teaspoons cloves

1 egg, slightly beaten

²/₃ cup molasses

¹/₂ cup canola oil

3 tablespoons sugar for topping

Stir together Quick Mix, sugar and spices. Add egg, molasses and oil; blend well. Refrigerate one hour or longer. Preheat oven to 375°.

For cookies: Roll dough into walnut-sized balls. Place 3 inches apart on lightly oiled baking sheet. Flatten balls with bottom of glass dipped in sugar. Bake 8 to 10 minutes until set but not hard. Cool on rack for 5 minutes; remove from baking sheet. Makes 36 cookies.

For bars: Lightly oil 12x18x¹/₂-inch jellyroll pan. Press mixture evenly into pan. Sprinkle with sugar and roll smooth with rolling pin. Bake 10 to 12 minutes or until set but not hard. Remove from oven; make 5 cuts (6 rows) each way and place on rack to cool 10 minutes. Remove from baking pan. Makes 36 bars.

In damp weather, freshen by heating 5 to 7 minutes in 250° oven. For soft cookies, keep in airtight container with slice of apple.

Hot Fudge Pudding

Satisfy your chocolate urge.

1¹/₂ cups Quick Mix (see page 47)

³/₄ cup sugar

2 tablespoons cocoa powder

¹/₃ cup chopped nuts

¹/₂ cup ¹/₂% low-fat or skim milk

1 teaspoon vanilla

¹/₃ cup canola oil

²/₃ cup brown sugar, firmly packed

¹/₄ cup cocoa powder

1¹/₂ cups boiling water

Preheat oven to 350°. In an unoiled 9x9x2-inch pan, combine Quick Mix, sugar, cocoa, nuts, milk, vanilla and oil. Mix well and spread evenly over bottom of pan. In a small bowl, stir together brown sugar, cocoa and boiling water. Pour over mixture, but do not stir. Bake 35 to 40 minutes until edges separate from pan. During baking, mixture rises to top and chocolate sauce settles to bottom. Makes 9 servings.

For a lower fat variation (5 grams less fat per serving), omit nuts and add 1 cup miniature marshmallows.

Nutrients per serving:

calories	324
protein	4 gm
carbohydrate	50 gm
total fat	12 gm
saturated fat	1 gm
monounsat'd fat	7 gm
cholesterol	0 mg
sodium	245 mg
potassium	190 mg
fiber	1 gm

% US-RDA

vitamin A	***
vitamin C	***
thiamin	10
riboflavin	7
vitamin B₆	5
folacin	2
iron	11
zinc	2
calcium	11

Applesauce Cake

Always a family favorite that you can do ahead.

1 cup brown sugar

$^1/_2$ cup tub margarine

1 teaspoon cloves

1 teaspoon cinnamon

1 teaspoon lite salt

$^1/_4$ cup egg substitute

$1^1/_2$ cup all-purpose flour

2 cups applesauce, divided

1 cup whole wheat flour

1 teaspoon baking powder

1 teaspoon baking soda

1 cup raisins (optional)

Nutrients per serving:

calories	*178*
protein	*2 gm*
carbohydrate	*29 gm*
total fat	*6 gm*
saturated fat	*1 gm*
monounsat'd fat	*3 gm*
cholesterol	*0 mg*
sodium	*140 mg*
potassium	*100 mg*
fiber	*1 gm*

% US-RDA

vitamin A	*5*
vitamin C	*****
thiamin	*8*
riboflavin	*5*
vitamin B$_6$	*3*
folacin	*****
iron	*7*
zinc	*2*
calcium	*3*

Preheat oven to 375°. Oil two 4$^1/_2$x8$^1/_2$-inch loaf pans or 24 muffin cups. In large mixing bowl, cream together brown sugar and margarine. Blend in cloves, cinnamon and lite salt. Mix in egg substitute, all-purpose flour and 1 cup applesauce. Add whole wheat flour; mix well. Add 1 cup applesauce, baking powder, and baking soda; blend thoroughly. Mix in raisins and assure they are well distributed through batter. Pour into loaf pans. Bake 45 to 60 minutes until a tooth pick comes out clean from center of loaf. Serve warm or at room temperature. Makes 12 slices per cake or 24 cupcakes.

The one bowl method avoids sifting and separate bowls, yet yields a moist, flavorful cake.

To maximize flavor development, make several days ahead, wrap well and refrigerate or freeze.

Pineapple Upside-Down Cake

Another quick to the oven treat.

¹/₄ cup tub margarine

¹/₂ cup brown sugar, firmly packed

1 can (20 oz.) sliced, chunked or crushed pineapple, in natural juice but well drained

1¹/₃ cups all-purpose flour

¹/₂ cup sugar

2 teaspoons baking powder

¹/₂ teaspoon lite salt

¹/₃ cup canola oil

²/₃ cup ¹/₂% low-fat or skim milk

1 teaspoon vanilla

¹/₄ cup egg substitute or 2 egg whites

Preheat oven to 350° (325° if cast iron skillet is used). Melt margarine in heavy skillet or square pan 9x9x2-inches. Blend in brown sugar and spread evenly over bottom of pan. Arrange drained pineapple evenly over margarine-sugar surface. Dot with pitted prunes, cherries and/or apricots, if desired.

In mixing bowl, combine remaining ingredients and blend well. Pour batter over fruit. Bake 40 to 50 minutes until inserted toothpick comes out clean. Turn bottom side up on large serving platter. Best when served warm. Makes 10 servings.

Most people like the taste and feel of a dessert with about two teaspoons of fat per serving. This recipe provides it as desirable monounsaturated oil.

Nutrients per serving:

calories	*236*
protein	*3 gm*
carbohydrate	*38 gm*
total fat	*8 gm*
saturated fat	*1 gm*
monounsat'd fat	*6 gm*
cholesterol	*0 mg*
sodium	*230 mg*
potassium	*190 mg*
fiber	*1 gm*

% US-RDA

vitamin A	*8*
vitamin C	*5*
thiamin	*9*
riboflavin	*6*
vitamin B₆	*7*
folacin	*4*
iron	*7*
zinc	*****
calcium	*7*

221

Grandpa Bob's Gingerbread

His favorite from his days on the boyhood farm.

1/2 cup tub margarine

1/4 cup sugar

1 egg or 1/4 cup egg substitute

1 cup dark molasses

1 cup boiling water

21/4 cups all-purpose flour

1 teaspoon baking soda

1/2 teaspoon lite salt

1 teaspoon ginger

1 teaspoon cinnamon

Nutrients per serving:

calories	257
protein	3 gm
carbohydrate	41 gm
total fat	9 gm
saturated fat	2 gm
monounsat'd fat	5 gm
cholesterol	32 mg
sodium	325 mg
potassium	1015 mg
fiber	1 gm

% US-RDA

vitamin A	8
vitamin C	***
thiamin	13
riboflavin	11
vitamin B6	4
folacin	4
iron	40
zinc	2
calcium	29

Preheat oven to 325°. Oil and flour a 9x9x2-inch pan. Blend together margarine, sugar and egg. Add molasses and water; mix well. Add remaining dry ingredients; beat until smooth. Pour into pan. Bake 40 to 50 minutes until cake pulls away from side of pan. Makes 10 servings.

Delicious when served hot from the oven with warm applesauce or Rum Hard Sauce (see page 36).

Any Fruit Cobbler

Twelve minutes and it is ready for the oven.

1 cup Quick Mix (see page 47)

1/4 cup sugar

1/3 cup 1/2% low-fat or skim milk

3 tablespoons canola oil

**2 cans (21 oz.) your favorite fruit pie
    filling**

Preheat oven to 425°. Oil a 9x9x2-inch baking pan.
Stir Quick Mix and sugar together in large mixing bowl.
Pour milk and oil into measuring cup; don't stir. Dump
oil and milk into mix; stir with fork to form a ball.
Knead ball 10 times. On waxed paper, press dough into
9-inch square. Pour pie filling into pan. Turn dough from
waxed paper onto the filling; cut 4 slits in dough. Bake
20 to 25 minutes until crust is golden brown. Makes 9
servings.

Perk up fruit flavors with these spices and extracts:

- *Apple, apricot or peach: add 3/4 teaspoon cinnamon or
  nutmeg.*

- *Berries: add 1/2 teaspoon cinnamon.*

- *Cherry: add 1/2 teaspoon almond extract and 1/4 teaspoon
  cinnamon.*

*To reduce very sweet flavor, stir 2 teaspoons lemon juice
into pie filling or omit 1 can pie filling and add 4 unpeeled,
sliced apples or other fresh fruit.*

Nutrients per serving:

calories	*177*
protein	*1 gm*
carbohydrate	*32 gm*
total fat	*5 gm*
saturated fat	*1 gm*
monounsat'd fat	*3 gm*
cholesterol	*0 mg*
sodium	*150 mg*
potassium	*100 mg*
fiber	*3 gm*

% US-RDA

vitamin A	*2*
vitamin C	*****
thiamin	*6*
riboflavin	*4*
vitamin B$_6$	*5*
folacin	*****
iron	*5*
zinc	*****
calcium	*6*

Strawberry Angel Treat

A basic recipe for mixing and matching fruits and toppings.

1 ounce angel food cake (¹/₈ of 8 oz. cake)

³/₄ cup frozen strawberries, sliced, partially defrosted, with juice

3 tablespoons Whipped Topping (see page 225)

To prevent juice from soaking into angel food cake, prepare this recipe immediately before serving. Cut wedge of angel food cake. Top with strawberries and juice. Add dollop of Whipped Topping. Makes 1 serving.

Angel food cake provides a nonfat base for low-fat puddings or fresh, frozen, or canned fruit sauces and low-fat frozen yogurts.

Nonfat toppings include Whipped Topping, fruit-flavored gelatin dessert powder, crushed peppermint or other hard candy or cake decorating sprinkles.

Nutrients per serving:

calories	260
protein	5 gm
carbohydrate	60 gm
total fat	0 gm
saturated fat	0 gm
monounsat'd fat	0 gm
cholesterol	0 mg
sodium	100 mg
potassium	270 mg
fiber	4 gm

% US-RDA

vitamin A	2
vitamin C	100
thiamin	4
riboflavin	10
vitamin B₆	3
folacin	14
iron	7
zinc	***
calcium	9

Whipped Topping

Use lavishly — it is fat free!

1 cup ice water

1 tablespoon lemon juice

1 teaspoon vanilla

1 cup instant nonfat dry milk

6 tablespoons sugar

Chill mixing bowl, beaters and water in freezer for 15 minutes. Set timer for reminder to remove. Add lemon juice, vanilla and dry milk; stir together. Beat 5 to 10 minutes or until stiff peaks form. Add sugar slowly while beating 1 to 2 more minutes. If topping separates, beat again just before serving. Makes 6 cups topping or twenty-four 4-tablespoon servings.

Frozen concentrated orange juice may be substituted for lemon juice.

Freeze in air tight freezer container for later use. Serve a scoop of frozen topping over any dessert.

Nutrients per serving:

calories	28
protein	1 gm
carbohydrate	6 gm
total fat	0 gm
saturated fat	0 gm
monounsat'd fat	0 gm
cholesterol	0 mg
sodium	20 mg
potassium	65 mg
fiber	0 gm

% US-RDA

vitamin A	24
vitamin C	***
thiamin	***
riboflavin	4
vitamin B_6	***
folacin	***
iron	***
zinc	***
calcium	6

Apricot Velvet

A creamy, nonfat dessert.

1 can (16 oz.) apricot halves

1 cup boiling water

1 package (3 oz.) apricot gelatin dessert
   powder

1½ cups Whipped Topping (see page 225)

Drain apricots; save liquid and add enough water to
make ¾ cup. Finely chop or puree apricots and
refrigerate. Pour boiling water into warmed large mixing
bowl; sprinkle dessert powder over hot water and stir
well to dissolve. Add apricot liquid; chill until syrupy
and thick. With mixer, beat gelatin until foamy. Fold in
Whipped Topping and apricots; chill until firm. Makes 4
large servings.

*For a special treat, serve in a parfait glass garnished with
fresh mint sprig or a colorful fruit. Use recipe with canned or
frozen berries, cherries, peaches, fruit cocktail or pineapple
and a complimentary gelatin dessert powder.*

Nutrients per serving:

calories	*200*
protein	*5 gm*
carbohydrate	*45 gm*
total fat	*0 gm*
saturated fat	*0 gm*
monounsat'd fat	*0 gm*
cholesterol	*0 mg*
sodium	*45 mg*
potassium	*285 mg*
fiber	*0 gm*

% US-RDA

vitamin A	*33*
vitamin C	*7*
thiamin	*3*
riboflavin	*9*
vitamin B$_6$	*5*
folacin	*2*
iron	*3*
zinc	*3*
calcium	*13*

Low-Fat
Candies and Desserts

The typical candy bar or serving of cake, pie, cookie or ice cream contains 200 to 300 total calories with 35 to 50 percent of those calories coming from 8 to 16 grams of fat, much of it saturated fat.

A low-fat candy or dessert has six grams of fat, or less, for each 200 calorie serving. About 27 percent, or less, of the calories are from fat.

To figure the percentage of calories from fat, multiply the number of fat grams by 9 (because each fat gram contains 9 calories), and divide by the total calories in a serving. For example: In a serving of chiffon cake, there are 4 grams of fat or, $4 \times 9 = 36$ fat calories. Divide 36 fat calories by the calories in one serving, 190, which yields 19 percent of the calories from fat.

By selecting from the low-fat candy and dessert chart, several selections can be eaten for a reasonable daily total of 5 to 15 grams of fat.

	Serving	Calories	Fat Grams	Percent Calories From Fat
CANDY				
Caramel, plain or chocolate	3 pcs	112	2.9	23 %
Gum Drops and Orange Slices	1 oz.	108	0.2	2 %
Hard Candy	1 oz.	108	0.3	3 %
Jelly Beans	10 pcs	66	none	0 %
Life Savers	15 pcs	117	0.1	1 %
Lollipop	1 med	108	none	0 %
Marshmallow	4 large	100	none	0 %
Mints, hard	14 pcs	104	0.6	5 %
Bit-O-Honey	1 oz.	121	3.6	27 %
Peppermint Patty	1 oz.	124	2.3	17 %

	Serving	Calories	Fat Grams	Percent Calories From Fat
DESSERTS				
Cake, not iced:				
Angel food	2 oz.	161	none	0 %
Chiffon	2½ oz.	190	4.0	19 %
Gingerbread	2½ oz.	210	6.0	26 %
Frozen Yogurt:				
Low-fat, 2%	1 cup	220	4.0	16 %
Gelatin:				
All flavors	1 cup	160	none	0 %
With fruit cocktail	1 cup	160	none	0 %
Ices:				
All flavors	1 cup	247	none	0 %
Fudgsicle	1 bar	90	0.2	2 %
Popsicle	1 bar	65	none	0 %
Sherbet:				
All flavors	1 cup	270	3.8	13 %
Puddings, Instant, made with skim milk				
Vanilla	½ cup	130	1.0	7 %
Chocolate fudge and milk chocolate	½ cup	140	2.0	13 %
Other flavors	½ cup	135	1.5	10 %

Packaged Low-Fat Cookies

Most cookies have a high fat content, with 40 to 50 percent of the calories from fat. The commercially produced varieties listed below provide only 17 to 33 percent fat calories. Read package labels and avoid cookies with animal fat, hydrogenated and tropical oils such as coconut and palm oils. If such cookies aren't available, choose the cookies low in fat and saturated fat. Our low-fat selections provide 1/2 to 1 teaspoon (2.0 to 5.3 grams) of fat per ounce of cookie.

Cookie	Number of Cookies	Calories	Fat Grams	Percent Calories From Fat
Animal	15	120	2.9	22%
Arrowroot	6	140	5.1	32%
Bars: apple, fig, cherry, raspberry	2	105	2.0	17%
Chocolate snap	10	135	4.5	30%
Coolers: cherry, lemon	5	120	2.8	21%
Gingersnap	7	120	2.8	21%
Graham Crackers: plain, cinnamon	2 squares	135	3.0	20%
Molasses	2	140	5.3	33%
Vanilla Wafers	8	135	4.8	32%

Water, Caffeine and Beverages

Water is the most essential of all nutrients, making up to 60 percent of the body's weight.

Severe dehydration can result with a water loss of six pounds (three quarts) in adults, and with a pint or less in infants. A person can survive days, even months without food and some nutrients, but only a few days without water as it is continually lost through the lungs, pores of the skin, kidneys and bowel. Water must be constantly resupplied to keep the body running smoothly.

Water provides the liquid needed in the blood, stomach, intestines and muscles for processing thousands of normal body reactions. Resulting waste is removed in fluids leaving the body. Other important functions include keeping the joints lubricated and body temperature regulated. Thirst signals depletion, and a glass of water delightfully replenishes that need. A well balanced daily diet includes two quarts or eight cups of water, and more if you are perspiring. Mineral and bottled waters are available, but tap water is an equally good choice. Although the best way to replace water is with water, many people prefer to meet their liquid needs with milk, juices, flavored drinks, soft drinks, coffee or tea. These are equivalent, cup for cup, with water. Water, however, is the zero calorie liquid.

From the good nutrition standpoint, water, fruit juices and milk are recommended. But, if you enjoy a steaming cup of coffee in the morning or after a filling meal, you need not give it up. It is wise to keep your daily caffeine intake below 400 milligrams or 2.5 milligrams per pound of body weight. Taken in moderation, caffeine isn't harmful for the average person.

However, more and more people are choosing to avoid caffeine, either by selecting beverages free of caffeine, or by drinking decaffeinated coffee or tea. When caffeine is present in a beverage, the law requires that it be stated. So, check the label carefully regarding caffeine content.

Caffeine is an ingredient in more than 1,000 nonprescription drug products as well as numerous prescription drugs. Most often it is used in weight-control remedies, stimulants to prevent drowsiness, headache and pain relief remedies, cold products and diuretics. When caffeine is an ingredient, it is listed on the product label along with the number of milligrams per dose. Some prescription medications, particularly those for headache, may contain caffeine. If in doubt, ask your pharmacist.

Be aware that caffeine in your diet, along with caffeine containing drugs, may push you to an excessive caffeine level. Caffeine is a stimulant and too much may cause problems. Nervousness, trembling, heart palpitations, diarrhea, severe headaches, insomnia and irritability may be symptoms of excessive caffeine consumption. People give children beverages containing caffeine and wonder why the children are "wired". Parents blame the sugar content, but caffeine is the more likely culprit. Caffeine is actually a drug, and those trying to kick the habit may suffer from headaches, sluggishness and irritability. So, gradual reduction of caffeine intake is best.

With any drug, the action varies from person to person. Some people have a low tolerance level or a medical problem that prohibits caffeine consumption. Many obstetricians advise pregnant women to limit its use. Caffeine can cross into breast milk causing babies to sleep poorly.

Recent studies have looked at coffee as a possible contributor to cancer and heart disease, but no strong links have been found. One study tried to show decaffeinated coffee caused an increase in blood cholesterol, but researchers agreed the rise was insignificant. Decaffeinated coffee stimulates the stomach to secrete acid as much as does regular coffee. The best bet for people with ulcers is to steer clear of any type of coffee.

The following chart showing the caffeine content of beverages and foods can help determine your caffeine intake.

Caffeine Content of Beverages and Foods

	Milligrams per 5-ounce cup	
	Average	Range
Coffee		
Instant	60	30-120
Percolated	117	
Drip, automatic	137	60-180
Decaffeinated, brewed	3	2-5
Decaffeinated, instant	2	1-5
Bagged tea		
Black, 5 minute brew	46	20-90
Black, 1 minute brew	28	
Loose tea		
Black, 5 minute brew	54	
Green, 5 minute brew	31	
Oolong, 5 minute brew	40	
Instant tea, 1 heaping teaspoon	30	25-50
Cocoa mix, 1 oz. packet made with water	5	

	Milligrams per portion	
	Average	Range
Chocolate milk beverage (8 oz.)	5	2-20
Milk chocolate (1 oz.)	6	1-15
Dark chocolate, semi-sweet (1 oz.)	20	5-35
Baker's chocolate (1 oz.)	26	
Chocolate favored syrup (1 oz.)	4	

	Milligrams per 12-ounces
	Average
Coca Cola, regular and diet	108
Dr. Pepper, regular and diet	96
Mountain Dew	130
Pepsi Cola, regular	91
Pepsi Cola, diet	86
Shasta Cola	100

Source: USDA Home and Garden Bulletin Number 232-7, 1986.

Alcohol in the Diet

A lcoholic beverages contain no fat and almost no nutrients. They are, however, high in calories with most, or all, calories coming from alcohol (ethanol). Each gram of pure ethanol yields seven calories, almost 200 calories per ounce. Although alcohol is fat-free, a drink or two before dinner can increase caloric intake by several hundred. The caloric contribution is shown in the chart on the next page. For those seeking to maintain or lose weight, such drinks should be limited or avoided. Instead, consume foods with needed nutrients.

Whether alcohol can be beneficial in preventing heart disease is a matter of on-going research. Some studies indicate that a limited amount of ethanol, one ounce per day, may be helpful. However, recent research data suggests that a few drinks per month, or total abstinence may be preferable.

Heavy drinkers may develop nutritional deficiencies, not only because alcohol replaces nutritious foods, but because it reduces the absorption of some vitamins and washes many minerals out into the urine. Drinking alcoholic beverages during pregnancy may damage the developing fetus; the more alcohol, the greater are the risks to the baby.

One hundred percent of the calories in gin, rum, vodka and whiskey (86 proof) come from ethanol. Carbohydrates and alcohol provide the calories in such drinks as beer and wine. If you are cooking with wine, some of the alcohol may evaporate and lower the calorie level slightly. Keep in mind that the calories are provided by the sugars and by the alcohol that does not evaporate.

The following table provides an idea of how different alcoholic beverages compare in alcohol and calorie content. Pay close attention to the serving size when comparing items.

Alcohol and Calories

DRINK	Serving Ounces	Alcohol Grams	Calories	Percent Calories From Alcohol
Beer				
Regular beer	12	12.3	150	57%
Light beer	12	11.0	92	84%
Liquor				
Gin, rum, vodka, whisky (86-proof)	1.5	15.1	105	100%
Wine				
Pink	5	13.8	105	92%
Sherry	5	22.5	210	75%
Sweet	5	21.3	224	65%
Red, Dry	5	13.9	118	87%
White, Dry	5	13.0	110	83%
Vermouth, sweet	1.5	7.6	70	72%
Vermouth, dry	1.5	6.4	45	96%
Cordials and Liqueurs	1.5	9.1	121	53%
Brandy				
Apricot	1.5	12.8	136	66%
California	1.5	14.9	104	100%

Source: USDA Agricultural Handbook 8.

Losing Weight

L osing weight has become a national pastime. It seems if you are not on a diet, you are almost out of fashion!

While getting to a desirable weight is important, many people are not realistic in their methods. In fact, 90 to 95 percent of those losing weight regain it. This book emphasizes the enjoyment of eating while reducing the consumption of fats, not the restriction of calories. We like to focus on celebrating good food and good eating habits, not on difficult diets and do-not-eat types of food. Recent research shows that food eaten in the form of fat is more likely to stay in the body as fat. By gradually reducing the amount of dietary fat, the slow, steady weight gain that often accompanies aging will be slowed for most people. Keep in mind that heredity does affect height, weight, fat and muscle distribution. Plump parents are more likely to have plump children. Partly, this is genetic and partly, it is the family eating and exercising habits which exaggerate fat gain.

Mother Nature spent millions of years helping our bodies regulate our appetites to correspond to our energy expenditures, but our sedentary lifestyle and rich food supply have upset this natural balance. We suggest that eating satisfying meals and finding enjoyable exercise will help you build and tone your muscles for a trimmer, healthier body.

Calorie-restricting diets leave a person feeling hungry, tired, irritable, deprived and focused on food. That is why many people who diet this way finally come to the point where they quit the calorie-cutting diets and gain back the lost weight. We propose that as you cut down on fats and increase your activity level, you bring your true caloric need and energy output back to a sound, normal balance. Food falls into its proper place. This method of weight loss is slower than that promised by the popular, trendy diet programs. With patience and thoughtful persistence, you will be creating new eating and exercising habits. You will feel energetic and satisfied as the scales show a slow, steady weight loss that is more likely to be permanent. You can then forever forget the "Guilt of Diets Failed"!

Healthful Eating Every Day

A good way to determine if you have eaten enough is to decide if you feel pleasantly satisfied, or stuffed and sluggish. If you feel full but still have energy to take a walk or run a quick errand, you are probably getting the right foods in the proper amounts. Translated into average calories on a daily basis, most women eat between 1,800 and 2,200 calories, while men eat between 2,000 and 2,600 calories. If you feel you need help in determining your caloric needs and in meal planning, see a registered dietitian, or a physician who specializes in nutritional guidance. Remember, appropriate food intake fuels an energetic body for mental and physical exercise.

Calorie levels in our sample meals are set to help reduce snacking. Based on thousands of observations of what people actually eat in homes, restaurants and in hospital dining rooms, we believe this is important. We have seen people skip meals or eat light, low calorie meals only to make up for missed calories with sugary, salty or fatty snack foods. Research has shown that eating three wholesome meals per day is excellent insurance against weight gain and insures a well nourished body.

It is important to divide your food intake over several meals throughout the day with each meal providing 1/4 to 1/3 of your caloric and nutrient needs. You will be less likely to store those calories as fat than if you ate the same number of calories at one meal. Each food group (see the Food Guide Pyramid information on page 4) contributes generous amounts of some nutrients but is low in others. Like a jigsaw puzzle, meals and the food groups within them fit together for picture-perfect nutrition. With this in mind, let us look at some benefits, and possible problems, associated with breakfast, lunch, supper and snacks.

Breakfast: A lively mind and active body require energy all day long. The late night eater often moans, "I'm just not hungry for breakfast". Keep in mind that heavy snacking dulls morning hunger, and increases the likelihood that the calories consumed in the evening will convert to fat. Skipping breakfast leads to a letdown and loss of energy at midmorning. To compensate, we fill up on high-calorie, high-fat snacks. We are not hungry for a proper, nutritious lunch; so we ignore it. By midafternoon there is a loss of pep along with hunger pangs. Again, we eat the wrong foods. We slight supper, still full of our high fat snacks. At bed time, we are hungry again and turn to snacks. This cycle deprives us of proper nutrition and leads to weight gain and energy loss. Treat your body to breakfast, lunch and supper and your mind-body connection will respond with a vigorous you. The sample breakfasts found on pages 238 to 244 are in the 400 to 600 calorie range.

Pleasant Lunches: A modest, low-fat lunch gives you a lift instead of an afternoon burden. Simple but filling, the high-carbohydrate, low-fat lunches outlined are low in cost, too, an additional benefit of eating grains, breads and vegetables. You are less likely to experience afternoon drowsiness after eating one of the sample 500 to 700 calorie meals found on pages 246 to 249.

Super Suppers: Evening meals prepare you for the 10-hour meal lag. Low-fat dinners, high in fiber and complex carbohydrates, contribute to a satisfied feeling that will last all evening. Our suggested suppers have 700 to 900 calories and are on pages 252 to 257.

If you prefer to eat your main meal at noon, try switching lunch and supper menus. If possible, it may be wiser to eat the larger meal at noon. This gives you more food in the middle of the day when it is more likely to be turned into energy.

Sensible Snacking: There is a place for nutritious snacks in the well-planned diet. Mindless snacking, however, can ruin an otherwise reasonable meal pattern. To avoid temptation, have on hand only nutritious snacks, such as those in our Low-Fat Snacking list on pages 258 and 259.

Today's Classic Breakfast

Take a look at the nutritional analysis; this meal really does the job!

Orange Juice
³/₄ cup (6 oz.)

Honey Fruit Granola *
¹/₂ cup (2 oz.)

Whole Wheat Toast
1 slice

Tub Margarine
1 teaspoon

Milk, ¹/₂% Low-Fat or Skim
1 cup (8 oz.)

*See recipe on page 54 or eat 2 ounces whole grain cereal.

More and more research is showing cereal breakfast eaters have lower blood cholesterol levels, especially those eating cereals with two or more grams of dietary fiber.

Speed the family breakfast by setting the cereal boxes, bowls, flatware and toaster on the table before you go to bed.

Calories from fat are 23 percent of total calories in this meal.

Nutrients per meal:

calories	*542*
protein	*21 gm*
carbohydrate	*83 gm*
total fat	*14 gm*
saturated fat	*3 gm*
monounsat'd fat	*8 gm*
cholesterol	*7 mg*
sodium	*350 mg*
potassium	*1530 mg*
fiber	*11 gm*

% US-RDA

vitamin A	*17*
vitamin C	*123*
thiamin	*23*
riboflavin	*13*
vitamin B₆	*73*
folacin	*58*
iron	*41*
zinc	*8*
calcium	*51*

Commuter's Breakfast

Delicious, satisfying liquid breakfast that has it all.

Breakfast Shake:

$1/4$ cup (2 oz.) egg substitute

$3/4$ cup (6 oz.) $1/2$% low-fat or skim milk, or low-fat yogurt

$3/4$ cup (6 oz.) orange juice

2 tablespoons ($1^1/2$ oz.) honey

2 tablespoons ($1/2$ oz.) wheat germ

Mix ingredients together, except wheat germ, in the order shown to minimize curdling. Blend 30 seconds. Pour into travel mug; top with wheat germ. Because the nutty flavored wheat germ tends to settle to the bottom, shake travel mug to keep it suspended.

Even a simple breakfast makes a major contribution to reduced fat intake for the day and will help to lower blood cholesterol levels. This filling drink contains only 9 grams of fat, leaving 58 grams of fat available for lunch, supper and snacks at the 2,000 calorie level. Most breakfast skippers are adults who give as their reason, "I'm trying to control my weight". However, it is known that skipping meals often promotes weight gain and higher blood cholesterol levels.

Calories from fat are 19 percent of total calories in this meal.

Nutrients per meal:

calories	433
protein	18 gm
carbohydrate	70 gm
total fat	9 gm
saturated fat	2 gm
monounsat'd fat	4 gm
cholesterol	6 mg
sodium	215 mg
potassium	925 mg
fiber	3 gm

% US-RDA

vitamin A	27
vitamin C	121
thiamin	31
riboflavin	24
vitamin B_6	64
folacin	70
iron	20
zinc	21
calcium	36

Fruit and Pancake Breakfast

Bring eaters to the table with fruit in season, hot pancakes and syrup.

Cantaloupe
1/4 **medium (1 cup cubes)**

Buttermilk Pancakes *
three 4-inch cakes

Hot Syrup
3 tablespoons

Tub Margarine
3 teaspoons

Milk, 1/2% Low-Fat or Skim
1 cup (8 oz.)

* See recipe on page 50 or prepare from commercial whole grain mix.

Here is another breakfast rich in complex carbohydrate, dietary fiber, and moderate in protein, fat and simple sugars. Eating a high fiber breakfast curbs the urge for midmorning sweet roll snacking.

Softer, tub-style margarines are usually higher in polyunsaturated and monounsaturated oils. Compare the labels to select those lowest in saturated fat and highest in monounsaturated fat.

Calories from fat are 27 percent of total calories in this meal.

Nutrients per meal:

calories	635
protein	18 gm
carbohydrate	98 gm
total fat	19 gm
saturated fat	5 gm
monounsat'd fat	9 gm
cholesterol	74 mg
sodium	890 mg
potassium	1250 mg
fiber	4 gm

% US-RDA

vitamin A	118
vitamin C	111
thiamin	21
riboflavin	21
vitamin B_6	77
folacin	30
iron	27
zinc	9
calcium	61

Easy French Toast Breakfast

Whatever the reason, common sense and science tell us we fare better with *breakfast than without.*

Tomato Juice
    ¹/₂ cup (4 oz.)

Easy French Toast *
    2 thick slices

Hot Cinnamon Applesauce Topping
    4 tablespoons (2 oz.)

Tub Margarine
    2 teaspoons

Milk, ¹/₂% Low-Fat or Skim
    1 cup (8 oz.)

* See recipe on page 52.

Sweetened berries or honey, plain or fruit flavored low-fat yogurt are other tasty toppings for your French toast.
    Breakfast may be the only family-time everyone can be together. Eating together is an ideal way to reach and enjoy family members. Grandmothers said it best: "touching and sharing meals are the most loving gestures".
    Calories from fat are 27 percent of total calories in this meal.

Nutrients per meal:

calories	*557*
protein	*30 gm*
carbohydrate	*71 gm*
total fat	*17 gm*
saturated fat	*5 gm*
monounsat'd fat	*8 gm*
cholesterol	*10 mg*
sodium	*1200 mg*
potassium	*1280 mg*
fiber	*4 gm*

% US-RDA

vitamin A	*59*
vitamin C	*43*
thiamin	*36*
riboflavin	*44*
vitamin B₆	*86*
folacin	*32*
iron	*37*
zinc	*12*
calcium	*63*

Today's Eggs and Biscuit Breakfast

Your family always enjoys this one.

Orange Juice
3/4 **cup (6 oz.)**

Scrambled Egg Treat *
1 serving = 2 eggs

Homemade Biscuits *
2 biscuits

Tub Margarine
1 teaspoon

Strawberry Jam
1 tablespoon

Milk, 1/2% Low-Fat or Skim
1 cup (8 oz.)

Nutrients per meal:

calories	600
protein	28 gm
carbohydrate	70 gm
total fat	23 gm
saturated fat	6 gm
monounsat'd fat	14 gm
cholesterol	116 mg
sodium	880 mg
potassium	1540 mg
fiber	3 gm

% US-RDA

vitamin A	60
vitamin C	122
thiamin	29
riboflavin	31
vitamin B₆	84
folacin	60
iron	25
zinc	13
calcium	59

* See recipes on pages 193 and 48.

Both of these recipes use traditional, favorite foods with small adjustments to create excellent low-fat alternatives.

Biscuits made from packaged mixes or purchased in deli tubes are high in sodium, total fat and saturated fat. Keeping Quick Mix on hand encourages the family cook to create these delicious, high fiber hot biscuits.

Calories from fat are 35 percent of total calories in this meal.

Yesteryear's Eggs and Biscuit Breakfast

This old-fashioned breakfast is high in fat and cholesterol; compare its nutritional analysis with that of "Today's Eggs and Biscuit Breakfast".

Orange Juice
3/4 **cup (6 oz.)**

Scrambled Egg
2 eggs cooked in 2 teaspoons bacon fat

Old-fashioned Biscuits
2 biscuits

Butter
2 teaspoons

Strawberry Jam
1 tablespoon

Milk, 3 1/2 % whole milk
1 cup (8 oz.)

Although this is not a recommended breakfast, we've included it here for comparison. Serve this breakfast only rarely, as an "old-time meal".

If 3 strips of crisp bacon are added to this meal, calories are increased by 100, total fat by 9 grams, saturated fat by 4 grams, cholestrol by 15 milligrams with 53 percent of the calories coming from fat.

Calories from fat are 49 percent of total calories in this meal.

Nutrients per meal:
calories	*787*
protein	*26 gm*
carbohydrate	*74 gm*
total fat	*43 gm*
saturated fat	*18 gm*
monounsat'd fat	*12 gm*
cholesterol	*485 mg*
sodium	*690 mg*
potassium	*920 mg*
fiber	*1 gm*

% US-RDA
vitamin A	*26*
vitamin C	*120*
thiamin	*31*
riboflavin	*66*
vitamin B6	*19*
folacin	*70*
iron	*19*
zinc	*14*
calcium	*54*

Nontraditional Low-Fat Breakfasts

T ake a break from the same old thing. Choose from these nontraditional foods for an unusual but wholesome breakfast. For good balance, include fruit, fruit juice or vegetable juice. If the item doesn't have a component from the bread/cereal/grain family, add a slice of whole grain bread. For a nutritionally complete meal, include low-fat cottage cheese, low-fat hard cheese or glass of low-fat milk.

Food	Amount	Fat Grams	Calories
Fruit juice	³/₄ cup	0	60
Fruit	1 serving	0	60
Tomato or V-8 juice	³/₄ cup	0	50
Breakfast pita:			
Pita pocket	1 each (1¹/₂ oz.)	¹/₂	100
Peanut butter	2 tablespoons	15	172
Chopped raisins	2 tablespoons	0	60
Chopped apple	¹/₄ small	0	15
Breakfast microwaved potato:			
Baked potato	1 medium	0	110
Low-fat cottage cheese	4 tablespoons	1	40
Tub margarine	1 tablespoon	11	100
Sandwich:			
Bread	2 slices	1	130
Mustard	2 teaspoons	0	10
Margarine	1 teaspoon	4	35
Lettuce	1 leaf	0	5
Low-fat cheese	2 ounces	10	144
Lean ham, turkey, fish or chicken	2 ounces	6	118

Food	Amount	Fat Grams	Calories
Fried Rice with Vegetables*	1 cup	7	200
Breakfast burrito	1 each (6 oz.)	15	350
Open-face sandwich with	1 slice	1/2	65
Bean Spread*	3 ounces	1	100
Pasta-vegetable soup	12 ounces	6	210
Toast	1 slice	1/2	65
Tub margarine	1 teaspoon	4	35
Whole grain bagel and	1 each (2 oz.)	1 1/2	163
Neufchatel cheese	2 tablespoons	7	74
Rice or Bread Pudding* made with skim milk	2/3 cup	4	275
Crispy Rice Bars*	4 bars, each 2X2-in.	10	346
Oatbran Muffins*	2 each	10	290

* See Quick Recipe Finder on pages vi to xvi.

Cottage Cheese Luncheon

A refreshing meal at work or at home, with variety added by changing the vegetables, crackers and fruits.

Vegetable-Cottage Cheese Salad*
1/4 recipe

Crisp Rye Wafers
2 triple wafers

Tub Margarine
2 teaspoons

Seedless Grapes
1 cup (20 each)

*See recipe on page 204.

Crackers and bread can be quite high in fat. Read the label to find those with 2 grams of fat, or less, in each ounce (28 grams). Some low-fat choices are bread sticks, graham crackers, plain croutons, matzo, melba toast, crisp rye crackers, oyster crackers, rice wafers, saltines, wasa crackers and zwieback. Wasa crackers are extra good, a favorite of children, and adults as well.

Calories from fat are 27 percent of total calories in this meal.

Nutrients per meal:

calories	420
protein	27 gm
carbohydrate	53 gm
total fat	11 gm
saturated fat	4 gm
monounsat'd fat	4 gm
cholesterol	14 mg
sodium	920 mg
potassium	960 mg
fiber	8 gm

% US-RDA

vitamin A	148
vitamin C	100
thiamin	22
riboflavin	32
vitamin B_6	28
folacin	30
iron	22
zinc	10
calcium	23

Filling the Brown Bag

Low calorie lunches soon leave you
hungry. Use this filling lunch pattern.

Ham'n Cheese Sandwich
>   **1 slice each whole wheat and enriched white**
>   **bread**
>   **1 slice boiled ham (1 oz.) or low-fat lunch meat**
>   **1 slice low-fat mozzarella cheese (1 oz.)**
>   **1 teaspoon mustard**
>   **2 teaspoons salad dressing**
>   **1 lettuce leaf**

Raw Vegetables in Season: tomato, cucumber,
**   radishes or summer squash**

Chocolate Instant Pudding
**   ³/₄ cup (6 oz.)**

   Many ready-to-eat low-fat foods are quite high in sodium.
A food low in fat and low in sodium does not sell well; this is
too much of a flavor change for many people. We also know
the hurried cook must get food into the lunch bag, or on the
table, fast. Time is not available to home-prepare the lower
sodium versions. Don't despair; switching your family to
lower fat foods is your primary goal. You can gradually ease
into lower sodium foods, and keep the total sodium per meal
at 700 to 900 milligrams, by diluting the sodium with
generous use of fresh vegetables, fruits and breads.
   Calories from fat are 28 percent of total calories in this meal.

Nutrients per meal:

calories	*541*
protein	*24 gm*
carbohydrate	*73 gm*
total fat	*17 gm*
saturated fat	*7 gm*
monounsat'd fat	*3 gm*
cholesterol	*53 mg*
sodium	*1000 mg*
potassium	*520 mg*
fiber	*4 gm*

% US-RDA

vitamin A	*29*
vitamin C	*27*
thiamin	*34*
riboflavin	*33*
vitamin B₆	*15*
folacin	*20*
iron	*18*
zinc	*14*
calcium	*54*

Soup 'n Sandwich

A classic American lunch on the table in 20 minutes.

Chicken-Noodle Soup
$^1/_2$ **of 10$^1/_2$ oz. can diluted with**
$^1/_2$ **can water**
Deli Roast Beef Sandwich
2 slices rye bread
1 teaspoon mustard
1 teaspoon salad dressing
1 ounce deli lean roast beef slices
1 lettuce leaf

Peppermint Milk*

Peach Slices in Natural Juice
$^1/_2$ **cup**

Nutrients per meal:

calories	622
protein	27 gm
carbohydrate	88 gm
total fat	18 gm
saturated fat	8 gm
monounsat'd fat	10 gm
cholesterol	56 mg
sodium	1500 mg
potassium	980 mg
fiber	7 gm

% US-RDA

vitamin A	39
vitamin C	13
thiamin	21
riboflavin	29
vitamin B$_6$	59
folacin	12
iron	33
zinc	24
calcium	41

*See recipe on page 209.

The huge selection of canned soups and luncheon meats attests to their popularity and ease of preparation. As mentioned on a previous page, lean deli meats and canned soups are high in sodium to compensate, in part, for the low-fat taste. Sodium intake can be reduced by having 1 or 1$^1/_2$ ounces of deli meat on a sandwich instead of 2 or 3 ounces. By selecting sodium free fruit and naturally fairly low sodium milk drinks, the total sodium for the meal is kept at a lower level.

Calories from fat are 26 percent of total calories in this meal.

Make-Your-Own-Soup Meal

A basic soup that invites refrigerator leftovers for even better flavor.

Bean-Vegetable-Ham Soup*
    1¹/₂ cups (12 oz.)

Hard Roll
    1 each

Herbed Yogurt (for roll)
    ¹/₄ cup low-fat yogurt with parsley, chives or herbs of your choice

Strawberry-Banana Gelatin*
    ²/₃ cup (5 oz.)

Lemonade
    1 cup (8 oz.)

*See recipes on pages 118 and 108.

Making your own soup is easy, economical and provides a soup lower in sodium than canned ones. Using the basic bean soup recipe, you can add pasta, potatoes, liquids drained and saved from cooking vegetables, fresh or leftover vegetables and lean meats. Although you can "heat and eat", longer simmering mellows and blends the flavors. If the soup pot is too much for one meal, cool and freeze the extra for an even tastier soup the next time.

Calories from fat are 8 percent of total calories in this meal.

Nutrients per meal:

calories	835
protein	38 gm
carbohydrate	155 gm
total fat	7 gm
saturated fat	2 gm
monounsat'd fat	2 gm
cholesterol	17 mg
sodium	1100 mg
potassium	2300 mg
fiber	15 gm

% US-RDA

vitamin A	30
vitamin C	150
thiamin	78
riboflavin	35
vitamin B₆	65
folacin	210
iron	65
zinc	29
calcium	51

Low-Fat Canned Soups

C anned soups, particularly the cream soups, may be high in fat. Fat content may vary for the same flavor from brand to brand. Read the label and select those that are 2 to 3 grams of fat per 4-ounce serving, before being diluted.

Regular canned soups are high in sodium. You may wish to buy the reduced sodium or low sodium soups. Make a quick, lower sodium, lower fat soup by adding $1/2$ to 1 cup water, $1^{1/2}$ cups finely diced potatoes or fresh or frozen vegetables to one can low-fat soup. Enhance flavor with herbs such as parsley, basil, garlic, oregano, nutmeg, marjoram or hot pepper sauce. Servings are now increased from 2 to 3 and sodium and fat per serving are reduced by 33 percent. Unused soup that has been boiled can safely be frozen for future use.

The values below are based on soup diluted with an equal amount of water.

	Amount	Fat gm	Sodium mg	Calories
Soup				
Bean/Vegetable and Black Bean	1 cup	2	1,000	100
Chicken, Beef, Turkey Broth base with rice, noodles and or vegetables	1 cup	2	800	70
Clam Chowder	1 cup	3	1,800	80
Golden or Beefy Mushroom	1 cup	3	900	90
Onion	1 cup	2	1,000	60
Potato	1 cup	2	1,000	70
Tomato, Bisque, Zesty	1 cup	2	800	90
Vegetable	1 cup	2	900	90
Soups Used As Sauces:				
Cream of Celery, Chicken or Mushroom, diluted with $1/4$ cup $1/2$% low-fat milk	3 oz.	2-5	565	52-72

Creative Low-Fat Sandwiches

Sandwiches are the mainstay for the busy cook. Traditional bread and meat combinations can be varied by adding vegetable dress-ups and low-fat spreads. Serve a buffet of unusual and family favorite ingredients and let everyone have fun building delicious creations. Served with a treat from the Low-Fat Milk Bar (see page 209), you will know the family is enjoying great taste and fine nutrition.

Rolls and bread: English muffins, hard or soft rolls, hoagies, submarines, tiny whole-wheat rolls, multi-grain rolls, kaiser buns, pita bread, soft flour tortillas, rye or pumpernickel bread, bagels; whole wheat multi-grain, sourdough, French and Italian breads.

Fillings: Roast Turkey Breast*, thinly sliced chicken, Roast Pork* or lean roast beef. Or select from an array of packaged luncheon or deli-meats and choose those with 2 or 3 grams, or less, of fat per ounce. Make your own Cheddar Cheese-pimento Spread*, Egg Salad*, Bean Spread*, Salmon Salad*, or lean taco mixture. Select cheeses with 5 or 6 grams of fat, or less, per ounce. Peanut butter contains 15 grams of fat per ounce, but it is the desirable monounsaturated oil; extend it with mashed bananas, fruit, honey, or jellies and jams.

Vegetable dress-ups: Bright green lettuce leaves or parsley sprigs, shredded lettuce, romaine or other lettuce; thin-sliced onion, tomato, mushroom, cucumber, zucchini, yellow squash, unpeeled apples, dill or bread and butter pickles, thin-sliced green pepper rings, chopped green onions, alfalfa or bean sprouts.

Spreads: Salad dressing has only half the fat of regular mayonnaise. Use it as is, or extend it half and half with low-fat yogurt or mashed cottage cheese. To spice up the flavor, add one or more: yellow, brown or Dijon mustard, horseradish, chives, dill weed, garlic or parsley. Tub margarine can be extended with mustard or horseradish. Salsa and cranberry are other tangy choices. One-half tablespoon herbed olive oil, drizzled over any sandwich, is good.

*See Quick Recipe Finder on pages vi to xvi.

Dinner's in the Oven

A special meal for the family with leftovers for delicious cold sliced turkey.

Roast Turkey Breast*
1 slice (3 oz.)

Golden Mushroom Sauce*
1/4 cup (2 oz.)

Perfect Baked Potato*
1 medium, and

Mock Sour Cream*
3 tablespoons

Herbed Broccoli*
1 serving

Garlic Bread*
1 slice

Peach Crisp*
1 serving

*See Quick Recipe Finder on pages vi to xvi.

Desirable high fiber complex carbohydrates are found in the baked potato (be sure to eat the skin), broccoli, garlic bread and peach crisp topping. Eating both bread and potatoes at the same meal, with a smaller serving of meat, is a big change for many people. Ideally, 50% or more of the calories should come from carbohydrates. In this meal 472 calories (118 grams x 4 calories per gram) or 53% of the 887 total calories are from carbohydrates.

Calories from fat are 27 percent of total calories in this meal.

Nutrients per meal:

calories	887
protein	43 gm
carbohydrate	118 gm
total fat	27 gm
saturated fat	7 gm
monounsat'd fat	13 gm
cholesterol	77 mg
sodium	1330 mg
potassium	1560 mg
fiber	11 gm

% US-RDA

vitamin A	140
vitamin C	250
thiamin	38
riboflavin	32
vitamin B6	73
folacin	66
iron	45
zinc	22
calcium	22

Crockpot Bean Supper

Make a big potful and freeze the extra for a future, speedy meal.

Many Bean Soup*
  1¹/₂ cups (12 oz.)

Buttermilk Cornbread*
  2 squares, 2x2-inches

Tub Margarine
  2 teaspoons

Any Season Fruit Salad*
  1 cup

Gingersnaps
  3 small

*See Recipes on pages 117, 49 and 111.

Less than one-third of our total fat intake should be saturated fat, more than one-third should be monounsaturated fat and less than one-third should be polyunsaturated fat. This meal is not only low in total fat (20 grams), it is also ideal with 4 grams (20%) of saturated fat, 10 grams (50%) of monounsaturated fat and 6 grams (30%) of polyunsaturated fat.

Calories from fat are 22 percent of total calories in this meal.

Nutrients per meal:

calories	828
protein	33 gm
carbohydrate	129 gm
total fat	20 gm
saturated fat	4 gm
monounsat'd fat	10 gm
cholesterol	32 mg
sodium	1110 mg
potassium	2300 mg
fiber	16 gm

% US-RDA

vitamin A	41
vitamin C	190
thiamin	78
riboflavin	26
vitamin B₆	56
folacin	100
iron	67
zinc	26
calcium	48

Skillet Dinner

Only one pot to clean after this meal!

Beef-Macaroni Skillet*
    2 cups (12 oz.)

Hot Herbed Roll*
    1 large roll with
    herbed margarine

Tossed Green Salad*
    1 cup, with

Buttermilk Ranch Dressing*
    3 tablespoons

Frozen Low-Fat Yogurt
    1 cup, and

Fruit Sauce*
    2 tablespoons

Nutrients per meal:

calories	945
protein	50 gm
carbohydrate	130 gm
total fat	25 gm
saturated fat	8 gm
monounsat'd fat	10 gm
cholesterol	113 mg
sodium	1310 mg
potassium	1400 mg
fiber	6 gm

% US-RDA

vitamin A	51
vitamin C	52
thiamin	37
riboflavin	53
vitamin B_6	44
folacin	58
iron	65
zinc	68
calcium	47

*See Quick Recipe Finder on pages vi to xvi.

Only 24 percent of the calories are from fat! Remember, the goal is to keep the total calories from fat to less than 30 percent of total calories.

Cooking an acid food in a cast iron pot causes small amounts of iron to dissolve in the food; this increases the iron available for the body to use.

Calories from fat are 24 percent of total calories in this meal.

Dutch Oven Dinner

Chicken, potatoes, carrots and gravy cooked sumptuously together.

Tangy Chicken Dinner*
  1 serving

Whole Grain Rolls
  2 each, and

Tub Margarine
  1 teaspoon

Spinach, Red Lettuce and Thinly-Sliced Radishes
  1 cup, and

Honey-Dijon Dressing*
  3 tablespoons

Easy Applesauce*
  2/3 cup

Fig Newton Bars
  2 each

*See Quick Recipe Finder on pages vi to xvi.

Enjoy fast, flavorful chicken meals made in a Dutch oven. Create your own dishes with skinless breasts, legs or thighs, low-fat sauces or canned soups blended with rice or pasta, and vegetables. As in this sample meal, add a salad, roll and dessert for a quick and perfect dinner.

Calories from fat are 24 percent of total calories in this meal.

Nutrients per meal:

calories	*810*
protein	*35 gm*
carbohydrate	*118 gm*
total fat	*22 gm*
saturated fat	*5 gm*
monounsat'd fat	*10 gm*
cholesterol	*80 mg*
sodium	*825 mg*
potassium	*1520 mg*
fiber	*8 gm*

% US-RDA

vitamin A	*175*
vitamin C	*82*
thiamin	*38*
riboflavin	*28*
vitamin B$_6$	*41*
folacin	*48*
iron	*36*
zinc	*19*
calcium	*26*

255

Fish and Chips

The English refer to a French-fried potato as a "chip".

Pan Fried Trout*
> **1 trout with**

Tartar Sauce*
> **1¹/₂ tablespoons**

Baked Potato Wedges*
> **4 wedges**

Creamy Coleslaw*
> **³/₄ cup**

Angel food Cake
> **1 slice (1¹/₂ oz.), with**

Clara May's Pistachio Sauce*
> **2 tablespoons**

Nutrients per meal:

calories	888
protein	37 gm
carbohydrate	122 gm
total fat	28 gm
saturated fat	4 gm
monounsat'd fat	15 gm
cholesterol	50 mg
sodium	840 mg
potassium	930 mg
fiber	5 gm

% US-RDA

vitamin A	20
vitamin C	76
thiamin	26
riboflavin	25
vitamin B₆	27
folacin	28
iron	34
zinc	7
calcium	57

*See Quick Recipe Finder on pages vi to xvi.

Fried fish on a low-fat diet? Yes! The secret is to use a very smooth, nonstick skillet with very little oil. Very hot oil cooks the fish fast and the amount of oil absorbed is minimized.

Baked potato wedges utilize the whole potato, skin and all, for a delectable, low-fat oven-baked French-fry.

Calories from fat are 28 percent of total calories for this meal.

Granny Smith's Pork Dinner

Pork and apples; perfect mates.

Granny Smith's Pork*
 1 serving = ¹/₄ recipe

Hot Noodles
 ³/₄ cup

Spinach with Onions*
 ¹/₂ cup

Sliced Tomatoes
 1 large, with

Salad Topping Mix*
 1 tablespoon

Apricot Velvet*
 ³/₄ cup

*See Quick Recipe Finder on pages vi to xvi.

Unfortunately, many people have been told that pork is high in cholesterol. The truth is that lean pork is no higher in cholesterol than poultry. Pork can be very high in fat; that in turn may cause your liver to produce more cholesterol. By selecting only the lean tenderloin or leg cuts, pork can be used in low-fat meals.

Calories from fat are 25 percent of total calories for this meal.

Nutrients per meal:

calories	885
protein	39 gm
carbohydrate	126 gm
total fat	25 gm
saturated fat	5 gm
monounsat'd fat	11 gm
cholesterol	90 mg
sodium	725 mg
potassium	1550 mg
fiber	8 gm

% US-RDA

vitamin A	172
vitamin C	78
thiamin	76
riboflavin	40
vitamin B₆	46
folacin	52
iron	40
zinc	25
calcium	38

Snacking the Low-Fat Way

Quick fixes for the nibbling urge.

Stocking the kitchen and refrigerator with ready-to-eat foods gets you half way to the goal of low-fat snacking. Choosing not to have undesirable snacks around is the other half. The following are suggestions for successful, satisfying low-fat snacking.

Keep a container of raw carrot and celery sticks, broccoli and cauliflower florets, radish and cucumber slices or other fresh vegetables in refrigerator	*and*	Vegetable Dip: Zesty yogurt dip made with 1 cup plain low-fat yogurt, 1 cup chili sauce and 1 teaspoon of horseradish
Wonderful, fresh, ripe fruits in season can be rotated through your refrigerator; eat as is, or slice and dip	*in*	Pineapple Dip: Combine 8 ounces low-fat Neufchatel cheese, 1 cup plain low-fat yogurt, 1 or 2 tablespoons honey and one 8-ounce can crushed pineapple, drained
Low-fat ready-to-eat cereals (see page 55)	*with*	Refreshing low-fat milk
Whole grain bread or toast	*with*	Your favorite jelly or jam and just a dab of tub margarine
Cinnamon graham crackers	*with*	Hot Cocoa* made with low-fat milk, topped with marshmallows
Graham crackers	*with*	Chilled or hot spiced apple cider or any fruit juice

Hot-air-popped popcorn	*with*	Small amount of margarine seasoned with garlic and onion powder, basil and oregano
Apple newtons heated in oven or microwave	*topped with*	Low-fat or nonfat frozen yogurt and sprinkled with cinnamon sugar
Frosty, bubbly, blended low-fat milk or yogurt selected	*from*	Low-fat Milk Bar*
Crispy saltines, rye krisp, melba toast, wasa bread, zwieback, matzo or plain bread sticks	*with*	Fresh low-fat cottage cheese or yogurt, or soup cup filled with tomato or broth soup
Crispy Rice Bars*, gingersnaps, vanilla wafers, fruit newton bars or lemon coolers	*with*	Any canned fruit packed in natural juices
Sherbet, low-fat frozen yogurt, low-fat frozen milk or Soft-Set Gelatin*	*scooped into*	Waffle ice cream cones

*See Quick Recipe Finder on pages vi to xvi.

Comparison of Vegetable Oils and Animal Fats

A tablespoon of dietary fat contains approximately 13 grams of fat or oil and 120 calories. The chart below shows the grams of total fat, saturated fat (sat), monounsaturated fat (mono), polyunsaturated fat (poly) and milligrams of cholesterol. Plant oils are naturally cholesterol free; only animal fats contain cholesterol. Selective oil-seed breeding can result in large differences in the proportions of fats from the figures shown below. Reading the labels will provide a more accurate assessment.

	Total Fat gm	Sat Fat gm	Mono Fat gm	Poly Fat gm	Choles- terol mg
Canola Oil	13.6	0.7	9.0	3.2	0.0
Safflower Oil	13.6	1.2	1.6	10.1	0.0
Corn Oil	13.6	1.7	3.3	8.0	0.0
Soybean Oil	13.6	2.0	3.2	7.9	0.0
Olive Oil	13.5	1.8	9.9	1.1	0.0
Peanut Oil	13.5	2.3	6.2	4.3	0.0
Vegetable Shortening (soy, cottonseed)	12.8	3.2	5.7	3.3	0.0
Chicken Fat	12.8	3.8	5.7	2.7	11.0
Beef Fat	12.8	6.4	5.3	0.5	14.0
Pork fat	12.8	4.6	5.4	1.2	12.0
Butterfat	12.7	7.9	3.7	0.5	33.0
Palm Kernel Oil	13.6	11.1	1.5	0.2	0.0
Palm Oil	13.6	6.7	5.0	1.3	0.0
Coconut Oil	13.6	11.8	0.8	0.2	0.0

Source: USDA Agriculture Handbook 8-4.

Nutrients in Milk, Yogurt and Cheese

Dairy product	Amt.	Cal-ories	Fat gm	Pro-tein gm	Cal-cium mg	So-dium mg	Potas-sium mg	Choles-terol mg
Skim milk	8 oz	86	0.3	8.4	302	126	406	3
1/2% low-fat milk	8 oz	91	1.3	8.4	301	125	394	4
1% low-fat milk	8 oz	102	2.6	8.0	300	123	381	10
2% low-fat milk	8 oz	121	4.7	8.0	297	122	377	18
3 1/2 whole milk	8 oz	156	8.5	8.0	288	122	351	34
1% low-fat buttermilk	8 oz	99	2.2	8.1	285	257	371	9
Nonfat yogurt	8 oz	127	0.4	13	452	174	579	4
2% low-fat yogurt	8 oz	144	3.5	12	415	159	531	14
Regular vanilla yogurt	8 oz	240	5.3	9	274	105	351	29
Frozen yogurt, vanilla*:								
Nonfat	1 cup	150	0	8	100	100	240	0
2% low-fat	1 cup	220	4.0	8	80	100	240	5
Regular	1 cup	240	6.0	8	70	100	240	25
Ice cream*:								
Reg. vanilla	1 cup	269	14.3	5	176	116	257	59
Cottage cheese:								
Dry	1 cup	123	0.6	25	46	19	47	10
2% low-fat	1 cup	203	4.4	31	155	918	218	19
Regular	1 cup	217	9.5	26	126	850	177	31
Cheese:								
Parmesan	1 oz	111	7.4	10	336	454	26	19
Feta	1 oz	75	6.0	4	140	316	18	25
Mozzarella; part skim	1 oz	72	4.5	7	183	132	24	16
Monterey	1 oz	106	8.6	7	212	152	23	20
Cheddar	1 oz	114	9.4	7	204	176	28	30
Proc. American	1 oz	106	8.9	6.3	174	406	46	27
Lo-cal proc. Amer.	1 oz	52	2.2	7.3	150	411	40	22
Cream cheese	1 oz	99	10	2.0	23	84	34	31
Neufchatel	1 oz	74	6.6	2.8	21	113	32	22

* 1/3 to 1/2 the volume of yogurt and ice cream is air whipped in to provide smoothness. Source: USDA Agricultural Handbook 8.

Dietary Fiber

Food Item	Serving	Total Dietary Fiber, grams
Baked Products		
Bagels, plain	1 bagel (55g)	1.2
Biscuit mix, baked	1 biscuit (28g)	0.5
Bread		
cornbread mix, baked	1 piece (55g)	1.4
mixed-grain	1 slice (28g)	1.8
oatmeal	1 slice (28g)	1.1
pumpernickel	1 slice (32g)	1.9
white	1 slice (24g)	0.5
whole-wheat	1 slice (25g)	1.9
Bread crumbs,		
plain or seasoned	1 cup (100g)	4.2
Cake mix, yellow, dry	1/12 box (43.5g)	0.5
Gingerbread, from dry mix	1/9 cake (63g)	1.8
Cookies		
butter	10 cookies (50g)	1.2
fig bars	4 bars (56g)	2.6
oatmeal	4 cookies (52g)	1.5
peanut butter	4 cookies (50g)	0.9
Crackers		
graham	2 squares (14g)	0.4
rye	2 wafers (13g)	2.1
saltines	4 crackers (12g)	0.3
whole-wheat	5 crackers (14g)	1.5
Doughnut, yeast-leavened,		
glazed	1 doughnut (42g)	0.9
English muffin, whole-wheat	1 muffin (57g)	3.8
Ice cream cone,		
sugar, rolled-type	1 cone (12g)	0.6
Pancake Waffle Mix, prepared	3 4" pancakes (106g)	1.5
Pastry, danish, plain	1 piece (42g)	0.5
Pies, commercial		
apple	1/6 of 20 oz. pie (94g)	1.5
cherry	1/6 of 20 oz. pie (94g)	0.8
lemon meringue	1/6 of pie (140g)	1.7
pecan	1/8 of pie (103g)	3.6
pumpkin	1/6 of 20 oz. pie (94g)	2.5
Taco shells	1 shell (11g)	0.9
Tortillas, corn	1 tortilla (30g)	1.6
Waffles, commercial,		
frozen, ready to eat	2 waffles (71g)	1.7

Food Item	Serving	Total Dietary Fiber, grams
Breakfast Cereals, Ready to Eat		
Bran, high fiber	⅓ cup/1 ounce (28g)	9.9
Bran flakes	¾ cup/1 ounce (28g)	5.3
Bran flakes with raisins	¾ cup/1.3 ounces (37g)	5.0
Corn flakes, plain	1 cup/1 ounce (28g)	0.6
Fiber cereal with fruit	½ cup/1 ounce (28g)	4.1
Granola	¼ cup/1 ounce (28g)	2.9
Oat Cereal	1¼ cups/1 ounce (28g)	3.0
Oat flakes, fortified	⅔ cup/1 ounce (28g)	0.8
Rice, crispy	1 cup/1 ounce (28g)	0.3
Wheat flakes	1 cup/1 ounce (28g)	2.5
Cereals/Grains		
Cornmeal, whole-grain	1 cup (122g)	13.4
Farina, regular or instant, cooked	¾ cup (175g)	2.5
Oat flour	1 cup (113g)	10.8
Oats, rolled or oatmeal, dry	⅓ cup/1 ounce (28g)	2.9
Rice, brown, long grain, cooked	1 cup (195g)	3.3
Rice, white		
long grain, parboiled, cooked	1 cup (175g)	0.9
medium grain, raw	1 ounce (28g)	0.4
Rice bran, crude	1 ounce (28g)	6.1
Wheat bran, crude	2 tablespoons (7g)	3.0
Wheat flour, white, all purpose	1 cup (137g)	3.7
Wheat flour, whole grain	1 cup (120g)	15.1
Wheat germ, crude	¼ cup/1 ounce (28g)	4.2
Wild rice, raw	½ cup (80g)	4.2
Fruits and Fruit Products		
Apples, raw		
with skin	1 medium (138g)	3.0
without skin	1 medium (128g)	2.4
Apple juice, unsweetened	8 fluid ounces (242g)	0.2
Applesauce		
sweetened	½ cup (123g)	1.5
unsweetened	½ cup (122g)	1.8
Apricots, dried	10 halves (35g)	2.7
Apricot nectar	8 fluid ounces (251g)	1.5
Bananas, raw	1 medium (114g)	1.8

Food Item	Serving	Total Dietary Fiber, grams
Fruits and Fruit Products *(Continued)*		
Blueberries, raw	1 cup (145g)	3.3
Cantaloupe, raw	1 cup pieces (160g)	1.3
Figs, dried	5 figs (94g)	8.7
Fruit cocktail, canned in heavy syrup, drained	½ cup (128g)	1.9
Grapefruit, raw	½ medium (123g)	0.7
Grapes, Thompson, seedless, raw	1 cup (160g)	1.1
Kiwi, raw	1 medium (76g)	2.6
Nectarines, raw	1 medium (136g)	2.2
Olives		
green	10 large (46g)	1.2
ripe	10 large (46g)	1.4
Oranges, raw	1 medium (121g)	2.9
Orange juice, frozen concentrate		
undiluted	1 fluid ounce (31g)	0.2
prepared	8 fluid ounces (249g)	0.5
Peaches		
raw	1 medium (87g)	1.4
canned in heavy syrup, chunks, drained	1 cup (200g)	2.2
dried	5 halves (65g)	5.4
Pears, raw	1 medium (166g)	4.3
Pineapple		
raw	1 cup pieces (155g)	1.9
canned in heavy syrup, chunks, drained	1 cup pieces (200g)	2.2
Prunes		
dried	10 prunes (84g)	6.0
stewed	½ cup (106g)	7.0
Prune juice	8 fluid ounces (256g)	2.6
Raisins	⅔ cup (100g)	5.3
Strawberries, raw	1 cup (149g)	3.9
Watermelon, raw	1 cup (160g)	0.6
Legumes, Nuts and Seeds		
Baked beans, canned, sweet or tomato sauce, with pork	1 cup (200g)	11.0

Food Item	Serving	Total Dietary Fiber, grams
Legumes, Nuts and Seeds (*Continued*)		
Beans, Great Northern, canned, drained	1 cup (177g)	9.6
Black-eyed peas (cowpeas), cooked	1 cup (171g)	16.4
Garbanzo beans (chickpeas), cooked	1 cup (164g)	9.5
Lima beans, cooked, drained	1 cup (200g)	14.4
Peanuts, dry roasted	1 ounce (28g)	2.2
Peanut butter		
chunky	2 tablespoons (32g)	2.1
smooth	2 tablespoons (32g)	1.9
Pecans, dried	31 large /1 ounce (28g)	1.8
Sunflower seeds, oil-roasted	1 ounce (28g)	1.9
Tofu	½ cup (126g)	1.5
Walnuts, dried, English	14 halves/1 ounce (28g)	1.3
Miscellaneous		
Preserves		
peach	1 tablespoon (20g)	0.1
strawberry	1 tablespoon (20g)	0.2
Soup, canned, condensed		
chicken with noodles or rice	7.27 ounces (206g)	1.2
vegetable	7.27 ounces (206g)	2.7
Pasta		
Noodles, egg, regular, cooked	1 cup (160g)	3.5
Spaghetti and macaroni		
cooked	1 cup (140g)	2.2
whole-wheat, dry	2 ounces (57g)	6.7
Snacks		
Corn chips	1 ounce (28g)	1.2
Popcorn, air-popped	1 cup (6g)	0.9
Popcorn, oil-popped	1 cup (9g)	0.9
Potato chips	1 ounce (28g)	1.3
Vegetables and Vegetable Products		
Beans, snap, boiled	½ cup (62g)	1.1
Beets, slices, boiled	½ cup (170g)	1.9

Food Item	Serving	Total Dietary Fiber, grams
Vegetables and Vegetable Products *(Continued)*		
Broccoli		
raw, chopped	1/2 cup (92g)	2.6
cooked spears, boiled	1/2 cup (92g)	2.4
Cabbage, green or red		
raw, shredded	1/2 cup (35g)	0.7
cooked, shredded	1/2 cup (75g)	1.5
Carrots		
raw	1 medium (72g)	2.3
cooked, slices	1/2 cup (78g)	1.2
Cauliflower		
raw, pieces	1/2 cup (50g)	1.2
cooked, pieces	1/2 cup (62g)	1.4
Celery, raw	1 stalk, 7.5 inches (40g)	0.6
Corn, sweet		
raw, cut off cob	1 ounce (28g)	0.9
yellow, canned	1/2 cup (82g)	3.0
cream style	1/2 cup (128g)	1.5
Cucumbers, raw, slices	1/2 cup (52g)	0.5
Lettuce		
iceberg	1 leaf (20g)	0.2
romaine, shredded	1/2 cup (28g)	0.5
Mushrooms		
raw, pieces	1/2 cup (35g)	0.5
boiled, pieces	1/2 cup (78g)	1.7
Onions, raw, chopped	1/2 cup (80g)	1.3
Onions, spring, raw, chopped	1/2 cup (50g)	1.2
Parsley, raw, chopped	1/2 cup (30g)	1.3
Peas, edible-podded, cooked	1/2 cup (80g)	2.2
Peppers, sweet, raw, chopped	1/2 cup (50g)	0.8
Pickles, dill	2 slices (13g)	0.2
Potatoes		
raw, flesh and skin	1 potato (112g)	2.0
raw, flesh without skin	1 potato (112g)	1.8
baked, flesh without skin	1 potato (156g)	2.3
baked, skin only	1 potato skin (46g)	1.8
Spinach		
raw, chopped	1/2 cup (28g)	0.7
boiled	1/2 cup (90g)	2.0

Food Item	Serving	Total Dietary Fiber, grams
Vegetables and Vegetable Products *(Continued)*		
Squash, summer		
all varieties, raw, slices	1/2 cup (65g)	0.8
all varieties, cooked, slices	1/2 cup (90g)	1.3
Squash, winter, all varieties,		
cooked, cubes	1/2 cup (102g)	2.9
Sweet potatoes, cooked	1/2 cup (164g)	4.9
Tomatoes, raw	1 tomato (123g)	1.6
Tomato products		
catsup	1 tablespoon (15g)	0.2
paste	1/2 cup (131g)	5.6
puree	1/2 cup (125g)	2.9
sauce	3/4 cup (229g)	3.4
Turnips		
raw	5 ounces (143g)	2.6
boiled, cubes, drained	1/2 cup (117g)	2.3
Vegetables, mixed, frozen, cooked	1/2 cup (108g)	4.1
Water chestnuts, canned, slices	1/2 cup (62g)	1.4

Source: USDA Provisional Tables (Matthews and Pehrsson, 1988).

About the Authors ...

As a registered clinical and administrative dietitian and as a home cook devoted to low-fat cooking, Pat saw a growing, unfulfilled need for practical, simple ways to switch from the typical high fat, high sodium fare to healthier foods and, at the same time, for methods to get nutritious meals to the table fast. Her on-going taste panels with hospital patients and staff evaluators confirmed that foods low in both fat and sodium, even though nicely seasoned with herbs and spices, are not well accepted. However, she found that even a modest increase in the fat and sodium content of foods boosted the taste evaluations considerably. Previously unacceptable foods became foods that patients and staff would accept and even enjoy.

Her co-author for the medical and informational sections is her son, William T. Stephenson, M.D., an oncologist in Kansas City. He majored in Medical Nutrition at Brigham Young University and is committed to healthy eating. He, his wife and children continue to enjoy tasty, low-fat eating and cooking.

*   *   *   *

If you have questions, suggestions, or comments on low-fat cooking and eating, write to:

Pat Stephenson, MS, RD
5600 NW Timber Edge Drive
Topeka, Kansas 66618-3122

General Index

Find recipes in Quick Recipe Finder, pages vi-xvi.

A

Alcohol, in the diet, 233
   chart, alcohol content, 234
Apples, tart varieties, 106
Atherosclerosis, 1, 2, 7
   fish, 133
   vegetables, 73

B

Bacon, occasional use, 70, 190
Beans, dried
   nutrition and cooking, 115
   preventing gas, 115
Beef
   nutrition, selecting and cooking,
     167, 168
   weight after cooking, 168, 175
Beta-carotene, 73, 75, 81
Beverages, 230, 231
   chart, caffeine content, 232
   low-fat milk bar, 209, 210
   water, 230, 231
Breads, nutrition and selecting, 44
Breakfast
   importance of eating, 236
   nontraditional, 244, 245
   sample menus, 238-243
Brown sugar, 213, 214

C

Caffeine, effects of, 230, 231
   chart, content of foods and
     beverages, 232
   in drugs and prescriptions, 231
Calcium (see dairy products)
   in vegetables, 199
Caloric need, 236
Cancer
   beta-carotene, 73, 75
   cruciferous vegetables, 78
   fiber, 42
Candy, commercial, 227
   calculating fat percentage, 227
   chart, low-fat commercial, 227
Canola oil, 1,3
   chart, comparison of fats and oils,
     260
Carbohydrate

health considerations, 39-41
   complex, 39-41
   foods, 41
   nutritional value, 39, 40
   simple, 213, 214
   recommended levels of, 214
   ways to increase, 41, 46
Cereals, nutrition, 44
   chart, Cereal Enhancers, 58
   chart, Hot, Quick Cooking, 57
   chart, Ready-to-Eat, 55, 56
Chicken (see poultry)
Cholesterol
   health considerations, 1, 2
   found only in animal products, 40
   HDLs: high density lipoprotein,
     "good", 1, 2
   LDLs: low density lipoprotein,
     "bad", 1, 2
Cocoa, low-fat syrup, 205
Cookies, discussion of,
   chart, low-fat packaged, 229
Constipation (see fiber)
Cruciferous vegetables, 78
Crystalized flour, 19

D

Dairy products, nutrition, selection,
     199, 200
   calcium requirements, 200
   chart of nutrients in, 261
   low-fat milk bar, 209, 210
   low-fat yogurt, 211, 212
   ways to include, 200
Desserts, general, 213, 214
   chart, low-fat desserts, 228
Dietary fiber (see fiber)
Dietary Fiber Chart, 262-267
Dietitian (see Registered Dietitian)
Dinner
   importance of eating,237
   sample menus, 252-257
Dressings,salad (see salad dressings)

E

Eggs and egg substitute

270

Order Form: *Easy Everyday Low-Fat Cooking*

☐ Check enclosed for entire amount payable to Easy Everyday Low-Fat Cooking
Mail check to: Easy Everyday Low-Fat Cooking, 5600 Timber Edge Dr., Topeka, KS 66618-3122
Phone: (913) 286-0734

SEND TO:

Name _____

Address _____

City _____

State _____ Zip _____

Phone # _____

TITLE	QTY	UNIT PRICE	TOTAL
Easy Everyday Low-Fat Cooking		19.95	
Shipping & Handling: ($3 for first book. Each additional book .50)			
In KS add 5.15% Sales Tax			
		Total	

Order Form: *Easy Everyday Low-Fat Cooking*

☐ Check enclosed for entire amount payable to Easy Everyday Low-Fat Cooking
Mail check to: Easy Everyday Low-Fat Cooking, 5600 Timber Edge Dr., Topeka, KS 66618-3122
Phone: (913) 286-0734

SEND TO:

Name _____

Address _____

City _____

State _____ Zip _____

Phone # _____

TITLE	QTY	UNIT PRICE	TOTAL
Easy Everyday Low-Fat Cooking		19.95	
Shipping & Handling: ($3 for first book. Each additional book .50)			
In KS add 5.15% Sales Tax			
		Total	